"When you look at a family, you [...] picture of the gospel. This has profo[...] [...] church and for society. *The Family Project* explores the theology of the family in an informative and accessible manner. I highly recommend it!"

—Dr. Russell D. Moore
    President, Southern Baptist Ethics and Religious
    Liberty Commission

"If you only read the papers, you'd think that 'family' was a plastic idea, to be bent and reshaped as the whims of contemporary culture demand. But in reality, the idea of family predates just about everything: democracy, the nation-state—even history itself. In fact, the only thing to predate the family is the Almighty. *The Family Project* is a reader-friendly, theological explanation of why you can't understand family without God. And vice versa."

—Jonathan V. Last
    Author, *What to Expect When No One's Expecting*

"After decades of emphasis on radical individualism we have come, not to freedom, but to an unspoken epidemic of loneliness. *The Family Project* traces the way homeward with intelligence, honesty, and depth."

—Frederica Mathewes-Green
    Author, *The Jesus Prayer*

"The bigger problem might be not that the family is under attack, as we often say, but that the family is just not understood. Glenn Stanton and Leon Wirth have done us all a tremendous service with this clear, cogent, and thoughtful explanation of what the family is and why it is central to God's work in the world. This is stuff that too many Christians just don't know, but hopefully will because of this book."

—JOHN STONESTREET
Speaker and Fellow, the Chuck Colson Center
for Christian Worldview
Senior Content Advisor, Summit Ministries

The Family project™

HOW GOD'S DESIGN REVEALS HIS BEST FOR YOU

GLENN T. STANTON
AND LEON C. WIRTH

TYNDALE HOUSE PUBLISHERS, INC.
CAROL STREAM, ILLINOIS

Dedicated to our beautiful, messy families: You have loved, inspired, and shaped us through our stumbles, trials, and imperfections to never give up.

Contents

Introduction

Births. Birthdays. Anniversaries. Love. Commitment. Abuse. Betrayal. Divorce. Death.

For all of us, most of our greatest joys—and deepest wounds—come from our family experiences. We all know that our own families matter, but can you explain to someone why family in general matters at all these days?

- To the weary single mom trying to keep her head above water—why does family matter?
- To the pastor struggling to keep his own marriage and family healthy while counseling deeply needy and hurting souls in his congregation—why does family matter?
- To the teen who wishes she could get away from her suffocating parents so she can be free to explore what the world offers—why does family matter?
- To the young man living in his parents' home, working nearly full-time to conquer new levels of the latest first-person-shooter video game—why does family matter?
- To the troubled Christian couple who carries more questions than answers about the marriage, its struggles, and the future—why does family matter?
- To the spouse wrestling with a text message or social media nudge from that old flame, wondering what harm could

come from it, feeling limited in life by the duties that come from family—why does family matter?

- To the young adult who wants marriage and kids but is afraid of doing it poorly or messing it up because all she has are unhealthy examples from her parents—why does family matter?
- To the family that seems to be doing pretty well in general—why does family matter?

We believe that many of the views held by many of us today regarding family, either as an ideal or in the practice of our everyday lives, have become weak and shallow. Conventional wisdom in many Christian and social circles has reduced family to either a culture-war landmine or merely a private, personal relationship.

We invite you to join us on a bold journey of rediscovery of some ancient truths about what family is in light of who God is, what He created us to be, and His unfolding story through history—*His*tory.

You see, God is revealing Himself—His character, His nature, His love, His grace, and His holiness—to the world. He has been doing that since He first created mankind, and He continues it today.

And God has been doing so in remarkably glorious and mysterious ways through family.

We will be moving through some very important environs that will probably be new to many readers. But they are not new. Many of the paths we will be taking are ancient roads that were well known and widely used a thousand or more years ago. Our rediscovery—and hopefully re-appreciation—of them will help us see and understand God, ourselves, our families, and hopefully the whole of our lives a bit differently than we do today. Christianity, as a 2,000-plus-year-old faith, has a rich storehouse of wisdom and insight into what God has taught and is teaching us through His

Word, given to us by faithful believers and leaders down through the ages. We will be guided along our journey by many of their insights and teachings.

As any important trip begins, it makes things more enjoyable and beneficial when the travelers go over the plan, direction, and highlights of the expedition ahead of them:

Where will we be going?

How will we get there?

What will we be seeing along the way?

Why are these particular points of interest worth paying attention to?

Such pre-excursion activities are exciting because they help us anticipate the trip, imagining what the actual experience itself will be like. This is what we will be doing in this introduction.

We hope it will serve to enrich your expedition, allowing you to see the larger meaning of high points such as weddings, births, baptisms, graduations, holidays together, vacations, etc. But the principles are also equally true in what we might see as the mundaneness of family life: preparing meals together, doing homework, washing clothes, disciplining, bathing the children, cleaning out the garage, grocery shopping, fixing the broken window in the bathroom, changing flat tires, etc. So much of your family's life is more divine than you might imagine.

Unfortunately, there is a troubling dearth of theologies[1] of family and humanity that help us gain a vivid, practical, and colorful picture of what lies ahead and to view it all in a more meaningful way. We hope to help overcome this problem with the materials presented in the following pages.

This is a very important perspective, for it bridges the gap between the technicality of classroom theology and the "tips and techniques" of self-help books. This project—both in this book and the

DVD curriculum, which is also available—cuts a middle way, painting a moving and meaningful picture of the story that God has been telling, and His invitation to all of us to participate in it with Him. And you will see how important the nature of marriage and family are to this divine story.[2] In many important ways, the human family is not just a special interest, some moral topic to fight over in the culture war, but a primary, ongoing narrative of God's story. And if we don't understand it this way, we cannot truly understand God's nature and His purposes and actions through history. That is a bold statement, but based on our long study of this topic we believe it is supported by a faithful examination of the Scriptures. See if you agree.

The tools we use and the trails we will go down are all founded on the truth of God's revealed word to us through the Holy Scriptures. But this will not be merely a study of lots of individual verses; for the Scriptures are not merely a collection of individual, quotable passages, but a story—God's story to us, from beginning to end. Seeking to be faithful to this narrative nature of God's Word, it will have a very strong cohering thread moving through it that connects these verses, stories, and instances that Scripture provides for us. And this thread moves through Scripture from the first verse to the last, as we will see. (Relax, though. We are not going to go through every verse!) It is more of a story than the typical sort of study you might be used to. But we will also see how these biblical truths are found and even revealed in

- the nature of our collective humanity—our deepest and most aching longings, universally felt among all people the earth over as well as throughout history;
- the way we live together in culture, despite all the unique differences we observe across the remarkably distinct societies around the globe;

- the investigations of philosophy and human psychology;
- the arts: painting, literature, poetry, and music;
- the surprising and sophisticated developments in today's cutting-edge sciences; and finally,
- the day-to-day ins-and-outs of both our interior lives—the deepest, most private crevices of our hearts and souls—and our exterior lives, the ways we live, relate to, and interact with those around us.

And we explore all of this unapologetically from the center of all reality: God and His character, nature, and essence, as well as His desire and purpose for us. Only in understanding who God is and what He is up to in the world can we understand ourselves, each other, and the connections between us.

An Important Intersection

Now we will be orienting ourselves from time to time on our trip by the intersections of two main thoroughfares. As in most cities, there are main roads by which we orient ourselves to all others places in the city. In our city of Colorado Springs, those roads are Union and Academy Boulevards. If asked, most people in your city could name yours and find widespread agreement. So the following are ours for navigational purposes.

Our East-West Pathway: Fuller Worldview Boulevard

This first byway is a larger Christian worldview, providing the full canvas upon which we will be drawing our picture of God's story from its beginning to its culmination.

Typically, Christians have understood the historical progress of a Christian worldview as a three-act play involving God and man. These are:

1. Creation

2. Fall

3. Redemption

Of course, these represent:

1. God's *creation* of the physical universe and humanity as male and female, made to serve as God's distinct and unique physical image-bearers in the world.

2. Man's *Fall*, where both male and female allowed themselves to be deceived by Satan and chose to go their own way, disobeying the one divine prohibition that God had given them. This rebellion severely devastated all of humanity, threatening to separate us forever from God.

3. *Redemption* is God's work to bring man back into right relationship with God through His boundless love for us, demonstrated through the giving of His Son for our sin. Because of this, our separation from God does not have to be forever.

Each of these is a key part of a Christian worldview, but there are more that cannot be overlooked as fundamental parts of the story as well. A full Christian worldview consists of four additional parts that not only add necessary things to the story but enrich our understanding of the story itself in important ways. A fuller worldview is understood collectively as follows:

pre-creation · creation · fall · incarnation · redemption · ascension · consummation

Here are the four added acts:

1. *Pre-creation*: While the start of creation is explained in Genesis 1:1, we are told of pre-creation in John 1 and numerous other places in the New Testament—as we will see later on. This part of our faith's worldview tells us what was there before there was any-

thing else. Actually, this is the starting point for the story that takes Christ as the center of it, isn't it? Read John 1:1-3 and 14. It tells us that Christ, the Word, existed before there was anything else, and He dwelt from eternity with the Father. We don't understand Christ if we don't understand this. And we cannot understand Christianity if we do not understand Christ. Have you ever thought about the significance of this? Most of us don't. But understanding and appreciating the nature of pre-creation will give you a much richer and truer view of the rest of God's story, for it sets the stage for everything else, as we shall see.

2. *Incarnation* is also an indispensable and dramatically game-changing part of the divine story. It is also connected to pre-creation as we read in John 1:14. God took on flesh and "dwelt among us," fully God and fully man. And it is not just crucial *that* He did, but also *how* He did. It is honestly impossible to overstate the significance of this as we will discover in our journey ahead. While incarnation initiates our Father's glorious redemption of the world from sin and death, it also speaks to the nature and relationship between heaven and Earth, the spiritual and the physical. It really brings these two together.

3. *Ascension* is perhaps the least appreciated part of this larger way of understanding a Christian worldview, for its importance is more subtle. We will not let the cat out of the bag here, because it is pivotal to critical points that will come up in later chapters. But it illuminates in significant ways the nature of both the spirituality of the physical body and the nature of fatherhood and sonship.

4. *Consummation*, as the name implies, is the conclusion of God's drama. It is what the whole story has been moving toward, and therefore speaks of God's purposes in our history and sets the stage for eternity. It tells us absolutely profound things about God's own nature and His eternal desire, so much so that we'll come to

wonder how we understood and appreciated God's movement in history without it.

A fuller Christian worldview is critical because it illuminates the fuller Christian story.

Our North-South Pathway: Definitive Statement Avenue
This second main street that will guide us to our destination recognizes four remarkable statements from God's own mouth that give meaning and understanding to everything else we might ever know or understand about what it means to be human. We refer to them throughout as God's *Four Definitive Statements*, for they establish fundamental truths in God's story.

The first three are the first statements God makes about the first two humans. As such, they are the most profound, consequential descriptions of what humanity is and what it means to be human in light of who God is. The fourth tells us how the story ends . . . or actually begins again.

Two are very good news, and two are very bad. The bad-news statements are sandwiched in between the two good-news statements. The first three appear in the first three chapters of the Bible. And they change everything. The fourth is *very* good news and speaks to humanity's only hope—and appears in the next-to-the-last chapter of Scripture. And all the rest of God's story is book-ended, if you will, by these defining statements.

So we should know about them and understand carefully what they are and what they mean before we begin our journey into understanding how family shows us the very image and nature of God Himself.

God's *First Definitive Statement* comes from the mouth of God as He's creating all that is. He's bringing into being the wonderful physical world and then comes to a place where He announces that

He will create something unique and special that stands in stark contrast to all the rest of creation. God says,

> "Let us make man in our image, after our likeness. . . ." So God created man in his own image, in the image of God he created him; male and female he created them. (Genesis 1:26-27)

This is the declaration from God about what we as humans were created to be and what we do: physically reflect and show forth the image of the invisible God in the world. And humanity does this in both male and female. As we will unpack throughout this book, a great gift to us from God is knowing who we are and what is unique about us, as well as understanding why we were created as we are.

While the first verse tells us who we are and what our purpose is, God's *Second Definitive Statement* tells us something very important about ourselves as well. Collectively, these are unarguably the two most definitive statements about being human in all the literature that man possesses. In explaining humanity's most fundamental problem, the second statement reveals something about us because it points to something important about God:

> Then the LORD God said, "It is not good that the man should be alone." (2:18)

In creation there is something that is not good, though God created it all. He does not make mistakes. He is incapable of it. This second telling of humanity's creation in Genesis 2 goes into more detail regarding our creation, explaining that Adam was created first. But God proclaims that Adam's solitude is not good for him. Adam is not as he was meant to be. Aloneness is neither natural nor good for anyone; it is not part of our divine makeup. It is man's original problem. And so God makes a partner for him, as we will see in greater depth in Chapter 3 of this book. In a very weighty statement about what it means to be female, God tells us that she is the answer to mankind's original and most significant problem.

God's *Third Definitive Statement* speaks to what most would typically think of as mankind's first problem. While his isolation is the first problem, this third statement from God indicates man's greater problem because of its devastating consequences:

> Then the LORD God said, "Behold, the man has become
> like one of us in knowing good and evil." (3:22)

Adam and Eve, by their own God-given free will, chose to disobey God's clearly given command—the only one given—and usher in the curse of sin and death upon themselves and all of humanity. As we know, this changed the whole game, setting the story on a whole different path. The rest of the story is about what God does to allow us to overcome this first and most grave mistake, which leads us to God's *Fourth Definitive Statement*.

God tells us in the last book of our Bibles what this whole story is finally pointing toward, what He is up to. It is glorious and profound:

> And I saw the holy city, new Jerusalem, coming down out
> of heaven from God, prepared as a bride adorned for her
> husband. And I heard a loud voice from the throne saying,
> "Behold, the dwelling place of God is with man. He will
> dwell with them, and they will be his people, and God him-
> self will be with them as their God. He will wipe away every
> tear from their eyes, and death shall be no more, neither
> shall there be mourning nor crying nor pain anymore. . . ."

And he who was seated on the throne said, "Behold, I am making all things new." Also he said, "Write this down, for these words are trustworthy and true." And he said to me, "It is done." (Revelation 21:2-6)

God will dwell with us, and we shall be His people. He will attend to our tears and pain, and He will end the death brought on by the original sin of Adam and Eve. He is "making all things new."

So these Four Definitive Statements are perhaps the most important statements in all of human telling and literature about what it means to be human, what we are, and where we are going—for they are far and away the most consequential, are they not? We will unpack the reality of these statements throughout the coming pages—in conjunction with understanding these additional critical parts of a complete and biblical worldview—because without a special appreciation of and focus on both of these intersecting roads, we cannot grasp the fullness of the larger story that God lives in and has been telling us.

So there we go. These are the basics of what each of us needs to know as we prepare for our investigative journey. So cancel the mail and the newspaper, have your neighbor Edna come feed the dog and cat, excuse the kids from school, get their make-up work, change the oil in the family car, and check the tires. We have a most excellent adventure to embark upon. Saddle up.

Note: Throughout this book, you'll see sidebars listing Internet locations where classical paintings referred to in the text may be viewed. Please note that some of these images, such as depictions of Adam and Eve, contain nudity. Certain other images, including those depicting the Crucifixion, may be disturbing to some.

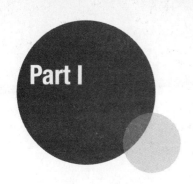

Part I

WHERE OUR STORY BEGINS

We want to know and understand what families are in a much larger way—in light of who God is in His larger essence and then what *we* are in light of this. These two—a biblical theology and anthropology—will merge together in a creative and true way, helping us appreciate what is taking place when families are formed and seek to live out the day-in, day-out routines of life together.

On our trek we will learn that family is so much larger, grander, and more mysterious than most of us have ever imagined. Most books that address the question of family in terms of biblical truth are either technical systematic theologies or advice books on how to solve family problems or improve general family life. This book is different. It seeks to explain *why* and *how* our families and humanness matter—and, most importantly, do so in light of who God is.

YOU ARE HERE

Davion Only was born in prison, spent years in and out of foster homes, and wanted a family—badly. He found his family of origin after learning the identity of his birth mother around the time that she died in June 2013. At her funeral, he discovered that he was loved by relatives that he didn't even know he had. But he still didn't have a family to call his own. So in September, the 15-year-old orphan took a rather bold step. He stood in front of a church congregation and asked for someone to adopt him.

"I'll take anyone," he said.[1]

That same year, Jackie Turner—a 26-year-old college student from an abusive home—put an ad on Craigslist, offering to pay a family to be hers for the holidays. She longed for the loving embrace of parents who cared about her and wouldn't hurt her. She was offering what little money she had: eight dollars per hour.

She told the media, "I've never felt the touch of my mom hugging me and holding me. I don't know what it's like to look in my dad's eyes and feel love instead of hatred."[2]

Here we will explore what we all have in common with Davion, Jackie, and so many like them.

What Is True of All People?

There are lots of different kinds of people in the world. No, not those who like the beach and those who like the country, or those who like Thai food and those who can't stand it. We're not talking about "cat people" and "dog people," but about much deeper and meaningful differences.

Look around at all the human cultures across the globe and throughout history. Think about those you learned of in *National Geographic* magazine through the decades. Many of them are so very different from ours, to the point of being difficult for us to understand and nearly impossible to relate to. They would have the same reaction to us. No matter what culture you come from, you can always find one that is just perfectly weird to you. *How can they find that kind of food tasty? Why do they wear those kinds of clothes? Why do they pierce their bodies with those things? Why* there? *Why don't* those *people ever pierce their bodies? Why would they choose those kinds of homes to live in? Why do they do that kind of work or play those kinds of games? Why do they dress and carry their babies that way? Why don't they just do it the* normal *way—you know, like* we *do it?* Paul Simon, on his album *Surprise*, has a wonderful song titled "How Can You Live in the Northeast?" on this very topic.

There are many curious differences among humans, just as there are many similarities. It is part of what it means to be human. We can choose our own lives, how we want to live. But given all these dramatic differences, we are all human—and there are things that all humans do because either they enjoy them or *must* do them. Anthropologists call these "human universals." They are things we find in all human cultures regardless of a culture's age, geographical or historical location, politics, religion, or economy. They are universal.

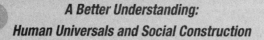

A Better Understanding:
Human Universals and Social Construction

When thinking and speaking about the ways humans act and why, one will often hear that all human behaviors—save a very few basic bodily needs like eating, drinking, staying warm, waste elimination, etc.—are "socially constructed." This is the theory, very popular among many academics and so-called progressives, that humans act as we do because our individual societies encourage, require, or shape such behaviors based on some need or power-play by that society's leaders—most often the men. Thus, such behaviors are artificially constructed by social influence. Typically we hear that term in comments like, "Well, we all know that gender difference is a mere social construct." Social construction theory assumes there is no universal human nature. This flies in the face of basic observation.

Marriage, parenthood, and siblinghood are all human universals, not socially constructed. They have been fundamental to human and social nature in all cultures since the beginning of time, through societies that have had no way of influencing one another due to geography, from the Agaw of Ethiopia to the Zapotec of Mexico. We address this social centrality of family more in Chapter 6.

Noted anthropologist Donald Brown[3] has long studied and outlined the beliefs, qualities, traditions, and practices that are humanly universal. It is a fascinating topic of study. Some of these everyday universals are very curious things, like a desire for sweets, singing and dancing, enjoyment of jokes and humor, the need for daily routines, the education of children, processes for cleanliness, gift-giving, thumb-sucking, playful tickling, rules of etiquette, gossip, customary greetings, use of hairstyles, etc. People in all cultures—and as far as we know, at all times—do each of these. Human universals.

For our journey in these pages, we must note that all humans universally have the following absolute needs, and these are each unique to humanity:

- *Question-asking.* No child needs to be taught to ask questions, as any parent knows. We have to be taught to keep our questions to a reasonable minimum or else parents go nuts. We are naturally questioning people. We wonder. We ponder. We ask. We seek. We always will.

- *Religious pursuit and practice.* People in all cultures naturally ask questions with religious meaning. We believe that there must be something over and in command of the world we live in. We are not inclined to accept ourselves as the ultimate part of reality. Atheism is not as natural.

- *Personal relationships.* People are fundamentally relational creatures. No one can become or live as a happy person without relationships. Brown calls this basic reality of all humans "triangular awareness"—the awareness of the self and at least two others one is in relationship with. Community is more than us and another person. We all must have others, a community. As we will see, people will fail to thrive physically and mentally without meaningful community and intimacy.

- *Sense of significance and meaningful work.* We must all feel as if we have some significance. This can come from our religious beliefs and understanding, our relationships, and our work. No person or society can become and remain healthy without meaningful work. We must have it to thrive, not just economically, but in every other way.

What is notable is that one can be impeccably cared for nutritionally and physically, but none of us in any time or culture can live in any measure of health and happiness without each of these four things in our lives. If we are deprived of them, very bad things happen. Examples in real human experience are as ample as they are sad.

In terms of question-asking and particularly queries of ultimate meaning, one unlikely and curious man asked three of the most important and fundamental questions that any of us can struggle with.

GAUGUIN'S QUESTIONS = EVERYONE'S QUESTIONS

The lonely artist had made up his mind. Today was the day he would end it all for good.

He climbed the dense, tropically wooded hill behind his Tahitian hut, more alone than he had ever been. He'd spent most of his life in loneliness—intentionally, some would say, for he seemed the only one who'd ever really mattered to him.

He took nothing with him on this short trip up the hill but his ever-pressing load of despair and a small tin of arsenic. His was a life of crushing debt, depression, emptiness, and debilitating disease, much of it the result of his world-class arrogance and unchecked sexual appetite. Desolation and failure would be his legacy.

Paul Gauguin had become a hopelessly pitiful man. He'd failed to achieve meaningful success as a painter in his lifetime. He'd abandoned his wife and children. He alienated every friend he ever had.

He'd headed to Tahiti in search of human purity, the authentic life untouched by the poisons of modernity, conventionality, greed, and power. He'd taken a "wife/servant" for himself in this paradise—a tall, dark-haired girl, perhaps 13 years old.

He subsisted on the rare and meager financial gifts that arrived from the mainland, in answer to his many begging and bitter letters home. His children never wrote their father. His wife did so only rarely.

Now he had come to the end.

Just days before, he'd completed one last painting, intended as his final testament to the world. He'd described its philosophical ambition to a friend as "comparable to that of the gospel" without the slightest appreciation of this ridiculous overstatement.

It was a massive, three-panel work depicting Tahitian women of all life phases engaged in various everyday activities and inactivities. Moving from right to left, as he intended, it showed the beginning of life in an infant and the end of life in a sad, old woman—and various stages between.

GET THE PICTURE

Paul Gauguin, *Self-Portrait with Halo* (1889)
National Gallery of Art, Washington, D.C.
Visit familyproject.com to see this painting.

Painted as a decoration for the dining room of an inn where Gauguin lived with one of his art students, this piece was completed on a cupboard door. Art scholars debate whether Gauguin was portraying himself as Christ or Satan. Perhaps it was both—portrayed in part by the twin apples of enlightenment and temptation alongside the temple of the artist—the enticing artist-savior of all those around him, calling them to a life of illumination and insight beyond what he condemned as the confining strictures of religion and art of his day.

Yet the greatest meaning of the painting was not found in the images presented, but in the title. It captured three of the most searching questions any human can ponder, and they appear in the section of gold in the upper left-hand corner. In French, as Gauguin wrote them, they were as follows:

D'où venons-nous? Que sommes-nous? Où allons-nous?

In English, they are:

Where do we come from? What are we? Where are we going?

And now, having finished his greatest work, Gauguin walked up the wooded hill and swallowed all the arsenic in the tin to make sure it accomplished its dark task. Finally he lay down, intending to sleep and never to awake in this life.

But even in this last act, the artist failed. He ingested too much arsenic, causing him to violently vomit the poison before it could take effect. He managed to find his way back down the hill—and to suffer a few more years of failure and emptiness. He would die at the early age of 54, his body appearing far older than it was, ravaged by alcohol abuse and syphilis.

So why are these particular questions significant, and what do they have to do with our exploration here? Let's look at them more closely.

1. *Where do we come from?* asks *What is the source of our being?*
2. *What are we?* wants to know *What is our nature? What are we made for?*
3. *Where are we going?* probes *What's our destiny? What is our existence and everything else moving toward?*

But curiously, these questions are not the brilliant insights of an artist freed from the stifling confines of traditional religion and Western society. Gauguin did not find them in the clarity of his atheism or in the "authentic" culture of Polynesia.

GET THE PICTURE

Paul Gauguin, *D'où venons-nous? Que sommes-nous? Où allons-nous?* (1897)
Museum of Fine Arts, Boston
Visit familyproject.com to see this painting.

This massive scape was completed on a large, three-part canvas of jute which Gauguin quickly cobbled together due to his material poverty. It is a beautiful piece of work, but offers no real answers to the nagging questions it poses in the yellow of the upper-left corner. It is curious that the scene consists of women in various activities and all stages of life, starting with birth at the right side leading to old age bordering on death at the left. And what of the two women coming from the cave, down the path toward the beginning-of-life side of this work? They are carrying a newborn child.

It cannot go without notice that the linear movement of human life from birth to death is book-ended by animal life with some kind of duck on the death side and a dog on the birth side. The only religious or spiritual hint in the piece is the curious pagan statue that the people seem to not only be ignoring but literally have their backs turned to. What is the meaning of this? A denunciation of empty pagan symbolism or religion as a whole? We are left to wonder. Does the lack of any clear answer to his questions mean that there are no answers to be had, or that Gauguin himself had none to offer? Or are the answers simply found in the beauty of the mundane everyday activities of life? If so, this meaning is apparently only found in the lives of women alone, for the painting features no males.

Even in his most brilliant moment, he was not original. Gauguin's questions came from someone who influenced him in the earlier years of his life, someone who knew why these questions were important to the human soul and what the right answers were. This someone drew from a much larger story than himself.

This man was Bishop Félix Antoine Philibert Dupanloup. Bishop Dupanloup was a brilliant intellectual, a member of the French Academy, and a respected and influential leader in the French church. He was a key advocate for the canonization of Joan of Arc, as well as a colorful and tireless Christian revivalist and a formational and distinguished educator of the young.

Gauguin studied under the charismatic bishop during most of his teen years at the Petit Séminaire, which Dupanloup founded in Orléans. Gauguin came under the influence of Dupanloup's catechism, with its repetitive contemplation of a variety of foundational questions regarding God, ourselves, others, and our collective existence. This system was driven by Dupanloup's conviction that once merged into the hearts and minds of the young boys, these questions—and their answers—would never be erased.

And they weren't, particularly in this one young student. No matter how far he roamed (or ran) ideologically, morally, or spiritually from God—no matter how he tried to shake his past—the passionate bishop's three questions, those he taught as more fundamental than all the others, could not leave the tormented and seemingly unyielding Gauguin.

They became the substance of his final testament.

ANSWERS

These questions plagued not only Gauguin but his whole generation—those before and those to come after, including our own. Can you think of a more important set of three basic questions that any soul can ask? Have you never thought about them to some degree? Do you think they have never occurred, in some degree or another, to any other human with a moderate level of intelligence? You know they are natural to all of us.

The good news is that there are answers—true and beautiful answers—found in glorious places. They are found in an exceedingly profound and breathtaking story. And where it takes you and how it answers these questions will likely surprise you.

So we have set a number of key foundation stones as we travel in our investigation, adding two to the two we established in the introduction:

- Seven parts of a fuller Christian worldview, beginning with pre-creation and ending with consummation
- Four Definitive Statements
- Four key human universals
- Gauguin's three questions

Keep these in mind, well noted in your travelogue as we start.

The Denarrated Life: Where Questions Go to Die

Each one of us must know that our lives are part of something bigger than we are, that the various parts of our lives—our work, our faith, our family and friends, our community involvement, our education—connect to some meaningful degree. This connection is the narrative of our lives. Just as in a story, it is the thread that carries things along. There can be good, healthy narratives that fill our lives—one person's life being about educating young people with Down syndrome, or another's about providing healthcare for cancer patients. And there can be poorer, unhealthy narratives—like wanting to become super-famous, crazy rich, or just to get your next bottle of Scotch.

David Hart, a contemporary Eastern Orthodox theologian, explains that we can know God in the way we do because "God is who He is because He has a story in which He acts."[4] Therefore, *we* must have a story to live in.

Famed moral philosopher Alasdair MacIntyre, in his book *After Virtue*, observed the essential nature of a storied context for each of us:

> I can only answer the question "What am I to do?" if I can
> answer the prior question "Of what story or stories do I find
> myself a part?". . . . Deprive children [ourselves] of stories and
> you leave them [us] unscripted, anxious stutterers in their
> [our] actions as in their [our] words.[5]

James Bryan Smith, a sought-after director and author in spiritual development, explains the importance of narrative to our lives in God:

> We are creatures who live by our stories. From early on, we
> are told stories by our parents, which help us interpret how
> life is or how life ought to be. We are naturally drawn to
> stories. . . . Narrative is the central function of the human
> mind. We turn everything into a story to make sense of
> life. . . . In fact, we cannot avoid it. We are storied creatures.[6]

Stories are a human universal but must be much more than tales we tell. Your story is that which ties your life together and gives it a cohering meaning. Douglas Coupland, one of the brightest contemporary novelists, observes and writes on the ways the last two generations—Xers and Millennials—see their place in the world. He inadvertently coined the term "Generation X" with his first novel by that name.

In his book of essays, *Polaroids from the Dead*, Coupland says that a primary disease of our age is the loss of stories, and as such, very bad things happen to us. We start to feel "lost, dangerous, out of control and susceptible to the forces of randomness," he says.

Sound like anything you observe today around you? Perhaps even within you?

This loss is where we lose the sense of our own lives, the feeling of belonging to something bigger, more meaningful, and more transcendent than ourselves. Just as basic as food and water are for our physical bodies, living within a life narrative is essential for our hearts' or souls' existence.

Coupland perceptively laments that it's now "possible to be alive, yet have no religion, no family connections, no ideology, no sense of class location, no politics and no sense of history. Denarrated."[7] Being "denarrated" is the bigger part of what we might call "not having a life."

The larger story which we live in and by should be worth living for and living out of. In fact, it should really be worth dying for. If it's not worth dying for, is it really worth living for?

So, we must ask: What are our stories today? What is it that gives our lives a sense of narrative, a greater backdrop of meaning to live against? And then is that story worth having? To be frank, is it worthy of you?

Consumerism, professional success, fashion and popular culture, sports, video games, social media, and entertainment are inadequate narratives for human beings. We are made for grander things. For too many of us, though, the narrative of our lives is work, school, trying to get to that next level. Our big life goal seems to be nothing more than making it through one more day, one more week with the kids' school, with the wash, with the bills, with work projects.

Each of these things is fine in itself, and even necessary. But all should be parts of our lives, not life itself. The great Southern writer Flannery O'Connor said, "It requires considerable courage at any time, in any country, not to turn away from the storyteller."[8] We are and have been moving away from the storyteller and therefore the story as well, perhaps precisely because we have lost our courage.

As Coupland said, if we cannot locate ourselves in a story much bigger than ourselves, we are lost.

Lost in meaning.

Lost in purpose.

Lost in motivation.

Lost in significance.

L-O-S-T.

So what is an appropriate narrative?

THE UNIQUE FULLNESS OF A CHRISTIAN NARRATIVE

It is our conviction that Christianity has the biggest, truest, fullest, and most compelling narrative for answering Gauguin's three questions. This book is an explanation of why and how this is, and does so through studying family. We will learn not just about how important family is but primarily how profound the Christian faith and God are.

Because, as you hopefully have seen, we are—every one of us—a Davion or a Jackie, searching for relationship, for meaning, for answers to questions that are found beyond ourselves.

THE BIG STATEMENT FOR REFLECTION

There is a universal human nature that is common to all people at all times in history. We are naturally born to be curious about the "big questions" of life. Each of us requires both intimacy and acceptance from others and a sense of significance about our lives, work, and place in the world. And we long to find meaning to our story, yearning to be part of a larger one.

QUESTIONS FOR CONSIDERATION

1. Many—Christians and non-believers—see Christianity as essentially a belief system that explains where we go when we die, and how to be good until we get there. Do you think Christianity is bigger or wider than that? In what ways? Why does this larger, fuller view matter?

2. Do you see individuals today as increasingly *denarrated*? How is that true of those around you at work, at school, in your family and neighborhood, and even in your church? Does this really matter?

3. What larger narratives did people have 100 years back and earlier? How did the following contribute to the narratives people inhabited?
   - Where they lived
   - How they supported themselves and their families
   - What they believed about ultimate reality

   Did farmers, for instance, live in a different narrative than city dwellers?

4. Consider our four fundamental human universals. What does it mean that people can be provided with adequate food, physical protection, and care, but if they don't experience intimacy and love and important work to do, they cannot thrive as human beings—even dying from such absences? Why do you suppose this is?

LET US MAKE MAN
(*IMAGO DEI*)

Where do we come from?

What are we?

How does God's First Definitive Statement answer these questions?

> "Let us make man in our image, after our likeness. . . ." So God created man in his own image, in the image of God he created him; male and female he created them. (Genesis 1:26-27)

Karl Barth, the great Swiss theologian many celebrate as the greatest Protestant theologian of the twentieth century—was asked during a sophisticated academic lecture to theology students at the University of Chicago if it was possible to capture his life's great learning and wisdom in one sentence. It's really kind of a silly question, but he thought a moment and answered that it was indeed possible. His answer was as profound as it was simple and good-humored. He said all he had learned, taught, and written throughout his long and illustrious career was summed up in the divine wisdom he learned on the lap of his humble Christian mother. It was found in a simple song that most of us know:

"Jesus loves me, this I know. For the Bible tells me so."

Truly, it doesn't get any simpler—yet more profound—than this. Everything else any of us will ever learn about God from the world's most sophisticated seminaries, brilliant sermons, or our local Sunday school class is all but a footnote to and explanation of this magnificent truth.

There is something curious about the biggest questions that humans can ask. The bigger and more meaningful they are, the younger we tend to be when we ask them. This is true of Gauguin's first two questions.

I (Glenn) remember as a seven- or eight-year-old child sitting in the backseat of our family station wagon on a long trip, trying obediently to be quiet. What was I to do but think? It hit me: If I was me, and I was pretty sure I was, I had to have come from somewhere beyond my mother's abdomen. I knew the explanation of my existence had to be bigger than that I "just happened." There had to be something *behind* my being who I was.

It is very likely that you had the same sorts of questions. And it wasn't because our parents had enrolled us at our neighborhood Little Tykes Socrates Academy. And the fact that we naturally ask such questions is a strong indication that there are answers. We outgrow questions like "Are unicorns really real?" or "Is there a Santa Claus?" even if no one ever told us (spoiler alert) that they were not real. But we don't outgrow our "Is there a God, and does He really care about me?" questions. These questions have been put into us for a reason. The apostle Paul, speaking to the greatest philosophers of the world in Athens, told them this:

God, who made the world and everything in it . . . made
from one blood every nation of men to dwell on all the
face of the earth . . . so that they should seek the Lord, in
the hope that they might grope for Him and find Him,
though He is not far from each one of us; for in Him we
live and move and have our being, as also some of your
own poets have said, "For we are also His offspring." (Acts
17:24, 26-28, NKJV)

Our two big questions in this chapter are related because what
we are is understood and gains its meaning from where or what we
come from, doesn't it?

If we come from the grime under the universe's fingernails, that
says something very significant about us—and it's not good news. If
we are simply someone else's dream—as René Descartes and other
philosophers considered—then we have no meaning at all, no real
being. We are just some illusion.

What if we come from some higher being with a purpose behind our creation, but are produced in a mere mechanical way,
spit out into the world as if coming off a factory assembly line?
We might have purpose and meaning, and there would be a higher
power, but it would be merely as a utility. You and I would be
utensils made of flesh and blood, but with no personal or unique
meaning.

But what if we are created by a higher, absolutely transcendent
being—the Creator and Master of the vast, powerful, and beautifully mysterious cosmos? What if we are created because of and out
of His love, character, and personality, to live in eternal relationship
with Him—even to be His beloved children and friends?

Could such a thing be true? Of all the possible options explaining our own existence, who wouldn't hope for that one? Regardless

of what any of us might think of its likelihood, this option is among the most attractive, is it not?

"Where Do We Come From?" The Unique Answer Christianity Offers

This option is the story that Christianity has to tell and has been telling for over 2,000 years. It has radically revolutionized billions of people through the ages and most of the world's societies for the better.[1]

So how does the Christian story explain where we come from and what we are? This is our focus in this chapter. To answer this question, we have to go back to the very beginning of the story.

All good stories begin precisely here:

- Once upon a time . . .
- It all started when . . .
- Long, long ago, long before you were born . . .

And the best and most important story in all of storytelling clearly starts at the beginning, opening with these three simple words: *In the beginning:*

In the beginning, God created . . . (Genesis 1:1)

The first sermon I (Glenn) ever preached to a congregation in my early twenties was on these five words, because this is the starting place of everything else. Before anything was created, before any action had been taken, before anything had been built, destroyed, eaten, or cared for . . . it is then that God's story to us starts.

Imagine staging this "in the beginning" scene for a dramatic play. How would you fashion it so audience members would get the power of it, so that they *feel* it?

The second line of Scripture ushering us into God's story helps our understanding:

The earth was without form and void, and darkness was over the face of the deep. (1:2)

Black, empty, cold, void, nothingness. Nothing . . . but God. Is this what the Christian story tells us?

It would seem like it, for there it is in black and white, plain enough for us to read right out of the gate. But there is more to the beginning of the Christian story than what we read in the first chapters of Genesis. There is more that God has for us in this story, and it makes a profound difference to the story of who God is and who we are.

It is precisely at this curious and perhaps even perplexing point where we must start our exploration of who we are and where we come from in earnest.

So let's begin with Paul Gauguin's first question.

Where Do We Come From?

This is not an everyday question like, "Where did the doughnuts go?" or "What are we doing for vacation this year?"

It's not just a curiosity question. It's a searching, aching question. As we saw in the introduction, in the typical Christian worldview understanding, we start with creation. But we must actually start earlier than that to get the fuller picture of where we came from. We must recognize that there was something there *before* creation, before Genesis 1:1!

How can that be? Well, let's see.

THE OTHER BEGINNING: PRE-CREATION REALITY

In considering the beginning, it is most important to recognize that Scripture gives us two seemingly different "In the beginnings."

Do you know what they are? (*Hint:* One is in the Old Testament. The other is in the New Testament.)

The first is the one that most of us know, the first words of the Bible that we just examined: "In the beginning, God created the heavens and the earth."

The second is central to the Christian story—the precise point that distinguishes it from Christianity's Jewish roots:

> In the beginning was the Word, and the Word was with
> God, and the Word was God. He was in the beginning with
> God. All things were made through him, and without him
> was not any thing made that was made. (John 1:1-3)

This John 1:1 "In the beginning" introduces and historically precedes the Genesis 1:1 "In the beginning"; it tells us about what was there before the creation of the world that Genesis 1:1 describes to us. John tells us about pre-creation.

Pre-creation. It is not something we typically think or talk about as we discuss the beginning. Before the creation of the world—the physical universe—there is something real going on that forever shapes the meaning and implications of everything else that comes after! It is impossible to overstate this. Jesus Himself tells us about it.

JESUS TELLS US SO

Rarely in Scripture do we get the glorious opportunity given us in John 17, where God the Son spends deeply personal, intimate, and passion-filled time talking to God the Father. We are given the honor of eavesdropping on two members of the Holy Trinity in dialogue.

Think about all the conversations you could listen in on and what special, privileged information you might learn from them. What were the last words Martin Luther King spoke to his colleagues before he died on the balcony of the Lorraine Motel in Memphis that tragic morning? What did the Beatles say to each other the moment they privately decided they would break up? What did the 9/11 passengers say to one another in their last seconds of life? Who wouldn't want to know?

GET THE PICTURE

Andrea Mantegna, *The Agony in the Garden*
(c. 1459)
National Gallery, London
Visit familyproject.com to see this painting.

Mantegna, a North Italian Renaissance artist (1431–1506) influenced by Donatello, became an influence upon the great Albrecht Dürer. Mantegna created many wonderful depictions of biblical truths and stories. This painting portrays Jesus the evening before His death, fervently communing with His Father regarding the trial that awaits Him and His love for His disciples. While the arresting party approaches, His disciples are fast asleep. The painting is a lower panel in the San Zeno Altarpiece triptych created for the Basilica di San Zeno, the main church in Verona, Italy.

As amazing as any of these words would be to listen in on, none can compare to the grandeur of being able to listen in on God the Son talking to God the Father. But here it is in the 17th chapter of John, open for anyone who has ears to hear and take it in.

Take some time now, or soon, to slowly read John 17 reflectively in this light.

In this conversation, the Son makes two profound statements that many of us who've read this chapter can tend to glance over—with little appreciation of their significance for our understanding of the Christian worldview of pre-creation. They are nothing less than a foundational metaphysical statement—both theological and philosophical—providing the Christian understanding on what is at the core of the universe, that which is behind, under, and over all reality. They're an insight into what was and is beyond "In the beginning."

A Better Understanding:
What Is Metaphysics?

Metaphysics is a branch of philosophy that extends back before Aristotle, but he is considered the first major metaphysicist. This school of inquiry is concerned with the nature of ultimate reality: What is it that is really behind the curtain that makes all we see and experience go? What is the ultimate nature of reality?

Obviously, we can see how we are doing the work of metaphysics in this chapter and that Christianity has real and profound answers to these questions. When a child asks, "Who made the world?" she is doing so as a student of metaphysics.

In this prayer to the Father, Jesus the Son says two things of particular interest to us here:

And now, Father, glorify me in your own presence with the *glory* that I had with You before the world existed. . . .

And . . .

Father, I desire that they also, whom you have given me, may be with me where I am, to see my glory that you have given me because you *loved* me before the foundation of the world." (John 17:5, 24, emphasis added)

BEFORE THE FOUNDATION OF THE WORLD

Before Genesis 1:1, there was something tremendous going on. Reality wasn't static. It wasn't dark. It wasn't cold. It wasn't empty. The *world* was all those things, as Genesis 1 tells us. But John 1 tells us that ultimate reality was not. Before Genesis 1:1, there was glory. There was love.

J. I. Packer explains,

Before the Creation ever appeared, God who is both singular and plural, unique and triune, solitary and social, existed and rejoiced in love—the love of the Father for the Son and the Son for the Father, love in which the Holy Spirit was and is somehow agent, the issuer, and sharer, all in one.[2]

This truth is further supported in the first chapter of John's Gospel, which explains that the Son has lived "in the bosom of the Father" from all eternity (John 1:18, KJV), an astoundingly vivid and beautiful way of describing the extraordinary intimacy of Father and Son that mysteriously is the core and foundation for everything else.

To appreciate the dramatic intimacy of this phrase, imagine being at a party and asking someone sitting alone or with others on a couch if you could sit with them. They might be quite happy, even honored you want to join them.

But what if you asked instead, "Might I sit in your bosom?" Would this simply be a different way of asking the same thing? Uh . . . no. You would get a very different reaction and a pretty permanent reputation—and it wouldn't be good. That might be the last party you ever got invited to. But this is precisely why John explains it this way. He wants us to not miss that it's not just a partnership or friendship. It explains the inordinate uniqueness and intimacy of this divine and primary relationship between the Father and Son. It is so intimate that it might even be difficult for any of us to look upon, if we could.

GOD IS LOVE: WHAT THAT MEANS AND WHY IT MATTERS

C. S. Lewis in *Mere Christianity* makes this universe-changing observation:

> God is love, and that love works through men—especially through the whole community of Christians. But this spirit of love is, from all eternity, a love going on between the Father and Son.[3]

Consider carefully what this means. The origin and source of the universe and everything we know, see, experience, or discover comes from one single source. What is it? If we just say "God," we are not being precise enough. It comes from, through, and out of a Father eternally and powerfully loving His Son and a Son loving His Father.

Therefore, reality, the universe, is not an impersonal place without meaning. It is profoundly personal, intimate, and loving, as is the relationship between the divine Father and the divine Son. This is a reality that should give us inexhaustible hope and comfort. There is no other belief system that has such a profound thing to say about the nature of all reality. But this is exactly what Christianity holds as a basic belief, and Jesus told us about it.

And it therefore says something profound about us: We are made inexplicably out of and for these qualities, as we shall see.

GET THE PICTURE

Peter Paul Rubens, *The Trinity Adored by the Duke of Mantua and His Family* (1606) Private Collection
Visit familyproject.com to see this painting.

Rubens was a true master and tirelessly active Flemish Baroque and counter-Reformation painter working from Antwerp. This beautiful work was completed for a patron, presenting a portrait of his family worshiping the Holy Trinity, which occupies the top half of the painting. This is a very rare work in its portrayal of the Trinity, with the pre-incarnated, pre-crucified, pre-ascended Christ in communion with the Father and the Spirit.

THE TRINITY: AN INTRODUCTION

The Christian story does not just hold that the center of all reality is the intimacy of the Father and the Son, as remarkable as that is. The early church father Gregory of Nazianzus (329–390) taught that "When I say God, I mean Father, Son and Holy Spirit." The Christian God is unique. He is not solitary. He is not a couple. He is a divine community. He is one, but also more, a *koinonia* of three divine Persons.

As Eastern Orthodox bishop Kallistos Ware explains,

> The Doctrine of the Trinity is not an embarrassing complication, a piece of technical theologizing of no importance for our daily existence. It stands at the very heart of our Christian life.[4]

As well, the late British theologian Colin Gunton notes,

> The Trinity has more often been presented as a dogma to be believed rather than as a living focus of life and thought . . . Because the theology of the Trinity has so much to teach about the nature of our world and life within it, it is or could be the centre of Christianity's appeal to the unbeliever, as the good news of God who enters into free relations of creation and redemption with his world. In light of the theology of the Trinity, everything looks different.[5]

Because of the Trinity, everything looks different indeed! But how? First of all, as Bishop Ware explains,

> From all eternity the First Person addresses the Second: "Thou art My Beloved Son" (Mark 1:11). From all eternity

the Second replies to the First, "Abba, Father; Abba, Father" (Romans 8:15, Galatians 4:6). From all eternity the Holy Spirit, "who proceeds from the Father and rests upon the Son" set the seal upon this interchange of love.[6]

When we read 1 John 4:8, God explains Himself with a simple eloquence:

God is love.

Three simple but deeply profound words, bottomless in meaning and implication. Similar in richness to the three words the Church first and continuously proclaimed about Christ: Jesus is Lord. Immensity in simplicity.

Notice what these three words say and what they don't say.

They say God *is* love.

They don't say "God *likes* love," "God *prefers* to love," or "God *enjoys* love."

Love is not just something He *does*—as we do—but love is what He *is*. And God being love's solitary source, and each of us being created in His image, we therefore know of love—and desire and require it intensely whether we recognize its source or not. It is one of humanity's most essential universal needs. Love does not define God, but God—as the source of everything—defines love.

So why is God as Trinity essential to understanding God's nature and character?

This brings up a very important theological truth that we must appreciate. Love, due to its nature, requires at least two: a lover and a beloved. It cannot exist in isolation, can it? And this existence and exchange of love is originally between our Father and the Son. Their love was and is so intense and powerful that from eternity it has poured out through a third, the Person of the Holy Spirit. Some theologians describe the Holy Spirit as the divinely personified love that flows from the intimacy of the Father and the Son. C. S. Lewis explains it this way:

> What grows out of the joint life of the Father and Son is a real Person, is in fact the Third of the Three Persons who are God. This third Person is called . . . the Holy Ghost or the "Spirit" of God.[7]

Love cannot exist without community; this is God's very nature and therefore the nature of reality. Reflect on this a while.

WHAT ELSE HAPPENED BEFORE CREATION?

There is something else that tells us that while we came onto the scene on the sixth day of creation, we actually entered the story eons before this—all the way back in pre-creation. Do you know how this is?

As Jesus told us important things about pre-creation in John 17, we learn more about what was going on in pre-creation in other places in the New Testament, besides John 1. In addressing the Ephesian church, Paul opens his letter by reminding the Ephesian Christians:

> Blessed be the God and Father of our Lord Jesus Christ, who . . . chose us in him *before the foundation of the world*, that we should be holy and blameless before him. In love he predestined us for adoption through Jesus Christ, according to the purpose of his will, to the praise of his glorious grace, with which he has blessed us in the Beloved. (1:3–6, emphasis added)

Before the foundation of the world, it was God's pure pleasure to choose us for Himself. In and through the love of the Father, Son, and Holy Spirit, we were adopted as God's children, even before we were ever created or the world ever came to be. That is the nature of God's love for us. It is eternal. Think of that!

First Peter 1:19-21 tells us that we were ransomed from our bondage to sin and dead religion . . .

> with the precious blood of Christ, like that of a lamb with-out blemish or spot. *He was foreknown before the foundation of the world* but was made manifest in the last times for the sake of you who through him are believers in God, who raised him from the dead and gave him glory, so that your faith and hope are in God. (emphasis added)

God had provided for and secured our salvation even before we were created through the ever-existing Lamb of God.

Titus 1:2 says God's gift of the "hope of eternal life" was "prom-ised before the ages began." This should be mind-blowing to us.

Of these "before the foundation of the world" statements that speak about the preparation of our salvation, Francis Schaeffer observes,

> This is very striking. How can a promise be made before the world began? To whom could it be made? The Scripture speaks of a promise made by the Father to the Son or to the Holy Spirit because, after all, at this particular point of se-quence, there was no one else to make the promise to.[8]

Our lives and destiny were considered and provided for in pre-creation by the divine community, from their love and care. Second

Timothy 1:9 assures us that it is God "who saved us and called us to a holy calling, not because of our works but because of his own purpose and grace, which he gave us in Christ Jesus before the ages began."

Wow!

So, before the creation of the world and humanity, the story was not just about the divine Trinity. We were there as well—as bit players—in the thoughts, work, and preparation of the Father, through the Son, by the Holy Spirit. God's story—and ours—begins well before Genesis 1:1. Pre-creation is no small part of the story.

So this larger understanding of the nature of God—who He is as Trinity and before the foundation of the world—answers Gauguin's first question, "Where do we come from?"

We come from God, who is a community of love, passion, personality, and communion who has provided for our salvation.

The second question, "What are we?" is where we go now. Its answer is also found in God's First Definitive Statement.

What We Are

God's First Definitive Statement is perhaps the most important statement because it is God's first statement about who we are. God is very clear in telling us exactly what we are, and He does so right out of the gate. It's there in the first chapter, on the first page of His story to us.

To set this stage, we must see how the whole creative process starts.

From His very first words, God explains that His creative work is a work of distinctions: "In the beginning, God created the heavens and the earth," one thing being unique from and complementary to another. There is this, and there is that, and they both relate to and contrast with one another. As we will see, this point is very important. In this first sentence of Scripture, God has specified three distinctions. Can you tell what they are?

The easy one is the creation and distinction of the heavens and the earth. They are different from one another, but they are what make up our world. We live on the earth and look to the heavens. The next two are not as easy.

This second one is found in the two words, "God created." In these words, God is distinguishing Himself from His creation. God is here. Creation is there. This sets Christianity and Judaism apart from pantheistic religions, which hold the worldview that God is made up of everything that makes up the cosmos, and everything together in the cosmos makes up God. Christianity and Judaism do not teach this. God is distinct from and rules *over* His creation.

The third distinction is actually so obvious, it is overlooked. It is the distinction between nothing and something. This is what the first verses of Genesis are telling us. Once there was nothing in creation. Then there was something. This is key because it explains for us that something could indeed come from nothing—God creating *ex nihilo*—and how it happened. Only God can do this, and He did.

So let's look at the creation story in Genesis 1 as a whole and appreciate the distinctions that God has created on each day of His work:

Day 1: Light and darkness, day and night, evening and morning

Day 2: Heavens and Earth, sky and Earth

Day 3: Land and sea; plants yielding seed and trees yielding fruit

Day 4: Greater light by day, lesser light by night

Day 5: Creatures of the sea, creatures of the sky

Day 6: Creatures of the land, and then . . .

What comes next is the answer to our "What are we?" question.

It is here that we see a turn in God's creative work. Up to this point in the creation process, God says it's so, and there you have it; it's so. Let there be light, and there's light. Let there be the cypress trees, seagulls, earthworms, mountains . . . and there they are. God speaks. It appears.

But when we get to God's description of His last piece of creative work on this last day of creation, we find something new in His creative declaration. It is here in our First Definitive Statement in Genesis 1:26:

> Then God said, "Let us make man in our image, after our likeness."

In contrast to God's speak-and-there-it-is process up to now, here we have something altogether different. God, for the first time, announces His intention before He acts. It's curious, but no small detail. It is almost as if the divine unity of the Trinity is both contemplating and announcing what will come next. This happens with no other part of creation. Let's look at what others, wiser in such things, say about this curious turn.

John Calvin, in his commentary on Genesis, says of this unique, God-spoken declaration,

> This is the language of one apparently deliberating. Hitherto God has been introduced simply as *commanding*; now, when he approaches the most excellent of all his works, he enters into *consultation* . . . [in] the plurality of the Persons in the Godhead.[9]

John Wesley makes a similar observation of this change in God's creative labors in his own commentary on Genesis:

> But now the word of command [in the rest of creation] is turned into a word of consultation.[10]

This moment in creation has a more personal, internal, reflective, or contemplative feel to it, doesn't it? Another very special kind of distinctness. But let's look more closely at what is happening here.

IMAGO DEI

This thing that God calls "man" will provide all of creation a visible, physical picture of the invisible and transcendent God.

Imagine that!

There are four very key words in this First Definitive Statement of God's, "Let us make man in our image, after our likeness."

The first two are related: "us" and "our," words of a plurality of Persons. The Trinity. The second two are related to each other as well as the first two: "image" and "likeness."

The English word "image" here comes from the Hebrew word *tselem*, which should put into our mind's eye the thought of a chiseled, crafted statue formed with the purpose of giving the viewer an idea of something larger and greater. Look at Michelangelo's *David*. That is not the actual David of Scripture. We know that. But it is a grand image the artist has created that points to him, showing us what he was like. It is something that unmistakably represents and points the viewer toward another greater thing.

The eminent scholar Leon Kass explains in his book on Genesis, written from the perspective of an observant Jew,

> Any image insofar as it is an image, has a most peculiar
> manner of being: it both is and is not what it resembles.
> The image of my granddaughter that smiles at me out of the
> picture frame on my desk is my granddaughter—not yours.
> But it is not really she—just a mere image.[11]

And the image itself has real meaning, a special value, doesn't it? Consider what Professor Kass's response would be if you took the picture of his granddaughter and tore it to bits on a whim. Anyone would take such an action as very hurtful and insulting. Now, suppose that Kass had, for some curious reason, a picture of his lawn chair on his desk, and you took *this* and tore it to shreds. He wouldn't be angry with you per se. He would just think you were nuts. And you might think the same of him for having such a picture prominently displayed on his desk. It's an image of something that doesn't really matter that much. The picture of his granddaughter is very different. Two pictures, the same action, very different responses.

Images matter because they convey meaning and value about the things they represent. This is certainly true about what this divine-image-bearing "man" will be and why God is offended at his destruction.

The English word "likeness" is similar but different from "image," as it comes from the Hebrew word *demuth*, which refers to something that literally resembles another. Think of a small-scale replica or model of a city or an amusement park. You can immediately see what it is supposed to be. And it is fascinating to look at, for it gives us detailed information and makes us curious to see its full-sized counterpart. That is why people like to build models and others like to look at them. A model is not the thing, but it resembles and thus tells us about the thing.

Now pretend we are reading this story for the first time and don't know what this God-image-bearing part of creation will be. We are eager to find out what will serve this important and singular place in creation. To get inside this drama, let's pretend that we can be any part of creation up to this point that we choose. Which part of the natural world are you?

We're going to be a beautiful, sleek, speckled sea trout and a great brown grizzly bear with crazy, six-inch claws. You pick what you want to be, and let's imagine our setting.

So here we are, midway through Day 6 of creation. We are nothing less than amazed at all the beautiful stuff that God has created and made us part of.

Look at that Great Barrier Reef, the Florida Keys, the beautiful columbine flower from the Rocky Mountains, the great African elephant, lightning strikes in the late evening, windblown deserts of the Middle East, blue-green algae, Victoria Falls.

Over there we see the sunset setting the sky ablaze; towering sequoias; waving wheat; white, billowing clouds that look like massive puffs of cotton candy. Look at those playful and beautiful rainbow dolphins up ahead.

The most eloquent words cannot even approach justice in describing all the wonder and beauty before us. We are breathless.

And in the midst of all this beauty, God ups the stakes—proclaiming He is going to now bring forth something unique, something that is even more profound, a picture or image of the magnificent and unceasing God who created all of this!

Wow, what created thing—as a physical representation of the invisible God of the universe—could do justice to what it represents? We all, as our pretend parts of creation, must be on the edge of our seats in delirious anticipation of what this next creation will be. It's going to have to be remarkable.

Well, it doesn't take long to find out what created thing will accomplish this divine task. God explains directly and plainly in the very next verse:

> So God created man in his own image, in the image of God he created him; male and female he created them. (Genesis 1:27)

So there they are, these two curious beings that show forth our God's image in the world, humanity in two models. They are both wonderful, but what are these creatures and what are they about?

GET THE PICTURE

Albrecht Dürer, *Adam and Eve* (1507)
Museo Nacional del Prado, Madrid
Visit familyproject.com to see this painting.

Albrecht Dürer was a German artist and one of the most talented of the Northern Renaissance painters. He did woodcuts, portraits, biblical scenes, and beautiful zoology paintings; the most celebrated and beautiful is his watercolor *Young Hare* (1502), demonstrating amazing technique. Dürer, a Roman Catholic, was at the center of the Reformation. In a 1520 diary entry, he wrote, "And God help me that I may go to Dr. Martin Luther; thus I intend to make a portrait of him with great care and engrave him on a copper plate to create a lasting memorial of the Christian man who helped me overcome so many difficulties." And he did, creating one of the best-known and enduring portraits of Luther.

Get a good look at them. Do they look familiar, like anyone you might know?

They are us. If you look anything like either of these creations, then you can know that you stand in significant contrast to all the other glorious parts of creation. And you do so in a most significant way, in fact the most profound way that one part of creation can be distinct from another. There is only one part of creation that can say three profound things:

1. "We are created to reflect and show forth who the invisible and divine Trinitarian God is in the world."
2. "In the Son's incarnation, there is a being like us who is also God."
3. "We have been given the invitation to become and be called the children of God."

The animals cannot say this. The mountains cannot say this. The beaches of the world cannot say this. Even the glorious angels cannot say this. Think about that! God is telling us that we—you, us, and every other person we share this world with—are more like God than we are like the rest of the creation.

This is only true of humans, each one of us.

John Wesley brings important and beautiful insight to this fact that we don't readily appreciate:

Man was to be a creature different from all that had been hitherto made. Flesh and spirit, heaven and earth must be put together in him, and he must be allied to both worlds. . . . Man is a little world, consisting of heaven and earth, soul and body. . . . the visible image of the Creator's glory.

Wesley continues:

And therefore God himself not only undertakes to make, *but is pleased so to express himself,* as if he called a council to consider of the making of him; Let us make man—The three persons of the Trinity, Father, Son, and Holy Ghost, consult about it, and concur in it; because man, when he was made, was to be dedicated and devoted to Father, Son and Holy Ghost.[12] (emphasis added)

Curiosity Point:
The Pioneer 10 and 11 Plaques

NASA placed very interesting six-by-nine-inch plates on both the early 1970s Pioneer 10 and 11 spacecraft. They were placed there in case either ship was intercepted by extraterrestrial life, in order to explain pictorially where the craft came from and who sent it. The plaques have many technical symbols and figures to explain where in the universe these missile-launching creatures live. And it has two interesting creatures presented on it. These primary figures on the plaque are not just two creatures, or even just humans—but a male and a female, the two kinds of humans the extraterrestrials would find if they were to visit our planet. And they would be welcome, judging by the inviting hand of the man who is depicted.

It is very significant that one of the most sophisticated efforts of science would present to the galaxy essentially what God presented to the galaxy on Day 6 of creation in order to reveal that which shows forth His image in the universe. It shows that these are the only two kinds of humans there are.

The plaques can be seen at familyproject.com.

Luther in his commentary on Genesis offers an important insight as well:

> Likewise, man is created according to the similitude of God; that is, the intellect is enlightened by faith, the memory is made confident through hope and steadfastness and the will is adorned with love.[13]

And given this bold description of who we are as humans, we must notice that this is the first thing the Scriptures say about us. When we introduce a speaker to an audience, don't we mention the most important and interesting things about him or her? This is precisely what God is doing with us in His First Definitive Statement: All human beings are special because each is a unique statue or picture of God in the world, distinct from every other human.

Physical icons of the invisible God.

This is no more or no less than what you are, and it's really the most profound statement about what it means to be human in all of literature. So, given this remarkable news in the creation story, we learn that we are like God, but not God! We did not conceive of or make ourselves or our world. We do not control our own destinies. We do not direct the motions of the earth. We are limited as parts of creation. But we are not nothing.

Theologians call humans the *Imago Dei* (E-mahg-O-day), for this is what it means: bearers of the image of God.

Of this, Francis Schaeffer correctly notes,

> For the [post-modern] man, this phrase, image of God, is as important as anything in scripture, because men today can no longer answer that crucial question, "Who am I?" . . . If anything is a gift of God, this is it—knowing who you are![14]

Indeed it is. It is what Gauguin and so many others have so painfully wrestled with—and, of course, found no reliable answers beyond what God has revealed to every person. And this is what God has given us in His love and grace toward us.

It is true of each and every man and woman—the man who collects your garbage as well as the woman who serves as mayor of your town. It is true of the folks who clean your bathrooms at work as well as the man who heads the largest corporation in your city. It is true of the person you disagree with politically. It is true of the person you love to spend time with as well as that other person over there who can irritate you to no end. It is true of "those" people from "that" country! It is true of the young and the old, the attractive and the unsightly, the talented and the feeble, the sick and healthy, the clean and the smelly.

Therefore, we must treat each person we meet with kindness, patience, and dignity. This is not a choice but a necessity because of what each person is. It is why those in Christian nations—or even post-Christian nations—tend to protect life, resist tyranny and oppression, and promote the dignity of all as much as possible.

It is one of the things that make Christianity and Judaism remarkably culturally and historically revolutionary faiths, for they call all people to care for and seek the well-being of others. It is not human nature to do this, but the personal and cultural influence that Christianity and its predecessor have had across the world is to take root in the hearts of people—dramatically changing the way each of us and our culture treat them.

As our First Definitive Statement declares, we are created from the divine union of the Trinity to exclusively bear the image and likeness of the Trinity in the world. No other philosophy or faith holds such a grand view and understanding of humanity. It is the foundational power of our story.

Francis Schaeffer captures the deep implications of this for our day: "The whole conception is rooted in the reality of the Trinity. Without the Trinity, Christianity would not have the answers that modern man needs."[15] This is indeed true if we fully appreciate these bigger implications of who our God is. Humans naturally ask big questions, and Christianity has very big answers.

When I (Glenn) started being interested in finding answers to these questions in light of an understanding of God specifically as Trinity, it blew my mind and soul to see how much larger and more robust it made our Christian faith. As a philosophy student in graduate school, I had made an in-depth study of how the various philosophies and religions of the world throughout history sought to make sense of man's largest questions. Having been a Christian for more than 10 years at that point, I had a strong enough understanding of my faith to be able to hang on to it robustly while at the secular university studying under contentious professors and with fellow classmates. But it was not until I started really understanding what it means that God is Trinity that I gained a much greater appreciation for how meaningfully Christianity answers these questions than is typically understood by both critics and adherents of this remarkable faith. It is so much more than an ancient theological mystery.

Christianity is a wonderful, simultaneously simple and complex faith. These strengths are found in its answers to the questions we all ask. *What are we?* and *Where did we come from?* We must look to the Trinity. *What is God's heart toward us?* We must look to the answer Karl Barth gave those learned seminary students: "Jesus loves me, this I know."

Who we are and where we came from beautifully illuminate God's Second Definitive Statement about humanity, which is where we go next.

THE BIG STATEMENT FOR REFLECTION

Every human is created in the image of God as a "picture" or "statue" of Him in the world; we reflect Him in a unique way that no other person has, does, or ever will. And the God we image is a divine community, a holy society. Each person therefore has the honor and dignity of being God's masterpiece, the only part of creation that bears God's image. This is where we come from, and it is what we are. And we understand this based both on the nature of pre-creation and creation, which is inherently loving and personal.

QUESTIONS FOR CONSIDERATION

1. How does the fact that our salvation was on God's mind and secured for us before the foundation of the world matter to the Christian story—to your story? How does that affect your own faith?

2. Some of the early fathers of the church explained that given that we are uniquely created in the image of God, we are therefore more like God than we are like the rest of creation. What do you think about such a statement?

3. What does it mean that the human body—in male and female versions—is created to show forth the likeness and image of the invisible God in the created world? How should we then view the physicality of the human body? Is it fundamentally good or bad?

4. Do you see your family members as "image-bearers" of God? How might this perspective—if it were ever-present in your mind and heart—change the way you think about them, interact with them, care for them, and love them?

Part II

REVEALED, RAVAGED, AND REDEEMED

We have now come to a very important point in our exploration, approaching the crest of this majestic mountain we have been climbing. From the introduction, we have ascended to this point that we're now approaching in Chapter 3. Every step has been leading us to this pinnacle. It brings together all we have learned so far and establishes both our footing and our view of everything else we'll experience in our expedition beyond.

It is not that everything will be downhill from there. But the distance we've traveled to now has brought us, chapter by chapter, to this approach of the summit that will then lead us along the heights we have achieved and along the spine of the mountain range that will appear before us, as shown in the graph on the next page.

Here are the major steps we've taken to get where we are:

- We are naturally question-asking beings. We don't need to be taught to do it.
- We all must have a meaningful sense of significance and intimacy with others.
- We live by stories, which is why Jesus told stories so often in His teachings. And we live in a story.
- We ask three key questions: *Where do we come from? What are we? Where are we going?*
- We embrace a fuller Christian worldview: pre-creation, creation, fall, incarnation, redemption, ascension, consummation.
- We are made with great love and intentionality to be the only part of creation that is the image and likeness of God in the world—one God in three divine Persons.

Now we go to our next step: how God completes the masterpiece of humanity, and in doing so creates the family, a group dynamic that uniquely completes the divine image of God in us and to us.

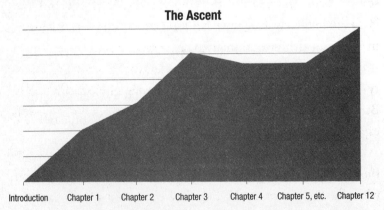

The Ascent

Introduction   Chapter 1   Chapter 2   Chapter 3   Chapter 4   Chapter 5, etc.   Chapter 12

It Is Not Good to Be Alone: How Family Completes the *Imago Dei*

There was no one like Emperor Frederick II, by most accounts the greatest in a long history of great Roman emperors. He was referred to by many as a "wonder of the world" and by others, the world's "astonishment." Not only a wicked-smart and cunning politician, he was a strong supporter of scientific advancement and the arts in early thirteenth-century Europe. He spoke six languages fluently, wrote poetry, played musical instruments, and composed many songs. A contemporary of the emperor described him this way: "Of faith in God he had none; he was crafty, wily, avaricious, lustful, malicious, wrathful; and yet a gallant man at times."

Disturbing in behavior and temperament, he once had a notary's thumb cut off for getting one letter wrong in spelling his name. But he is perhaps best known in history for his curious scientific experiments.

Salimbene, an Italian Franciscan and careful historian of the time, explained that Fredrick doubted a man's soul left his body when he died. So to test his belief, he entombed a living man in a secured casket, save only for a small hole drilled in its cover. He had attendants wait and watch for the man's life to slip away and then observe if his soul did indeed rise through the hole and up to the heavens. Care to guess his conclusion? Yes—irrefutable scientific proof that there is no rising of the soul after death, for none was seen. There seemed to be an obvious oversight in his assumption about the nature of souls.

Another experiment had to do, curiously, with digestion. Salimbene tells us Fredrick "fed two men most excellently at dinner." After the feast, he ordered one man to take a nap, the other to go on a hunting expedition. He wanted to find out whether post-meal rest or activity better aided digestion. How could he measure the progress, or lack thereof, that each would make? Well, nothing was as precise as actual observation, so he had the two men disemboweled later that night in his presence. Salimbene reports that "it was judged by the physicians in favour of him who had slept." So there you have it.

But his most noted experiment touches dramatically on our topic in this chapter. Fredrick wanted to find out what the "natural" human language was, that which Adam and Eve spoke. Was it Hebrew, Latin, Greek, or some other language? So he gathered a group of newborns who would be raised from birth without any kind of verbal interaction whatsoever. They would be bathed, fed, changed, and otherwise cared for, but not interacted with in other ways, verbally or otherwise. They would not even hear others talk amongst themselves, but be raised in absolute human silence. Salimbene said of this unique experiment that Fredrick "labored in vain because the children all died," since "they could not live without the petting and joyful faces and loving words of their foster mothers."[1] Such tragic experiences have been seen in certain orphanages around the world where children are physically cared for but never actually engaged emotionally, physically, or visually. Their hearts remain beating, but their minds and spirits don't develop. They no longer cry; they rock themselves and have a catatonic gaze to them.

Indeed, humans need intimacy as much as they need food, water, shelter, and protection. If all these others are provided, but intimacy is lacking, the young will likely die—just as if they were deprived of all the other necessities for life. Adults who are deprived of intimate interaction tend to go crazy, literally.

And this human developmental reality is spoken of by God. Do you know where He says such a thing?

This Can't Be Good

We just examined in great detail God's First Definitive Statement found in Genesis 1:26. It is the first and most consequential thing that God says about humanity:

> Then God said, "Let us make man in our image, after our likeness."

While this declaration speaks dramatically to who and what we are as humans, God's second declaration is the second most profound and consequential statement about what it means to be human. As such, it speaks as well to Gauguin's second question: *What are we?*

In fact, it is not only the second most profound statement in Scripture about us, but all the other ideas anyone has ever had about the nature of being human are secondary to this truth. It speaks to man's most fundamental problem.

Do you know what that might be? Most would say it's the Fall and the entry of sin and death into the world. Yes, this is a devastating,

all-affecting event in human history—and we address the serious-
ness of this in Chapter 5. But this is not man's *first* problem. That
revealed itself prior to the Fall.

It's the first thing that God says is not good in His creation. We
find it in the second chapter of Genesis, the second account of God's
creation of man. It announces the most fundamental problem of
being human and is basic to an adequate theological anthropology:

> Then the LORD God said, "It is not good for the man to be
> alone." (Verse 18, NIV)

Better Understanding: What's a Christian Anthropology and Why Does It Matter?

Is there such a thing as a Christian anthropology? Is it Christians studying anthropology? Is it looking anthropologically at
Christian practices, beliefs, and culture, as we might study the
anthropology of a primitive culture?

Well, not quite. A Christian or theological anthropology is
something every Christian must have. It is essentially an understanding of what it means to be human: why we do what
we do, are what we are, and desire the things we desire. It is
the Christian's answer to Gauguin's second question: "What
are we?"

In fact, the subtitle of this book and *The Family Project*
as a whole could be *A Christian Anthropology*, for this is exactly what it explores and seeks to know. What is it that God
created humans to be and do? The answers we find for this
question make up our Christian anthropology.

We typically don't spend much time contemplating the meaning and richness of this statement from God, for it seems to just set up the last part of God's creative process. But it does much, much more than that.

ORIGINAL SOLITUDE

Genesis 2:18 is God's Second Definitive Statement, and we are going to investigate the significance of it in this chapter. Three key phrases in this statement deserve our attention:

1. *"The LORD God said . . ."* Because God said it, we know it's true, trustworthy, and meaningful.
2. *"It is not good . . ."* There is something very powerful, profound, and really troubling in this statement. God says something is not good in His creation. Stop and think about that.

Let's set the scene for this statement so we can really understand what's going on:

- God has created Adam from the dust of the ground and breathed into his nostrils the breath of life. That seems really, really good. Could we say even *great*? Adam is certainly a carbon-based life-form, but so much more than that.
- Eve has not been created yet. It is only Adam with God.

But God says something is not good in this picture. What could not be good?

- Adam has a beautiful home in the garden God made wonderfully for him.
- Adam has greater intimacy with and access to God than any other human since Adam, save for Christ.

Who wouldn't be totally satisfied with that? But amazingly, God says it is not good. This is indeed a profound statement.

So, what's not good? We are told in this last key phrase:

3. *". . . for the man to be alone."* We must see and think about this as the fundamental problem of man. We are not made to be alone. And this does not mean that only Adam, the male, is not to be alone. Major players on each side of the Reformation explain this.

John Calvin comments,

But although God pronounced, concerning Adam, that it would not be profitable for him to be alone, yet I do not restrict the declaration to his person alone, but rather regard it as a common law of man's vocation, so that everyone ought to receive it as said to himself, that solitude is not good.[2]

And Pope John Paul II explains:

The complete context of this solitude, about which Genesis 2:18 speaks, can convince us that here we are dealing with the solitude of "man" (male and female) and not only the solitude of the man-male, caused by the absence of the woman.[3]

LONELINESS IS DESTRUCTIVE

Isolation is not a natural state for man. Now, of course, sometimes it is nice and necessary to get away by ourselves. When we speak of isolation or aloneness here, we are not talking about getting away for the weekend for a solitary hike through the mountains or curling up alone with a good book. Jesus Himself regularly got away by Himself. We must all "get away" from time to time. We cannot isolate ourselves, though, and remain healthy.

Consider the remarkable story of Christopher McCandless that is told in the book and film *Out of the Wild*. In the early 1990s, this young man from a well-to-do family in the United States decided after college to give all of his money away to charity, hop in his old beater of a car, and head off into the world by himself—leaving all of his possessions, family, and friends behind.

Traveling the country, he finally made it to his destination, the desolate wilds of Alaska. He had long desired to head out into the wilderness and make a life for himself—all by himself—wanting no contact anymore with anyone. His dream only lasted about four months, when he realized that the romanticism of life alone in the wild was deceptive. Nature was not his friend; it was uncooperative and it wanted him dead. He realized—while reading *Dr. Zhivago*—that no human can survive such isolation, even if he could provide food and shelter for himself. True happiness, he came to learn, is experienced only in relationship with others. He decided to head back to his old life, to people.

But the harshness of winter had set upon him and his part of the world. He was trapped by a now-raging river which was, when he arrived in the spring, easily passable. It was impossible now. So he had to settle for the winter back into the old, abandoned bus he had been living in. Through a series of unfortunate circumstances and unwise choices, his life painfully and tragically ended in that bus due to cold and sickness leading to starvation. His diary, the companion he kept right up to the end, revealed that his last thoughts were of his family.

Isolation is a most devastating force. And this is humanly universal.

Consider as well what we do with the most heartless, depraved criminal: put him in prison for life, perhaps even on death row. But if he continues to act in "unsociable" ways, what do we do with him? Solitary confinement. All prisons everywhere do this because they know it's not good for man to be alone. No person, even the most psychologically deranged, can whistle through solitary. It will undo even the most soulless, hardened criminal.

Penitentiaries, which were originally very different from general prisons, were founded with the Christian goal of helping criminals come to terms with their evil deeds and sins, to help them become penitent. Each prisoner was placed alone for long periods of time in a small, bare cell. All he had was four walls and a window in the ceiling of his cell, giving him a view only to the heavens above so he could think about nothing but the sins that put him there—and God, who alone could save him.

Such an experience was expected to bring an inmate to a right state of mind, becoming penitent for his sins and dependent on the grace and correction of God. But guess what? This arrangement only made the prisoners more savage . . . or dead. Wardens and psychologists came to realize that this isolation had a torturous effect on these prisoners, turning them more into angry animals than repentant human beings—because this is what isolation does to a person. They discovered it was not good for man to be alone. This practice was abandoned, even though the name "penitentiary" stuck and is still used generally for large prisons.[4]

Consider something more common to all of us. It's your first day at a new school. You know no one, and of course you're anxious. You have your lunch and are looking for a table. You see some kids who look interesting and go over to see if you can sit with them. As you approach, they all spread out, taking up any free space, and tell you, "These places are taken." Snubbed!

How does this make you feel? And this is not simply because you've been raised in a culture that taught you such experiences should make you feel bad. It's deep within each of us the world over. And it is not just because *today* you don't have a place to sit, is it? It's not about loneliness but rejection, alienation, emotional isolation. This is an important difference.

We all deal with loneliness, for it is a normal part of life. God's statement about being alone is more about a deeper kind of isolation, a deeper, more permanent solitude. Loneliness hurts. Isolation can either kill or drive us mad.

Now, let's set the same scene in a different way. You're looking for a table to join, and some kids wave you over. You approach them, perhaps cautiously, and one says, "Hey, you're new here, aren't you? The first day here can be a bit frightening. Would you like to sit with us?" Does this situation create a different kind of feeling? Your heart both jumps with happiness and then settles in the comfort and affirmation of their welcoming. This is a humanly universal reaction also.

- Isolation—alienation, exclusion, abandonment—is a universal poison to humans.
- Intimacy—acceptance, invitation, inclusion—is a universal tonic to humans.

Both are powerful beyond understanding, but in very different ways.

DID GOD MAKE A MISTAKE?

If it is not good for man to be alone, we might we ask, "Well, who's responsible for that? Who created him that way? Did God make a mistake?"

That would be the wrong question, though. It's not that God made a mistake but that He desires to teach us something about how He made us, about our anthropology. There are two key lessons here, and the first might seem heretical.

First, God declares that Adam is alone. But is he really? *Who was it that just told him he was alone?*

That would be God. So in a very significant way, Adam is not technically alone, is he? If Adam were super-spiritual, he would respond, "But God, I'm not alone. I have You. And You are all I need!" But there's no use in trying to be more "spiritual" than God. (That's what the Pharisees were all about!)

God is not confused here; it's as if He's saying, "Adam, given the way that I made you, in My image, you need another." So what is God's answer to this primary problem?

God gives Adam a job to do: Name all the animals. This was important work, because to name something is to give it meaning, isn't it? What is the first thing we do when we meet people? We give them our name, another human universal. This is not just habit, but giving others our name is welcoming them in getting to know us. It is the first step in getting to know "who we are." And when we meet them again, it is special to us when they remember our name, isn't it? We know we matter to them.

Consider as well having a mysterious ailment that causes you pain every day and saps your energy and joy. Every doctor you have seen has no idea what's causing your illness. But you finally get to the right specialist, and he tells you your condition is called "something-or-other-itis." He hasn't given you the cure yet, but just the fact that he knows it has a name is tremendously encouraging to you. You feel like a new, hopeful person, just knowing this. You feel understood and validated.

When people tease us, we say they are "calling us names." And we try to convince ourselves that the childhood ditty "names will never hurt me" is true, but it isn't. It hurts all who experience it. This shows us the power of names and naming things.

But did God really think naming the animals would solve Adam's aloneness problem? Of course not. The animals were not duct tape to Adam's problem, a cheap emergency fix. In fact, it is not unfounded to think that God had Adam name the animals so that Adam could recognize something important about himself in noticing something interesting about them. They have mates, and Adam does not. And these mates are very much like each other. But where's Adam's mate, this other that is just like him, but different? It does not take him long to realize it's not good for him to be alone. Precisely!

Curiosity Point: Who Is in the Center of the Sistine Chapel?

Art history quiz: What is the painting at the center of the Sistine Chapel's ceiling? Most would guess that very famous one, *The Creation of Adam*. Well, they would be wrong.

In the very center of this very important chapel, housed in this place called the Vatican—a major center of Christian history and experience that many naysayers claim is all controlled by male power and dominance—is this central painting.

What is this a picture of? The creation of Eve.

She is the center of the story that Michelangelo is telling across this famous ceiling, the story of divine history from creation to the flood and the shameful drunkenness of Noah.

We must know—and be able to explain to critics of Christianity who claim that it is an anti-woman faith—that it is extremely *pro*-woman. Remarkably so!

Scripture teaches us this, in that Eve was the answer to humanity's original problem, and that she is a unique image-bearer of God in the world. God chose for His own Son to leave heaven and enter our realm through the most intimate "woman-ness" of a very real, historic, flesh-and-blood woman. Women are central to Christianity in very powerful and consequential ways.

You see, this Second Definitive Statement is not just the lead-up to the creation of the other created human that we read about in Genesis 2. It is a fundamentally important statement in itself—a statement about what it means to be human. And as we shall see, it has enormous implications for who we are, where we come from, and what we must have in order to live physically, spiritually, and emotionally. Well, God is going to provide the solution to humanity's original problem by bringing out of Adam—out of his very side—something new and unique. What is it?

It's not an *it*. It's something the world has never seen. It's a *she*.

WHY SHE'S THE ANSWER

God's answer to this original human problem is not a buddy for Adam—someone to hang with, a fishing pal. God's answer to our primary human dilemma is explained in Genesis 2:

> So the LORD God caused a deep sleep to fall upon the man,
> and while he slept took one of his ribs and closed up its
> place with flesh. And the rib that the LORD God had taken
> from the man he made into a woman and brought her to
> the man. (Verses 21-22)

She, being suitable for Adam, is given by God because she is precisely what Adam has needed. As a distinct, feminine God-imager, Eve is Adam's answer, and she is his—because she is a human person, the same as Adam but importantly different.

She is female, woman.

This gives meaning and purpose to Adam's maleness. She completes him. He completes her. God takes her hand in His and introduces her to Adam. He is very excited about God's answer to the problem of his solitude. He doesn't need to be told that she is special and warm up to her. His response—the first human words recorded in Scripture—is joyful and immediate:

GET THE PICTURE

Three mosaics (1174 and 1267)
Adam Entering Eden
Creation of Eve
Adam and Eve Being Introduced by God
Cathedral of Monreale, Polermo, Sicily
Visit familyproject.com to see these mosaics.

The magnificent Cathedral of Monreale in Sicily, built in the late 1100s, is arrayed in its entire interior with astounding Byzantine mosaics of biblical and holy scenes. The first image presents what we are learning now—that man was created as a solitary being—in *Adam Entering Eden*. This was "not good," so in *Creation of Eve*, the viewer gets to see where Eve comes from and who it is that brings her forth.

Finally, we see God taking this amazing creature by the hand and bringing her to the man as his completion. Adam is raising his arm as if preparing to exclaim, "There she is, bone of my bone, flesh of my flesh." These works are amazing sermons to us, housed in one of Italy's greatest national treasures and perhaps most finely decorated building.

Then the man said, "This at last is bone of my bones and
flesh of my flesh; she shall be called Woman, because she
was taken out of Man." (Verse 23)

Notice something interesting here. God does not correct Adam
for his "carnalness" as he notices her physicality, her distinct and
beautiful body. He is glad Adam gets it, for He wants him to. But
also, Eve is his equal, right by his side, figuratively and literally. She
is his mate; she is human. They are both made to rule over creation
together and solve each other's problem of original solitude. And
this matters more than you might imagine.

Are you female? Then this is what you are, a uniquely feminine
divine image-bearer. Never let anyone diminish who you are as a
girl or a woman. Your femininity means something divinely and
inexhaustibly profound! Eve is woman, not just in her spirit, her
psyche, or soul, but in her flesh as a distinct, embodied God-imager.

Are you a male? Then that is who you are, a uniquely mas-
culine divine image-bearer. You cannot allow anyone to diminish
who you are as a boy or a man. Your masculinity means something
inexplicably extraordinary. As parents of little boys and little girls,
it is our job to teach our children how much this means, because
of whose image we bear, which is explained in Glenn's book, *Secure
Daughters, Confident Sons.*[5]

This is what we are told clearly and boldly by God in Genesis 1:27:

So God created man in his own image, in the image of God
he created him; male and female he created them.

There is no greater statement of what it means to be both
human and gendered in all of literature. And the importance of

what it means to be male and female is a foundational part of God's story to us.

Now, in God's presentation of the one human to the other, He does it through their bodies. Adam takes note of Eve physically with excitement and joy, not to God's rebuke, but to His delight. These are the first recorded words of humanity, and they are about this creation called "woman" and her woman-ness:

> This at last is bone of my bones and flesh of my flesh.
> (Genesis 2:23)

Our bodies, male or female, are statements we and God make to ourselves, to each other, and to the rest of creation about who we are. Our bodies matter; God is saying something profound to us though our bodies, as we see in the creation story. Christians are not gnostics who believe the body is evil. As God's children, we embrace, celebrate, and cherish what God has taken great joy to create and to give us. In fact, as John Paul II explained,

> We can deduce that man became the image of God not
> only through his own humanity, but also through the com-
> munion of persons, which man and woman form right
> from the beginning. . . . Man becomes an image of God
> not so much in the moment of solitude as in the moment
> of communion. This is obviously not without significance
> for the theology of the body, but constitutes perhaps the
> deepest theological aspect of everything one can say about
> man.

Indeed it does. He continues,

The body, in fact, and only the body, is capable of making visible what is invisible: the spiritual and the divine. It has been created to transfer into the visible reality of the world the mystery hidden from eternity in God, and thus to be a sign of it.[6]

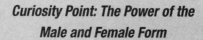

Curiosity Point: The Power of the Male and Female Form

We must consider what theologians call "embodiment," the fact that humans are not just souls or minds but bodies also—a trinity of key essences of what it means to be human. Our bodies, our physical flesh, bones, and organs are a key part of who we are. And our bodies make two primary communications about us to even the dullest observer. They come in two models: male and female. They are unmistakably different and distinct. No one needs this explained. But we must also understand that in this physicality, these bodies have great power—not just as humans, even though our bodies are the physical picture of the invisible God in the world, but as male and female bodies.

Often we have difficulty seeing unclothed male and female images in classic art. This is natural but happens because there is a tremendous power and meaning to the male and female physical form. We don't get that feeling when we see images of male and female ducks, horses, dogs, or cockatoos. As wonderful as these creatures are, they don't possess the visual, physical, and even divine power that male and female humans do. They are consequential figures because they both mysteriously image God in the world. Our Christian anthropology tells us so.

And we must appreciate that now, at Eve's appearance, Adam's nature now makes sense physically, emotionally, psychologically; before now he was a physical oddity. He couldn't really be "male" without her. And that is certainly not just about sex, because maleness is so much more. She gives definition, meaning, and purpose to the fullness of his maleness. And he gives definition, meaning, and purpose to her femaleness. This is captured in what the phrase "helper" or "helpmeet" used in Genesis 2:18 means.

The Hebrew is `ezer kenegdo`, which the noted Hebrew scholar Robert Alter tells us "is notoriously difficult to translate" into English. It essentially means one who actively intervenes on behalf of another, to assist by coming alongside, to support as a counterpart.[7] Of course, it's not a precise illustration, but think of the wings of a plane. The plane requires two wings to work as counterparts, but not two identical wings. If the manufacturer sent the assembly crew two left wings, they would have big problems, requiring them to return one of the wings. Both must be designed and shaped so that they correctly work alongside each other in cooperation and contrast. They are very similar but also importantly unique and different. And either wing by itself is really meaningless, isn't it? So the meaning of this term "helpmate" does not mean that Eve is Adam's "little assistant" any more than one wing of a plane would be the "helper" of the second. They help each other do what they do but do so in their unique and essential design.

Art Study: Michelangelo's Creation of Adam

One of the most famous images in all of art history, and certainly the art of Christianity, is Michelangelo's *Creation of Adam*. Nearly anyone can tell you what this painting is, usually saying something along the lines of, "Isn't that the painting where those two fingers are touching?" Of course it is, and it is the image of God's hand touching Adam's in His creation of Adam. And of course we see the focus of the painting being the touching fingers.

But if this is all we really see, we miss something very powerful about the painting and what Michelangelo is seeking to teach us. One very significant thing is happening on the left side of the piece, the creation of man. But there is also something just as important on the right side.

Look at that creature tucked tenderly and protectively under God's left arm. It is not an angel or some other heavenly being. She is rather both heavenly and earthly, because that is exactly what she is: *she*. God is creating Adam, and He has Eve there under His arm. And look at her left hand grasping securely onto God's left arm. He will later give her to Adam to solve his problem of original solitude.

If you're a woman, how does it make you feel when you see this powerful portrayal of God's mind and heart toward you, holding you until the right moment in His creation as His special answer to the fundamental problem of humanity? If you're a dad, what do you think if the creature under God's arm represents your daughter—and God has handed her over to you to be her earthly protector, just as He is now Eve's?

Michelangelo's art talent is just as sharp and magnificent as his theology. He knew what he was communicating to the believers of his day and for millennia to come. It is a beautiful story of what it means to be human, male and female, and of God's view of us as such.

GET THE PICTURE

Michelangelo di Lodovico Buonarroti Simoni,
***Creation of Adam* (1508–1512)**
Sistine Chapel
Visit familyproject.com to see this painting.

Commonly known as Michelangelo, he was an Italian
Renaissance painter, sculptor, architect, poet, and engineer,
as well as a peer and rival of Leonardo Da Vinci. Commissioned by Pope Julius II, his Sistine fresco contains over
300 figures. It is centered, along the ceiling of the chapel,
on key parts of the Genesis story, divided into three large
paintings of three groups each, depicting the creation
of the universe, the creation and fall of Adam and Eve,
and Noah and the flood—for a total of nine scenes from
Genesis.

So, in a very real sense, Adam becomes male only when God
introduces him to Eve. It is now good for him as it is good for her.
And this is God's perfect desire for us, His design and plan.

HUMANITY IN TWO STREAMS: WHY GENDER MATTERS

We now move to the next part of our exploration of the *Imago Dei*
in the world. It's missed by many because it seems so obvious, but
it's being vigorously challenged—if not outright denied—in various
sectors of society today. And there is a deep spiritual reason behind
this that we must recognize. We will get to that in a moment.

In such self-important places as the gender and women's studies departments at some universities and colleges, it is a confidently held premise—their pre-suppositional foundation, really—that humanity doesn't exist in two sexes, but rather in a spectrum of possible genders. For instance, medical professor Anne Fausto-Sterling famously asserted in a prestigious paper published by the New York Academy of Sciences that, as the subtitle declared, "Male and Female Are Not Enough."[8] When she laments that "Western culture is deeply committed to the idea that there are only two sexes," it makes one wonder whether she's contending that nations outside the Americas and Europe experience multiple sexes in the everyday. If that is the case, those cultures are doing an excellent job of hiding these additional genders; from all appearances, they seem pretty committed to doing the male-female-only thing, just like the West.

The title of her paper boldly announces her discovery of "The Five Sexes." Seven years later Fausto-Sterling would apologize in a follow-up article for being too short-sighted, claiming we should bump her original number up by one. *Six* different genders! And the otherwise professionally respected journal *Sciences* determined her observations were worth publishing. If you're having a hard time imagining what the extra four genders might be, it's not because you haven't gotten out enough. It's that they are merely rare variations on the binary (a four-letter word in the gender studies world) male-female makeup of humanity.

But Fausto-Sterling was being *far* too conservative in her estimation. In fact, as we are writing this, Facebook just added—get this—50 different expressions of gender(!) that their users can choose in their personal profiles beyond the boring "male" and "female." In fact, many of these folks astonishingly say there are as many genders as there are people—which is closer to the truth if you adhere to the radical notion that we each "interpret" our own genders, and there are no objective standards for the way we see ourselves sexually. Taking this approach seriously, you can say you are "trans-fem/butch, hetero-asexual," and if you truly believe that, no one can tell you you're wrong. And for someone to impose their categories on you is oppressive and dismissive of you as a person, according to this theory. As such, male and female are really false social constructs—all too much ado about nothing.

In fact, many years ago I (Glenn) participated in a large public debate on the topic of the same-sex family hosted by Wisconsin Public Radio at the University of Wisconsin-Madison. I began my remarks with what I knew would be a match to a powder keg for that audience. See how radical you think it is. I announced, "I come here tonight operating from a basic view that humanity is universally divided into different sexes, male and female, and that both are fundamentally important for each other and society." I tell the truth, the auditorium *erupted* in equal measures of laughter, as if I'd said I believed in unicorns; boos, as if I'd said one race was not as human as all the others; and hisses (my first time ever being hissed!) as if I'd said their campus's mascot Bucky Badger was in the habit of pushing down old ladies and taking candy from babies. In fact, after the event, campus security insisted they escort me safely to my car. True story. We are not in Kansas anymore.

But this understanding of humanity is sheer ideology flying in the face of universal human experience and any sort of science. There are no third, fourth, fifth, or sixth genders to be seen on the streets and trails of the world or even in the locker room; we wouldn't know what to call them if we saw them. To speak of humanity is to speak of male and female.

Yet, there are a zillion ways to be and live as an unmistakable male: Russell Crowe is not Yo-Yo Ma is not Nelson Mandela is not Mr. Rogers is not Gandhi is not Paul McCartney is not Muhammad Ali is not Bill Gates is not Andy Warhol is not Clint Eastwood is not Richard Simmons. There are very different types of men, but each one is a man. And there are just as many ways to be a woman: Margaret Thatcher is not Oprah is not Mother Teresa is not Annie Lennox is not Emily Dickinson is not Amelia Earhart is not Jacqueline Kennedy is not Eleanor Roosevelt is not Rachel Ray is not Odetta is not Ellen Degeneres. There are still only two general makes and models of humans, gender-wise, but countless ways in which they express themselves. And this humanity is very interesting and delightful.

But in thinking of male and female as "mere social constructs," isn't it ironic that one will only get the idea that there might be more than two genders not by observing people in all their different forms, but by submitting oneself to a few semesters of gender studies classes? That is where pure androgyny and gender-spectrum theories, ideological constructs that don't exist in nature, can be found. They are constructed by a "progressive" few. Even the liberal French feminist philosopher Sylviane Agacinski notes the obvious—but knows she needs to spell it out for many in her camp—in her important book *Parity of the Sexes*:

> Humankind does not exist outside this double form, masculine and feminine. . . . The human species is divided into two, and, like most other species, in two only. . . . In other words, every individual who is not a man is woman. There is no third possibility.[9]

So, given our unique and even exalted place as God's image-bearers in creation, why and how do male and female as the two different kinds of human beings matter? Why do we exist as two and two only? And why is this understanding of humanity being questioned at best and so viciously attacked at worst today?

These are big questions related to one of Gauguin's: *What are we?* And the answer is found in another: *Where do we come from?*

They must be answered for us to more fully understand what it means to be created in the image of God. And this comes from understanding God's nature better.

Better Understanding: What Are Persons?

In having a strong Christian anthropology, we must understand and have an appreciation of what a person is. Throughout philosophy and religion, there are many explanations that try to define what a person is and isn't. Christianity has something to say here.

Persons are beings designed with minds and wills, able to love, able to create, and able to serve others. This does not mean that humans who cannot do any of these things because of physical, emotional, or psychological limitations are not human. These qualities are true of human persons in general, not individually. In a Christian understanding there are three different kinds of persons:

1. Divine Persons, the three Persons of the Trinity: Father, Son, and Holy Spirit.

2. Heavenly persons, angels who have wills and minds. Satan had the will and freedom to rebel against God. Angels can create in that they compose their heavenly songs of adoration to the threefold God.

3. Human persons, who include all human beings from conception into eternity. All are unique, God-created, and God-imaging.

THE CHOREOGRAPHY OF THE TRINITY

In the last chapter, we began to examine the reality of the Trinity and what that tells us about the character and nature of God, whom we image. Now we will examine more closely how the Trinity further reveals—and defines—reality, humanity, and the family.

Let's look carefully again at the divine relationships within the Trinity. Pastor Tim Keller explains plainly and clearly what the Trinity reveals about the nature of God when he writes,

> Each of the divine persons centers upon the others. None demands that the others revolve around him. Each voluntarily circles the other two, pouring love, delight, and adoration into them. Each person of the Trinity loves, adores, defers to, and rejoices in the others. That creates a dynamic, pulsating dance of joy and love.[10]

"A dynamic, pulsating dance of joy and love"! Isn't that so beautifully worded? What Keller is describing here is found in a fancy but extremely important theological word that we must all know about: *perichoresis* (perry-core-EE-sis). Say it with us, class: perry . . . core . . . EE . . . sis. Gold stars for everyone!

In Latin, the word *circuminsession* (sir-cum-IN-session) refers to the same thing.

In its earliest form, it comes from the ancient patricians of the church: Basil, Gregory of Nazianzus, and Gregory of Nyssa—the Cappadocians—and later John Damascene. It explains the essence and mystery of the one-ness and three-ness of God, sharing its roots with our word "choreography." It refers to the beautifully close interrelatedness of the three Persons where they are clearly distinct as Father, Son, and Holy Spirit, but also one in their own eternal and intense love for each other. Like dancers who are many but appear as one in their movements and relation to each other. This is what the word is beautifully getting at. Hilary of Poitiers, one of the earliest and strongest defenders of correct theology in the church, explains in his major work *On the Trinity*,

> These Beings can reciprocally contain One Another, so that One should permanently envelope, and also be permanently enveloped by the Other, whom yet He envelopes.[11]

Each is wrapped up in and taken in the love of the other two, while still being distinct and unique. This divine interpersonal envelopment is the fundamental and eternal nature of the trinitarian God, helping us understand in some way how they are actually one and three, three in one.

Perichoresis and *circuminsession* are what Christ is speaking of when He explains to His disciples that "I and the Father are one," "Whoever has seen me has seen the Father," and "I am in the Father and the Father is in me" (John 10:30; 14:9-11). Now, clearly, they are two. First Christ, whom we can see is speaking to us—and pointing us to His Father, whom we cannot see. But they are also one because Jesus tells us emphatically that they are.

In *Mere Christianity*, C. S. Lewis explains the absolute significance of this:

> Perhaps the most important difference between Christianity and all other religions: that in Christianity God is not an impersonal thing nor a static thing—not even [just] a person—but a dynamic, pulsating activity, a life, a kind of drama almost, if you will not think me irreverent, a kind of dance. . . . It matters more than anything else in the world.

The whole dance, or drama, or pattern of this three-Personal
God is to be played in each one of us.[12]

Don't pass over that explanation too lightly, for it is magnificently
rich. Read it again slowly and soak it in, for in saying something
profound about God, it says something so important and consequential about us as well.

And as one of Lewis's good friends Charles Williams once said, in
an interesting and completely orthodox turn of Scripture, "It is not
good for God to be alone."[13] God alone—for the Christian—is not
God, as He cannot be eternal love. Jonathan Edwards, the great colonial American preacher and the third president of Princeton University, who was considered one of the most intelligent men in the New
World, understood that "God is within Himself a holy society."[14]

It's precisely what Jesus speaks of when He says this in John
14:11:

Believe me that I am in the Father and the Father is in me.

So Exactly Why Does This Matter?

So we've had a nice theology lesson about the Trinity.

But is this metaphysical proposition about the very nature of
our God and all reality too esoteric for you, too philosophical, too
ethereal? Are you asking, "What difference does it make?"

It's natural to ask such questions at this stage in our exploration;
for most of us, this is new ground we are covering.

We must appreciate that this essential Christian reality is really
over no one's head, because it's greatly imbedded in each of our
hearts, in the depths of our being. We have been given in Christianity and hold in our souls a very profound faith.

As Colin Gunton explained in the quote noted earlier,

> Because the theology of the Trinity has so much to teach
> about the nature of our world and life within it, it is or
> could be the centre of Christianity's appeal to the unbe-
> liever, as the good news of God who enters into free rela-
> tions of creation and redemption with his world. In light
> of the theology of the Trinity, everything looks different.[15]

Can you see this from what we have just learned? We really
cannot understand God unless we understand what it means that
He is Trinity. And this is fundamentally related to our topic in this
chapter, because we cannot truly understand ourselves unless we
know where we came from.

It answers Gauguin's question, *Where do we come from?* We come
from the divine Trinity. We cannot miss how this has dramatic and
weighty implications for how we understand and know ourselves.

Christian philosopher Francis Schaeffer observes,

> Modern man is deeply plagued by the question, "Where do
> love and communication come from?" Many artists pour
> themselves out in their paintings, who paint bleak messages
> on canvas, many singers, many poets and dramatists are
> expressing the blackness of the fact that while everything
> hangs upon love and communication, they don't know
> where these things come from and they don't know what
> they mean.[16]

And so they are hopeless and in despair. In comparison with all
other religious faiths and philosophies known to man, Christianity
answers such deep, searching questions in the most beautiful and

profound way—even far more than most Christians can even consider. And it is true to the motions of the world and the human soul. You can live the rest of your life drawing deeply from the richness and substance of what we've been discussing and never come close to exhausting it. In short, it is captured here:

> *Before "in the beginning" there was*
> *a Father loving a Son and a Son loving a Father,*
> *and their love flows forth in their Spirit.*

It explains the larger part of the answer to Gauguin's first two questions:

1. *Where do we come from?* We come from God—one God in three distinct Persons who live in divine relationship, in *perichoresis*.

2. *What are we?* We are human beings—our sexes distinct as male and female—uniquely, lovingly, and mysteriously created to show forth the unspeakable, unfathomable image and likeness of the trinitarian God in the world.

This is what it means to be human.

- We are male and female, made from Love, for love.
- We are male and female, made from Intimacy, for intimacy.
- We are male and female, made from Community, Communion, and Communication, for community, communion, and communication.
- We are male and female, made from Cooperative Creativity, for cooperative creativity.
- We are male and female, made from Life-Giving Persons through their love, to be life-giving persons through our love.

So when God says it is not good for man to be alone, this is not some simple statement that sets the scene for the creation of Eve. It is a dramatically important anthropological and theological statement that holds all the meaning and consequence in the world for what it is to be human.

And it is not just a humanly psychological truth, but is rooted in divine reality. It explains to us that the need for intimacy with others is as basic as food and water. We cannot live without it, and as our scientific discoveries and understandings advance in remarkable ways, they continue to reveal how true this is for each of us (see Appendix A, "'It Is Not Good': The Scientific Support"). God put it so deeply into the smallest parts of us because we are created in His image. Fortunately, He has also provided a wonderful way for that image—and for us as creatures who require community—to be whole.

HOW FAMILY COMPLETES THE IMAGE OF GOD

Walk through the hallways and rooms of most homes in our culture and you'll see a familiar sight on the walls, or perhaps displayed on tables or dressers: family portraits. But you probably won't see those in which Dad blinked, Mom sneezed, or the kids looked away. We tend to go for those that present us at our best.

Easier said than done, right?

It was a cold and stressful night a few Octobers ago for my (Leon's) family as we ventured out for an annual tradition: the Christmas portrait. Since our family is a bit larger than most, we have a lot to coordinate so that we end up with that perfect Christmas-letter photo. But this night seemed harder than usual.

One of our daughters had forgotten her shoes. Yes, that's right:

We somehow managed to get in the car and drive across town on a snowy night without noticing that she had bounced into the car without footwear.

I carried her into the studio on my back, determined to stay patient and calm. But her anxiety skyrocketed when she noticed a sign that said, "No Shoes, No Shirt, No Service." She was sure she'd be kicked out despite my assurances that she would be fine.

Her anxiety, and my impatience, grew steadily. When the photographer showed the signs of someone who'd rather be anywhere else but there, I knew we were in for a long night.

The bottom line: We were not at our best, the photographer was not at her best, and the pictures were unusable. A rescheduled appointment with a different photographer gave us a great picture—and a practical lesson.

We all want to get our picture right (unless we aspire to get our faces on one of those awkward-family-portrait Web sites). Family pictures matter to us. As we noted earlier, images matter because they convey meaning and value about the things they represent. They are not just incidental.

Each of us is created in the image of God. With God's First Definitive Statement, each of us can build a meaningful life—a philosophy and understanding of life—that can provide us with all the sense of significance that we will ever need. But wouldn't it sound heretical to say this grand truth alone is insufficient for us as humans? Indeed it would, but God's Second Definitive Statement tells us this is true. We need others besides God. This is due to God's own design.

The early leaders and teachers of the church understood and illustrated for the largely unlearned and illiterate faithful a very important understanding of the Trinitarian God that matters for our discussion of sex difference. It is represented in an old teaching tool called the Trinity Shield.

It shows us that . . .

- The Son, while fully and completely God, is not the Father. He is the Son.
- The Holy Spirit, while fully and completely God, is not the Son or the Father. He is the Holy Spirit.
- The Father is fully and completely God but is neither the Son nor the Holy Spirit. He is the Father.

Each is neither more nor less God than any other. The Father is not more God than the Son or Spirit. This essential but perplexing truth and beautiful mystery has been taught throughout the history of the Christian church in the Trinity Shield. Design-wise, there are many different, remarkable types down through the ages—but they all teach the same thing.

The Trinity Shield

The Trinity Shield was and is a very interesting visual tool used by clergy to teach their congregations about the mystery of the Triune God. It explains that the Father, Son, and Holy Spirit are all fully God by linking each of the outer circles—representing the divine Persons of the Trinity—to the center circle, which notes God with the three connecting lines in which is written "IS."

Hence, the Father IS fully God, the Son IS fully God, and the Holy Spirit IS fully God.

The outer lines connecting the three have written in them, IS NOT. Hence, the Father IS NOT the Son or the Holy Spirit, the Son IS NOT the Father or the Holy Spirit, and the Holy Spirit IS NOT the Father or the Son.

They are all fully and completely God, one not more than the other. But they are also importantly and characteristically unique from one another.

What does this curious lesson about the Trinity and these ancient symbols have to do with our subject? Can you make the connection? It helps us understand the nature of the God-image-bearing humans. Consider this same shield as the "Human Shield," as we do below.

One of the earliest images of the Trinity Shield is from the writings of Peter of Poitiers, a French professor of theology in the late 1100s. A presentation of the Trinity Shield is found in an ancient chronicle written in the early 1200s by John of Wallingford, a writer, historian, and monk. Another Trinity Shield by a Spanish artist from the sixteenth century, along with the two just mentioned, can be viewed at familyproject.com.

Each is God. But each is distinct from the others in His divinity. Both similarity and distinction are found in the very nature of God.

Now let's apply this to the nature of being human. Can you see what truths about humanity this might be leading us to?

- Adam is fully human. Eve is fully human. Each in equal measure, no more, no less than the other.
- But Adam is not Eve. Eve is not Adam.

So, just as the members of the Trinity are distinct from one another, yet each wholly God, this same mystery is present in these two beings created to show forth His divine image in the physical world. This is why Eve was needed for Adam, and no other being would do. They had to be similar in their humanity but importantly distinct in their sex difference in order for them to be precisely what God intended them to be as His images in creation. Their difference brought meaning and significance to the difference and uniqueness of the other. Anything that requires a counterpart cannot really be understood without reference to its counterpart. Consider a bow without the violin, a cart without a wheel, or a piece of stationery without a pen. They are all very different, but one is incomplete apart from the other.

This is one of the most primary reasons why Adam and Eve reflect something very deep, beautiful, and profound about the unique God of Christianity. As we are told clearly in the first chapter of Genesis:

So God created man in his own image, in the image of
God he created him; male and female he created them.
(Verse 27)

This is really remarkable when we reflect on it.
- *Fact one:* Man (humanity) is created in God's own image.
- *Fact two:* In the image of God, he is created. (Same point, but God is just making sure we get it!)
- *Fact three:* In this image of God, humans are created male or female.

Humanity. Male and female, female and male. Both are divine in their fundamental quality and essence, but differently so. We don't know *how* this is so, for it is too profound. But we know that it *is* so.

And it is for this reason that Christianity must take what it means to be a male or female very seriously, more so than any other faith or philosophy does. We cannot reverence one gender over the other, either, for to do so is to misunderstand what either or both actually are.

THE TWO AS GOD-IMAGERS—TOGETHER

So the male cannot be fully human without the female. The female cannot be fully human without the male. These may seem like two very brash and unorthodox statements. But they are not. We only become what we are in relation to another. The famous Jewish philosopher Martin Buber explains this in a unique but important way.

Martin Buber and the Other

Born and raised in Vienna near the dawn of the twentieth century, Martin Buber (1878–1965) was a widely celebrated Jewish social and religious philosopher and translator. The tumultuous divorce of his parents when he was a small child brought him to live in the more peaceful, idyllic, and wealthy home of his paternal grandfather, a famed scholar in Jewish literature who influenced him greatly. Buber's most celebrated work is *I and Thou*, expressing his philosophy that relationship is the center of what it means to be human. In this important work, Buber holds that man lives between two essential standings.

One is his fundamental nature to stand *I-It*, meaning that he understands himself in relation to and in distinction from things. Man's other, and more important nature, which has everything to do with our subject in this chapter, is *I-Thou*. *I* is me (or self) and *Thou* is you (or Other).

We are defined by and gain meaning in our relationship with an Other. Buber explains in a curious poetic style in the first paragraph of his book, "For the *I* of the [starting] word *I-You* is different from that in the basic word *I-It*." We are a different being when we relate with a thing than when we relate with another person. One makes us more fully human; one does not.

This is why he explains, "The basic word *I-You* can only be spoken with one's whole being." *I-It* cannot because it doesn't engage us at our core, at our full humanity. Of course, what Buber is telling us is that "It is not good for man to be alone." For it is only in relationship with an *Other* that we become what God originally intended us to be—truly human.

Buber wants us to catch that "the concentration and fusion into a whole being can never be accomplished by me, can never be accomplished without me. I require a You to become [me]."[17]

And you require a Me to become a You. It is what Scottish philosopher John Macmurray explained simply and directly in his 1954 Gifford Lecture at the University of Glasgow, titled "Persons in Relation": "It is only in relation to others that we exist as persons. . . . We live and move and have our being not in ourselves, but in one another. . . . Here is the basic fact of our human condition."[18]

In a sense, there are no truly individual persons. Our humanity is founded on our need and desire to relate to other persons. This is a profound message of God's Second Definitive Statement.

As Eastern Orthodox theologian John Zizioulas explains in simplicity: The human person can only be rightly understood as "being as communion."[19] We can only really become ourselves in relation to others.

While God's *Other* for Adam in answer to the problem of his original solitude was Eve, his wife, everyone else's primary "others" after this moment are known as "parents." For it is in and through these two people that our most basic needs for love, touch, care, belonging, and intimacy come to us. And it is not just some societies that mourn the news that "this baby's mother or father has abandoned him" or "she has no living parents." We know that children without loving parents are severely short-changed, and this is a human universal. Our road begins at the particular intersection of a specific male and a particular female. And our journey continues best when this same male and female stay together as our mother and father through life and invest their time, energy, love, resources, instruction, correction, and encouragement (sometimes to the point of exhaustion) in this new God-imager who is each of us. This is why it is God's intent that "a man shall leave his father and his mother and hold fast to his wife, and they shall become one flesh" (Genesis 2:24).

It is here that each of us starts out. And many of us go on to eventually form this type of union ourselves with another and start the cycle all over again. It's been all the rage for quite some time. It's what creates each new generation, and one way or another, we all have the privilege of participating in it. Until there are clones, we come *from* the love of our parents *into* the love of our parents; this is true even of adopted children. Theologian Michael Downey explains this in his book *Altogether Gift*. In a truly Christian anthropology, we must know that

the human person is not an individual, not a self-contained being who at some stage in life chooses or elects to be in relationship with another or others. From the first moment of existence, the infant is toward the other, ordinarily the mother or father, who in turn is toward the infant. From our origin, we are related to others. We are from others, by others, toward others, for others, just as it is in God to exist in the relations of interpersonal love.[20]

This is how, in our God-given human wiring and creation, it is family that truly completes the image of God in humanity; for that image is not *just* in our individual selves but in our relation to others. Study the painting *A Married Couple Receiving a Child from the Holy Trinity* (see "Get the Picture" sidebar). It is very important for our study, perhaps the one image that brings all that we have been learning into one place as no other does. It shows us in a remarkable way how the Trinity Shield has meaning for each of us. Just as the Father, Son, and Holy Spirit are all one but different, so is the most basic core of humanity.

Man and woman become one flesh in their marital union. And in this one flesh union, they become so close in their love that a third can come forth. That third—children—is of their common flesh and is one with them, yet remains *other*.

GET THE PICTURE

A Married Couple Receiving a Child from the Holy Trinity
Miniature from *The Book Which Among Other Matters Deals with the Birth of Our Lord Christ, His Life, His Passion* . . . (**vol. 2, fifteenth century**)
Visit familyproject.com to see this painting.

A dramatic and captivating image showing us the mysterious connection between the nature of the divine Trinity and the earthly trinity of family is in this wonderful and little-known painting. Here we find a modest husband and wife enjoying a time of intimacy in their house, all prepared to keep out the cold of the evening with heavy blankets and curtains that will surround the bed. Their heads are sufficiently wrapped to encourage warmth if not sensual desire.

As they have shared their special love as only husbands and wives can (or should), we see a little special-delivery package coming to and through the love of this man and woman from the love and intimacy of the Trinity. Eternal intimacy is lovingly sending this special and unique new life through the human intimacy of husband and wife—which will now create a new earthly trinity of husband and wife welcoming the child of their very flesh.

This is what humans do, and the painting suggests how it is orchestrated each time by God—whether we realize it or not—to cooperate with Him in the most profound ways that humans can love each other.

Every new life flows forth from the Trinity, from their immense and overflowing love, and into the world through the love and intimacy of a mother and father. However, while each child in the world may not come from the pure love of a mother and father—for selfishness is too often at work in human relationships—every child does come from the purity of the Trinity's love. God-ordained humanity seeks to replicate this godly love in our marriages and family lives.

For just as the Nicene and Athanasian Creeds tell us that the Holy Spirit proceeds from the Father and the Son[21] essentially as their fully divine and personified Love, each of us proceeds from our parents' love as a fully human embodiment of that love. It is a remarkable and beautiful mystery that is true of each of us.

The mystery of the Trinity is reflected in creation in the mystery of the family. And every one of us is a part of this as someone's child as well as perhaps someone's husband or wife and someone's mother and father.

IMAGO DEI AS FAMILY

So we must appreciate that if the mystery and image of the Trinity are shown forth exclusively in humanity in communion, they do so not exclusively but most fundamentally through the family. This is a very profound and bold statement, so consider these foundational truths of humanity's creation and purpose, which we have explored to this point:

1. From the beginning, it is not good for man to be alone.
2. Woman is the answer to this original human problem, thus completing and fulfilling the man and his humanity.
3. God's first command—His first work and delight for the man and woman—is for them to engage each other in this most loving, intimate, intensely physical marital embrace. (We explore the nature of marriage and sexuality more deeply in the next chapter.)
4. They are commanded to do this so that their love might bring forth little boys and girls who will serve as the next generation of God-imagers.
5. The prophet Malachi tells us that this is what our God is seeking: "godly offspring" (Malachi 2:15).

Picture This:
The Earthly and Heavenly Trinities

In considering the beautiful and mysterious relationship between the divine Trinity and the earthly trinity of father, mother, and child, many artists have portrayed this connection in magnificent and stunning ways—showing the heavenly Trinity vertically with the Father and Holy Spirit taking the viewer's eye down to the divine Son, who is and has become the fully flesh-and-blood child of the natural family, standing between His earthly parents, Joseph and Mary.

Visually, it is a very creative device to teach us the connection between the earthly family of mother, father, and child and the nature of the triune God; the earthly family of Jesus helps us appreciate this earthly and heavenly realities. This connection or similarity is not accidental or mere happenstance.

Here are the most notable examples. To view them, visit familyproject.com.

> Bartolomé Esteban Murillo (1617–1682)
> *The Heavenly and Earthly Trinities* (1681–1682)
> Oil on canvas; National Gallery, London
>
> Jacob de Wit (1695–1754)
> *Holy Family and Trinity* (1726)
> Oil on canvas; Amstelkring Museum, Amsterdam
>
> Giovanni Battista Pittoni
> *The Nativity with God the Father and the Holy Ghost* (1740)
> National Gallery, London

At the very moment that God creates the fullness of God-imaging humanity in both male and female, He also creates a family. This is what both creation narratives in Genesis 1 and 2 tell us. The creation of the one is the creation of the other.

> So God created man in his own image, in the image of God he created him; male and female he created them. And God blessed them. And God said to them, "Be fruitful and multiply and fill the earth and subdue it." (1:27-28)

> And the rib that the LORD God had taken from the man he made into a woman and brought her to the man. Then the man said, "This at last is bone of my bones and flesh of my flesh; she shall be called Woman, because she was taken out of Man." Therefore a man shall leave his father and his mother and hold fast to his wife, and they shall become one flesh. And the man and his wife were both naked and were not ashamed. (2:22-25)

The creation of humanity as the image of God in the world is the creation of family; as one makes its debut on the stage of God's creation, the other does at the same moment. The creation of Adam and Eve is the creation of the first husband and the first wife. They really cannot be separated, can they? And as unique and distinct God-imagers, they are called by Him to come together in love and allow their love to be life-giving—or better yet, life-bringing.

Pope John Paul II explains this work of families, which began with the first couple at their creation:

> The fundamental task of the family is to serve life, to actualize in history the original blessing of the Creator—that of

transmitting by procreation the divine image from person to person.[22]

Big Statement for Reflection

We are made for relationship, not isolation. This is evidenced by our beginning in Adam, where each of us comes from the overflowing, limitless love of the eternal community of three divine "Others." This allows us to become "Others" to them as well as those around us, more fully reflecting God's image. In this we become who we were lovingly made to be.

It is in family that each human first and most deeply experiences and shows forth the fullness of our God-imaging nature, because it is here that we first and most fully become part of a flesh-and-spirit trinity reflecting the divine Trinity as someone's child, spouse, or parent. No human is excluded from this. And because we are all created this way, it is the universal human ideal that this human triad remains connected and relationally close—for humans mourn when it fails to form or breaks down.

Questions for Consideration

1. How has this chapter changed the way you understand the idea that it's not good for man to be alone? What proof of this truth have you seen in your own life? How might this affect the way you interact with co-workers, your spouse, your children, and those in your community?

2. Reflect on a time when isolation was a comfort or a refreshment. How was that time a preparation for engagement, or reengagement, in your relationships? Now think of a time when isolation was a detriment, obstacle,

or discouragement. How did relationships with others, especially family, affect you in each of those circumstances?

3. How have you seen the nature and importance of male and female challenged in today's culture? Do you think it really matters? Why or why not?

4. What do you think of the idea that the image of God is most fully revealed in family? How could it influence your understanding of your own family and those around you? What practical difference can this big truth make in your family's day-to-day life?

FOR THIS REASON

Honey . . . will you marry me?

Have you noticed that people love to tell—and hear—stories about how couples got engaged? Think back on some of your favorite engagement stories in your family or among your friends. They are usually great social icebreakers, especially when the tale seems especially romantic, unique, or creative. Sometimes the stories of others' reactions are as fun and instructive as the story of the engagement itself.

When Michelle and I (Leon) got engaged, we celebrated with our good friends Chad and Laurie over pizza. We laughed about how I had to sing the last line of the song I had written to propose to her ("Michelle, will you marry me?") *three times* before she realized it wasn't just a song but an actual question seeking an actual answer!

But the excitement of our impending marriage was tempered by the struggles of some extended family members who questioned our wisdom and timing. And the early years of our marriage, while fun and exciting, were also marked by the dissolving marriages of some folks very close to us. Our enthusiasm was certainly sobered by the reality that marriage is not for the faint of heart.

Engagement—and marriage itself—can bring great happiness

and its opposite. The two people involved are humans in all their wonder, frailty, love, bitterness, and wounds. In our 32-plus years of marriage, Jackie and I (Glenn) have experienced pains and challenges. That is the effect of sin, and it exists in every marriage and family to various degrees. It's part of the deal.

But it was not always so. God had—and has—something else in mind.

This apex of our journey, as we just learned in the previous chapter, is that it's in family where we first and most fully bear the image of God. This certainly sounds like an overinflated statement, because most of us have been taught that we bear the very image of God within us simply by nature of being created as human beings. This is absolutely true, but it doesn't really tell the whole story. A truly Christian anthropology must affirm that while we image God in our humanity, we cannot fully realize our humanity as pure individuals, independent of others—can we? To be human is to be in relationship. To be divine image-bearers is to be in relationship. This is true because of who God is. And by God's lovingly personal and holy design, it is in family that we first come to be in relationship with others—and do so most intensely and longest. This is a profoundly important and consequential truth, that which most dramatically illuminates for us the nature of both God and man.

We must remember that a full and true Christian anthropology can never overlook God's Second Definitive Statement that it is not good for man to be alone. And so now we look at the place of marriage in God's story.

While it would be wrong to conclude that marriage is everyone's answer to the "it's not good for man to be alone" problem, it is humanity's answer in general—and was indeed the institution that God gave us to solve this dilemma. But we also become fully human in our relationships with others as well. And as we learned at the end of the previous chapter, it is and has been God's delight and design that each of us come into His world through the communion, love, and commitment of a husband and a wife who become mother and father because of us.

So let us take time here to study the nature of marriage more fully so we can appreciate what it is that God has done and is doing through this most divine of all human bonds.

What Is Marriage?

In the Christian worldview and anthropology, it is not possible to consider what it means to be human without considering what marriage is. In God's creation of Adam and Eve, we do not see just two people—two independent individuals. It may seem this way, but if we pay close attention to God's narrative, we find they are something much more. They are a union. And in this union they become something that they cannot fully be in their individuality.

Italian theologian Angelo Scola explains this concisely: "The image of God is completed in interpersonal communion."[1] Austrian theologian Michael Waldstein elaborates in his introduction to *Man and Woman He Created Them: A Theology of the Body*:

> According to Genesis 2, the creation of human beings
> reaches its *perfection in the communion of persons between*
> *man and woman*. According to Genesis 1, the image of God
> belongs to human beings precisely in their perfection. . . .
> It follows that the communion between man and woman is
> part of the divine image.[2] (emphasis added)

Contemporary Orthodox theologian John Zizioulas adds to this in the recognition that our God is Trinity:

The being of God could be known only through personal relationships and personal love. Being means life and life means communion. . . . God is a relational being: without the concept of communion it would not be possible to speak of the being of God. . . . The substance of God . . . has no . . . true meaning apart from communion.

This has big implications for being human:

There is not true being without communion. Nothing exists as an "individual," conceivable in itself. . . . The person cannot exist without communion.[3]

If we understand anything about what it means to be human, we must know this, as we studied in Chapter 3. This is precisely what the deeply serious Christian writer John Donne meant in a famous piece of his poetry, "Meditation 17" from *Devotions upon Emergent Occasions and Death's Duel*:

No man is an island, entire of itself;
every man is a piece of the continent,
a part of the main.
If a clod be washed away by the sea,
Europe is the less . . .
any man's death diminishes me, because I am involved in mankind;
And therefore never send
to know for whom the bell tolls;
it tolls for thee.[4]

The happy human life is lived in relation to others. This is a human universal and a profoundly Christian truth.

And so, the start of all this?

God places the first man and first woman in a relationship right from the beginning, as Jesus tells us (Matthew 19:4-6; Mark 10:6-8). It is the most powerful and fundamental relationship that humans can experience, for it initiates all other relationships, doesn't it? God doesn't start humanity out as partners in a church or ministry. It is not as business colleagues or as teammates in sports. He doesn't have Adam and Eve join together in starting an institution of higher learning or a book group, as wonderful as all those might be. Those will come later; but for now, from the beginning, He has something else in mind for them.

The first things we read about Adam and Eve as persons after their appearance in creation are in the following statements:

And God blessed them. And God said to them, "Be fruitful and multiply." (Genesis 1:28)

And . . .

Therefore a man shall leave his father and his mother and hold fast to his wife, and they shall become one flesh. The man and his wife were both naked and were not ashamed. (2:24-25)

GET THE PICTURE

Jean Corbechon, *The Marriage of Adam and Eve* (1415)
Print illustration from Des Proprietes De Chozes
Fitzwilliam Museum, University of Cambridge
Visit familyproject.com to see these works of art.

Very little is known about Jean Corbechon, other than he was a celebrated illustrator of the day, his work appearing in numerous books in the 1300s and 1400s.

Jean Fouquet, *God Introducing Adam and Eve* **(1476)**
Illustration from Antiquites Judaiques
Bibliothèque Nationale, Paris, France

Jean Fouquet, a leading French painter and illustrator, was influenced in his work by the Italian Renaissance and brought that influence to France. He is credited with creating portraiture in miniature.

What is notable about these two works is the positioning of Adam and Eve as a couple, between God the Father who brings them together in His creation and introduction, performing their wedding ceremony as the angels and the rest of creation witness and celebrate the grand event. These images put a new kind of trinity in our minds: God the Creator with the two beings He crafted to show forth His image in the world. He is the One who signifies them, and He is the One who brings them together, giving them both unique meaning and communion.

Jesus beautifully and powerfully affirms these early words in Matthew 19:4-6 as trustworthy historical truth and not just some quaint flannelgraph Sunday school stories. He says,

Have you not read that he who created them from the be-ginning made them male and female, and said, "Therefore

a man shall leave his father and his mother and hold fast to
his wife, and the two shall become one flesh?"

So they are no longer two but one flesh. What therefore
God has joined together, let not man separate.

To speak of Adam and Eve is to speak of a husband and wife.
You cannot separate the two, for the only time they were not spouses
was prior to Eve, when God said it was not good. But when Eve ar-
rives, Adam becomes something he was not: a husband. And Eve, a
wife. And it is good, very good. They have become as God intended
them to be. So let's consider what we know about Adam and Eve
so far in God's story.

First, God tells us that Adam and Eve are God-imagers in creation, the only parts of this glorious creation that are honored with
this distinction and serve this purpose.

Second, these two humans are profound in their sex distinction.
They are both human but are beautifully and importantly different
as male and female humans, an essential duality. And this gives a
unique power and responsibility to each that the other does not and
cannot possess.

And third, they are two, but also one flesh: husband and wife,
a mystery.

In fact, God teaches us that each of these points is not only
true of Adam and Eve, but for all those who come after. God says
the man shall leave his mother and father and cleave to his wife.
Adam doesn't have a father and mother to leave, but the rest of
the human race will, and "for this reason"—this holy and mysterious union where the two will become one—a man will leave his
mother and father and cling to his wife. And if he is to leave his
most important of all relationships (with his mother and father),
he is to forsake all other relationships as well (with his buds, his

co-workers, his siblings, etc.) and give all to his wife. This is how humanity is to work in general.

Marriage is the first and most fundamental human relationship, the first divine and social institution. It is this coming together of male and female in the spousal union that serves as the bedrock, the foundation, the wellspring of both human experience and human culture. And God has these newly human newlyweds join together and start their own family, through their love producing another divine human image-bearer to expand their own love and community. As we will see in Chapter 6, no society anywhere has found a better way than marriage to regulate human sexuality and create a new, healthy, thriving next generation that contributes to the community good. It is unquestionably irreplaceable.

GET THE PICTURE

Hendrick Goltzius, *The Fall of Man* (1616)
National Gallery of Art, Washington, D.C.
Visit familyproject.com to see this work of art.

Hendrick Goltzius was a Dutch artist. At a very early age, he burned his hand badly—leaving it dramatically malformed, allowing him to very skillfully hold the tools he used as an engraver, enhancing his ability as an artist. He married an older widow, and her wealth allowed him to found his own business. But she was of ungracious character—so he traveled widely, coming under the influence of Michelangelo's work in Italy. This beautiful painting shows Adam and Eve as a husband and wife enjoying their tender intimacy.

GOD'S DELIGHT IN MARRIAGE

John Calvin taught that creation has been sustained moment by moment since its beginning by God's sheer delight in it. The fact that the first thing He does with the first two humans is to join them as spouses says a great deal about the pleasure God derives from seeing a man and woman come together in every way in marriage. This is true of your marriage (if you're wed), and the marriages of your parents, siblings, grandparents, friends, co-workers, and neighbors. This is why the church has taken a uniquely serious and intense interest in marriage through the ages, to the point where many believe that marriage is a Christian institution. But it is not. While created and ordained by God, it is a common grace—as is water, sunshine, or friendship—made for all people in all lands at all times. If it were a Christian institution, it would have existed only after the founding of Christ's church and only in those lands where Christian missionaries have gone and established the faith. But this is not the case. Where God puts humans, He puts marriage, because of our design.

This is no small truth.

This was God's intention from the very beginning, as Jesus tells us in Matthew 19:4. It is what He does with humans by His own sovereignty and holy delight. How does this mold the way you should view your own marriage, those of your children, and the others around you? We must be passionate about and delight in what God is passionate about and delights in. Marriage is one of these things, and why God's Word tells us that marriage should be "held in honor among all" (Hebrews 13:4).

Whether we realize it or not, we change to an important degree as we enter marriage and issue forth from the union of our mother's and father's marital love. This is what the great church father John Chrysostom is saying when he makes this bold and stunning proclamation:

> When husband and wife are united in marriage, they no longer seem like something earthly, but rather like the image of God himself.[5]

And this is because, as Theophilus of Antioch, in his *Apology*—an ancient effort to show how the Christian story of creation was superior to the pagan creation myths—taught,

> God created Adam and Eve that there might be great love between them, reflecting the mystery of divine unity.[6]

It is only in Adam's union with another human that he comes to really bear the image of God. And this union is not any kind of human-to-human union, but a marriage to a very different kind of human being: Eve. It is a grand work of arrogance to say this union between the two distinct parts of humanity does not necessarily have to be for life, or that it can be replaced by any two humans regardless of sex simply because some want it that way. It denies God's image in marriage. God is answering the fundamental human dilemma of Genesis 2:18, showing us that it is only in Adam's life-long, forsaking-all-others union with Eve that man is "good."

Now, this does certainly not mean that no man (or woman) is good unless married, for Christianity teaches a real and definite virtue in chastity and singleness. This is a general statement for humanity, for not all people need to be married to be whole, but all *peoples* need marriage. Whether we are involved in it or not, the marriages around us affect each of us in very profound ways.

If you don't believe this, do away with marriage in any culture and see what happens. It is why we see marriage demonstrated in every single human culture at every time.

In fact, anthropologists cannot find a time when marriage started in human experience. To them, it just seems as if it always was. In fact, one of the most significant anthropological historians of marriage says it seems to have "developed out of primeval habit."[7] Almost as if it started with the first two humans to come along. Does that sound familiar?

MAN'S DELIGHT IN MARRIAGE

As we've mentioned before, the first biblically recorded words of humanity are from Adam, describing this new creation.

Let's appreciate what Adam notices first about her. It's what any healthy man would notice: her physicality, bone of his bone, flesh of his flesh. And God does not chastise him for the observation as if he is being too "fleshly." She's a person, like him. But as a woman, she's very much *not* like him! And she is stunning in this difference. He is fascinated by her in many ways because of who she is, and because now his own masculinity makes sense and can be understood.

At Adam's celebratory proclamation, God makes a really wonderful statement, which we've also noted before:

> For this reason a man will leave his father and mother
> and be united to his wife, and they will become one flesh.
> (Genesis 2:24)

"For this reason," God says.
For *what* reason? Do you know?

God is telling us that the man and woman have been made especially for each other, to complete one another. That is the *why* of "leaving and cleaving."

This is God's universal plan for marriage: that the husband leaves all his other allegiances, including the most basic and fundamental with mother and father, and cleaves, clings, holds fast to his wife. He trades one "closest of all relationships" for an even closer one. It is interesting that God speaks this command to "leave and cleave" to the man, not the woman. This is because He made women more relationally wired. Their romantic and mothering relationships are more central to how they are generally. Men are the ones who are most likely to roam. This is true of men and women in all cultures.

The wife becomes the center of the husband's personal, social, and domestic life. She becomes his new allegiance and belonging-place. Man and woman leave behind the old and form a new central relationship, starting the whole process over again in their own union. We call it a generation because marriage is both unitive and generative. It restarts the process of humanity anew.

And here is the big punchline: God's Word teaches us that this is not just a mere biological process but a divine orchestration of generation-to-generation God-imaging that all humans get to participate in, and that results from cooperating with the triune God. As Eve said, "With the help of the LORD I have brought forth a man" (Genesis 4:1, NIV).

This is both our purpose and our origin, including all of us as someone's child.

This is what family is. *This* is what humanity is. And it's no small thing.

It is the first and most basic thing God gives humans to do.

Soak this in. Reflect on it, for it tells us much about both God and man. This is the meaning the Christian story brings to being human and a member of a family, either as a partner in a marriage or the product of a husband-and-wife union.

And as a conclusion to the original wedding, this simple, beautiful observation is made in Genesis 2:25:

> And the man and his wife were both naked and were not ashamed.

Here we are to think of nakedness more in terms of vulnerability and security than morality.

Have you had the horrific dream in which you are completely naked in a group of people and you have nowhere to hide? Most of us have. There really is something deeply human and theological here. It is frightening to us because it means we are devastatingly exposed to all those we know in all of our vulnerability. Our psychological protection and security are gone.

For Adam and Eve in their original God-given state, it was different. They felt no shame, no vulnerability, no need to hide themselves. They were free and secure to be who they were, able to fully glory in each other. The absence of shame tells us they were just as they were meant to be, with nothing left out or hindering their union with God or with each other. Nothing to hinder their own perception of themselves, and no reason to hide. They could know and reveal themselves to each other fully, with total intimacy. But it is sadly not so today, as we will see in the next chapter.

MARRIAGE AND THE NARRATIVE OF GOD

Given what we have observed, it is important for us to think in a larger context about what Scripture—God's revelation to us of His divine story and history—says about marriage. If asked how marriage is talked about in Scripture, many of us might think of the few places where marriage is specifically mentioned—with Adam and Eve, Abraham and Sarah, Isaac and Rebekah, Samson and Delilah, etc. Then we might look to Jesus' few mentions of it, as well as Paul's major teachings on it in 1 Corinthians and Ephesians 5—and those of Peter in 1 Peter 3. Other than that, marriage doesn't really seem to be a big part of the story itself, does it? Many other things are going on.

But such a view is an example of poor hermeneutics, the means by which we understand a text. It uses proof texts over the narrative itself, which far too many Christians do. It gives us only an elementary understanding of Scripture, like thinking one understands a movie only by studying all the individual scenes and missing the bigger picture—as if the movie *Forrest Gump* were just about a dim-witted Southern boy who likes chocolate and happens to stumble into some of the most important historical events of his lifetime.

The divine story is so much bigger than the individual parts. Those who really know the story God is telling through Scripture know that while marriage is not talked about as much as, say, the holiness of God, it is central in the overall narrative God is and has been telling us.

Alice Mathews and M. Gay Hubbard explain this in their book, *Marriage Made in Eden*:

> What God says about marriage lies embedded in the whole story. Even more, God has integrated his case for marriage not only in the whole story, but in the meaning of the whole story. Marriage in God's story cannot be sectioned out into an appendix or a footnote. . . . Instead, God presents mar-

riage as a part of the complex business of being God's people both with God and with each other.[8]

Indeed. As we will see in Chapter 11, Mathews and Hubbard are exactly right! Given this, we have to understand what marriage really is, what it is about, why God created it, and what it does as a part of God's story.

God absolutely delights in His first two humans, in this husband and wife. As Mathews and Hubbard explain,

> Marriage is not an accommodation to human limitations. It springs from the very character of God.[9]

This is precisely what the Christian story of creation and humanity explains to us, and the church has held this from its earliest days.

SEX: THE FIRST FULLY HUMAN ACT

God and *sex*.

We read somewhere that the two founders of Google said these were their two most consistently entered search terms.[10]

But are we uncomfortable with those two words side by side? Do we think they even belong together? Perhaps most Christians would say "no," but that is because we tend to have a skewed view of both God and sex. But a careful reading of the narrative God has given us in His Word offers us a fresh perspective here. These subjects are matched together in the first chapter of Scripture.

What is the Christian "take" on sexuality? What is it that faithful Christians believe about sexuality? It is important that we get this right because of the special view God takes of it, as well as the dramatic consequences of getting it wrong. Consider the place sexuality plays in so many of our most important human and social problems:

- abortion
- unmarried childbearing
- fatherlessness
- shame
- the sexual objectification of women and children
- sexual addiction
- infidelity
- pornography
- rape and sexual abuse
- homosexuality
- human trafficking
- AIDS and so many other sexually transmitted diseases

What we do with and how we view sexuality is very consequential, in extremely deep ways. This is because God made it so.

But tragically, the Christian message on sexuality often consists of only two parts: the prohibitive and the instructive.

1. *Prohibitive:* "Sex is for marriage. Otherwise, don't do it!"
2. *Instructive:* "Once married, both husband and wife should enjoy sex. So here are some helpful marriage manuals on how to make love masterfully."

Try to think of any books you've read by Christian authors that don't stick to either of these two roads on this topic. There's nothing wrong with either of these messages, for they are both true and good. The problem is that this is all evangelicals really have to say about this important topic. Is this all God wants us to know about sexuality? "Stop, don't, wait," and "Green light now, so be skillful"?

God has such a dramatically more beautiful story to tell us on the matter. And the place to start is in understanding again what God created us to be.

As we have observed so many times through these pages, we must appreciate that to be human is to be an embodied God-image-bearer made for relationship with others. Much of this interaction happens with our bodies long before we become sexually interested or involved. Our bodies carry us toward, present us to, and interact with others. It is through our bodies that we recognize others. It is with our bodies that we decide to shake someone's hand or give someone a hug or a pat on the shoulder. If we refuse to do one of these things when meeting another person, that means something very significant too, doesn't it?

Humans act through their bodies. And embodiment comes in two forms, male and female; this shapes how we do and don't interact with one another in so many non-sexual ways. Men might punch another guy on the shoulder. This is a male-to-male greeting and is seen as such by guys. Women, not so much. Younger and older women will sometimes walk with each other holding hands without any indication of same-sex sexual attraction. Men and women only hug each other socially when they know each other well. Sexuality is a different kind of bodily interaction. In fact, it is far more than just bodily; it is emotional, spiritual and soulful. It is overtly inherent in our God-created nature. God's first act with these first humans after blessing their creation is to officiate their wedding.

The first command God gives our new bride and groom within this spousal union is something they are quite happy to fulfill. It comes very naturally for them because of how God created them. They need no instructions to talk them through it. God's statement to them is a blessing and encouragement. It is not a command to do something that requires intentionality and purpose. It is no burden. It is on the first page of God's Word: "Be fruitful and multiply."

For humans, being fruitful is necessarily an action of passion and intimacy that makes them distinct from the animals. It is not just an instinctual act of physical sensation but something much more. Man and woman come together in the most intimate physical, emotional, and spiritual way that two people can connect. It is a total giving of self and receiving of the other as to become literally one flesh, a human *perichoresis* of sorts.

Think about this. This is the first act to which God calls the first two humans. Their first act is both sexual and divine.

Perhaps the holier among us might have called them to something more . . . uh . . . appropriate, wholesome, or godly. Maybe we'd have started a prayer group. Or a farm. But C. S. Lewis had this kind of false holiness in mind when he explained,

> I know some muddle-headed Christians have talked as if
> Christianity thought that sex, or the body, or pleasure were
> bad in themselves. But they were wrong. . . . Christianity
> has glorified marriage more than any other religion: and
> nearly all the greatest love poetry in the world has been
> produced by Christians. If anyone says that sex itself is bad,
> Christianity contradicts him at once.[11]

Sex is no small part of the Christian story. As the man and woman embraced each other in this loving, intimate, and bodily communion, who do you think gained the greatest delight and happiness from this union?

The man? The woman, perhaps?

Or God?

Note that your answer may tell you a great deal about your view of God. Sex, after creation, is the first part of the human story; it is that way because God wanted it that way. God no doubt took the greatest delight in it because this was the completion of His image-bearing creations. Can your view of God make room for that? It must.

As C. S. Lewis said, it is no use trying to be more spiritual than God. And the early church fathers wisely corrected gnosticism by explaining that we have no business being ashamed to talk about what God was not ashamed to create.

And it is here, from the beginning, that God allows the man and woman the opportunity to become lovers—not just in a romantic, valentiney kind of way, but as God-imagers, those made to reflect a God who is a very passionate, life-giving, and sustaining Love.

Of course the love that Jesus shared with the Father before the foundation of the world is not the kind of love between a husband and wife. We are very different kinds of beings; most notably we are embodied and they are not; we are humans and they are divine. But make no mistake: This wonderful, seemingly transcendent love between husband and wife is a deep and beautiful mystery in the image of the love of God. We don't know precisely *how* it's true, but we do know and can trust that it *is* true.

WHAT IS THIS UNION FOR?

This marital union is indeed for intimacy, union, and mutual enjoyment for husband and wife, but it is also about more. God's first instruction to the husband and wife in Genesis 1 highlights the procreative purpose of marital union. His statement in Genesis 2 highlights its unitive purpose.

This union adds to and strengthens us in the fully free and secure giving and receiving of one another. When this loving embrace between husband and wife is what it can be, there are few other times when we feel as fully and euphorically alive. When the sexual embrace is merely a taking from one for the other, it makes us feel less than we are, like an object. It is life-robbing, not life-giving. Theologian Karl Barth expressed this well when he declared, "Coitus without coexistence is demonic."[12]

The marital union also has power to give life to new persons, new eternal souls. That is no small thing; it is actually the most powerful thing in the world, for it literally shifts the balance of the universe each time it happens, as one more eternal God-imager comes into the world. It is exclusively in the loving, bodily sexual union of the two streams of humanity that this happens. Nature is very narrow in this regard, and it is because of how God chose to do it in His delight. According to His design, it is only in this mysterious and unique union of husband and wife that the unfathomable wonder and mystery of a child is produced.[13]

So what does it mean for a couple to be open to life in its sexual union? Various Christian traditions—Catholic, Orthodox, and Protestant—differ in answering this question. But generally, all assert that it at least means that a married couple should be open to the blessing of fertility. While they might delay childbearing for a season of life through non-abortive contraception or natural family planning, married love should flow forth into coming generations by participating with God in creating new image-bearers. This must be understood in the truth that the loving communion of the Trinity issues forth in new life as Genesis 1:26 plainly tells us. So should our marital unions as God-imaging unions.

THE BEST PLACE FOR SEX:
CONTEXT MATTERS

Saying sex is nothing to be ashamed of—as Christianity does—is different from saying sex is *never* something to be ashamed of. It is all a matter of what you are talking about and in what context it takes place.

As many have observed, sex is like fire. They are two of the most powerful forces in the world. The first is a human force, the second a natural one. Both are able to do profound good and essential things. They can produce great pleasures. Without either, human life would not be possible.

But handled improperly, outside of safe confines, both can cause untold damage. How we use each makes all the difference in the world, between living happily and productively and facing great harm. Context matters.

Consider a couple in a hotel room downtown on a Wednesday afternoon, engaged in sexual intercourse. Is this the Christian ideal of sexuality? Well, it depends, doesn't it?

What if it's . . .

- two unmarried co-workers cheating on their spouses?
- a prostitute and client?
- an adult man harming an underage girl?
- a drunk college student forcing himself on a coed?
- two men or two women?
- two actors filming a vile kind of movie?
- an engaged couple?

Each is wrong, but to differing degrees.

However, what if it's . . .

- a virginal couple nervously engaging each other on their honeymoon?

- a married couple with three small children at home, and the wife's parents gave the spouses a special time away alone?
- a couple celebrating their 60th wedding anniversary?

Each is engaging generally in the same kind of physical activity, but its significance and goodness are very different in each case. Some of the situations are downright evil; some are also misguided or foolish. Some are quite beautiful and divine in their own unique way.

What are our criteria for determining which is which? Every mentally capable human needs to be able to answer this question, for human sexuality is a deeply value-laden thing. Human sexuality never "just is." Many would put each of these under various moral categories depending on their view of what sex is and what the human person is created for. The Christian view of sex is determined by how we view God, how we view others, how we view ourselves—and what God created us for.

Sex is not just a physical activity but a host of very different activities coming together in very specific settings. And the setting and relationship between the people matter immensely.

A Christian view of human sexuality is all about context—making sure we don't separate some parts of the thing from all the others that are intended to make it complete. *The Message*, Eugene Peterson's paraphrase of the Bible, states it this way:

There is more to sex than mere skin on skin. Sex is as much spiritual mystery as physical fact. As written in Scripture, "The two become one." . . . We must not pursue the kind of sex that avoids commitment and intimacy, leaving us more lonely than ever—the kind of sex that can never "become one." There is a sense in which sexual sins are different from all others. In sexual sin we violate the sacredness of our own bodies, these bodies that were made for God-given and God-modeled love, for "becoming one" with another. (1 Corinthians 6:16-18)

That is what makes sex so wonderful. It becomes polluted and diminished when this intense sexual embrace is separated from the total self-giving and other-receiving of each in the protective confines of marriage. C. S. Lewis had it right in saying,

> The monstrosity of sexual intercourse outside of marriage is that those who indulge in it are trying to isolate one kind of union (the sexual) from all the other kinds of union which were intended to go along with it and make up the total union.[14]

It is no mere coincidence that the best social science research consistently finds that the most sexually fulfilled people, physically and emotionally, are the faithfully married—particularly those who come to marriage as virgins. And interestingly, sexual satisfaction and contentment tend to diminish as the number of lifetime partners increases. The most comprehensive study on sexuality ever done was conducted at the University of Chicago's National Opinion Research Center, and these scholars explain what their research concludes:

> We are left with a picture (of sexuality) that does not fit any of the popular images. . . . Those who are having the most partnered sex and enjoying it most are the married people. The young single people who flit from partner to partner and seem to have a sex life that is satisfying beyond most people's dreams are, it seems, mostly a media creation. In

real life, the unheralded, seldom discussed world of married sex is actually the one that satisfies people the most.[15]

And this is true for two important measures of sexual satisfaction, both physical and emotional. Specifically, married people have greater numbers and intensity of orgasm, as well as greater emotional satisfaction from their sexual experiences, compared with the unmarried in any other relational category. And what is more, it was found that religious and non-religious married men had orgasms per sexual engagement at about the same rate—which was most of the time—but conservative Protestant and Catholic women had orgasms with their husbands at notably the highest rates compared with wives with no particular religious faith.

These scholars report,

The association for women between religious affiliation and orgasms may seem surprising because conservative religious women are so often portrayed as sexually repressed. . . . And despite the popular image of the straitlaced conservative Protestants, there is at least circumstantial evidence that the image may be a myth as it pertains to sexual intercourse.[16]

Marriage and faith impact sexual satisfaction for great good. Who knew?

Well, God did.

It is only through the exclusive, protective marital giving of body, mind, and soul that real intimacy can take place. And it is only in a relationship where someone is not being used as a sexual object, but rather where the other is giving completely of himself or herself and can be completely received and loved as a total person.

In this type of sexual union we see the best image-bearing qualities of the Trinity, and in no other. We are not true to our natures as image-bearers when we are just a physical body to be used, and this is true whether in marriage or out. There is a reason why such relationships not only leave us feeling worse than unsatisfied, but used and shameful.

HUMAN SEXUALITY AS A PICTURE OF THE INNER LIFE OF GOD

God gave us marital intimacy and sexual communion as a gift. How do we honor Him with this gift? By making sure we reflect the nature and qualities of the relationship shared by the Trinity, the image we and our lives were created to reflect. This requires that we understand some primary characteristics and qualities of the Trinity:

- The Trinity is a community of loving Persons who are relationally active, not static. They are, throughout eternity, giving to and receiving from one another in unconditional, loving intimacy. It's their very nature to do so. It's who they are! And so should we be.
- This community of loving Persons is permanent, for they have always exhibited this giving and receiving of love for each other and always will. These are not merely convenient or passing relationships. They are not opportunities. We can count on their relationship lasting.
- This community of loving Persons is committed, for their relationships are not dependent on how fulfilled they are or on what they can get out of the relationship.
- This community of loving Persons is exclusive, for there have always been three distinct members and there always will be three. No more, no less. They don't invite other gods into their intimacy, nor do they swap partners. They are each for the others.

- The Persons of this community are self-giving, for they seek to serve and to give to one another and glory in doing so. They're not self-seeking. While they glory in receiving love from one another, it's not about what they can get but what they can give. That is their intrinsic nature in their divine relations.

- This community of Persons is one, but also distinct and complementary. This means that while the members of the Godhead are one in essence (each is fully God), they are also distinct from one another and complement one another. Each person of the Trinity can't be fully appreciated apart from the other two. Each needs the others because each is distinct from the others. All complement each other in their uniqueness.

- This community of divine Persons is life-giving—for this is exactly what we are, the offspring of their eternal love. Husband and wife must also be life-giving in their union, for their sexuality is not just a cul-de-sac for their own pleasure, but is to be poured out into another that becomes their own flesh and blood.

What are we?

We are made in this image, for this image. And again, this is not required of every person, for not all are called to marriage. This does not mean they are any less human, because we all are always a part of this human trinitarian nature as someone's child.

And just because our marriages can be messy, imperfect, and often painful, that takes nothing away from this magnificent truth as we will surprisingly see in vivid detail in Chapter 11. It still remains true about every marriage that is and ever was.

That is very good news.

BIG STATEMENT FOR REFLECTION

As image-bearers, we are marital and sexual creatures. It is a human universal because humans are universally created as divine image-bearers whether they realize it or not. Mysteriously, both marriage and sexuality reflect something of God Himself—and humans exclusively get to participate in that in total human form, bodily, spiritually, and emotionally.

QUESTIONS FOR CONSIDERATION

1. Before reading this chapter, had you ever realized that the creation of man was the creation of marriage? What does that say about the nature of marriage? What difference could knowing this make regarding your own marriage, or that of your parents?

2. If someone asked you what Jesus said about marriage, would you be able to answer? What do you think was the most profound and foundational thing He had to say on the subject?

3. Do you agree that sexuality lies at the root of many of our most damaging social and personal problems? If so, why? If not, why not?

4. When you hear that sexuality is such a foundational and primary part of the Christian story on what humanity is, how does it make you feel? Troubled? Interested? Uninformed? Embarrassed? Grateful? Does this challenge your assumptions in some ways? If so, how?

THE MAN HAS NOW
BECOME LIKE ONE OF US

Paul McCusker is a friend and colleague who has earned his living by writing novels, plays, and radio dramas all his professional life. As one who understands how to tell a good story, he explains that every tale must have a villain and a dramatic crisis. The villain could be a character who does not like green eggs and ham, or the wolf in "Little Red Riding Hood," or that ominous killer tanker truck in Steven Spielberg's first movie, *Duel.*

There is a reason this is true of all stories, and it has to do with God's own story.

For the last four chapters, our story has been a remarkably happy and life-giving one. It's been idyllic, has it not? So far God has created something to represent His divine and invisible nature in the created order. That would be humans—you, me, all of us. He's provided a solution for our original problem of solitude and loneliness. He's given us relationships—marriage, sexual communion, parenthood, family, friends, community, and society.

It is all very good. Adam and Eve are happy in it, and blessed, just as God intended.

But things don't stay this way.

They turn overwhelmingly tragic, changing the whole nature of the story itself, as well as nearly all of the participants. In fact, it is nearly impossible to find the words to describe how bad it gets. It is in this chapter that we learn the nature of this downward turn of the story.

God gives Adam and Eve all of creation to care for and enjoy. There is only one part of creation that God puts boundaries around:

> And the LORD God commanded the man, saying, "You may surely eat of every tree of the garden, but of the tree of the knowledge of good and evil you shall not eat, for in the day that you eat of it you shall surely die." (Genesis 2:16-17)

God is clear, is He not? Obey this one rule, and all is perfect. Later God would give us 10 commandments, but here in the Garden, there is only one. How difficult could it be to color inside God's lines? His prohibition is not a negative, but positive in that His concern is our protection and well-being. Like any good parent, He says, "Don't do this, because the consequences will be harmful to you." This protection is God's loving grace to us.

But . . .

Man and woman chose to listen to another voice. They came to doubt God's word at the encouragement of that angel who, in vicious and self-absorbed jealously, chose to turn his back on God's goodness. He wanted to be God, and therefore became God's enemy. This fallen angel tells Eve through the mouth of a serpent,

> "Did God actually say, 'You shall not eat of any tree in the garden'?" And the woman said to the serpent, "We may eat

of the fruit of the trees in the garden, but God said, "You
shall not eat of the fruit of the tree that is in the midst of
the garden, neither shall you touch it, lest you die." But
the serpent said to the woman, "You will not surely die.
For God knows that when you eat of it your eyes will be
opened, and you will be like God, knowing good and
evil." . . . So she took of its fruit and ate, and she also gave
some to her husband who was with her, and he ate. (3:1-6)

Satan made God out to be something He certainly was not and
is incapable of being: a liar and a deceiver. Satan, the arch-liar-and-
deceiver, pretended he knew better, appearing to be the truth-teller,
having Adam and Eve's best interests in mind. This is how he oper-
ates; Adam and Eve allowed themselves to be deceived. They chose
to disobey and to create their own reality. And we have been doing
it ever since, each one of us.

And what happened? We are told immediately:

Then the eyes of both were opened, and they knew that they
were naked. And they sewed fig leaves together and made
themselves loincloths. (Verse 3:7)

This did not bring Adam and Eve beautifully together as their
obedience to God did. This misguided obedience to the wrong
authority created a devastating division between them. There was
separation and alienation, the third part of our fuller Christian
worldview.

Before we look at the consequences of their actions, we must
examine why Satan struck at these people. There is an important
reason; it is found in what these two were created to do and be.

GET THE PICTURE

**Lucas Cranach the Elder, *The Fall of Man*
(detail from *Paradise*, 1530)
Kunsthistorisches Museum, Vienna**
Visit familyproject.com to see this painting.

Lucas Cranach the Elder, the father of (you guessed it) Lucas Cranach the Younger, was a celebrated painter in his time, working in the Catholic tradition. But he came under the influence of Martin Luther's teaching, embracing it with enthusiasm. In time Cranach and Luther became great friends, with Cranach becoming the godfather of Luther's first son—and painting one of the most famous portraits of Luther known today.

WHAT WAS SATAN AFTER?

Satan wanted to sabotage God's plan for creation because of his absolute and all-consuming hatred for God. But if Satan's interest was in leading humanity astray in rebellion against God, he could have approached Adam after the man got the basic direction about the tree. Easier to try to mislead one than two, right? Misleading a human is not what Satan was really after. We know what he was after if we consider what we've learned about God and man in the previous chapters.

Satan's interest is not just in getting a human to disobey God, but more meaningfully and profoundly in attacking the human couple. Note that "the eyes of both were opened" after they had eaten the fruit. They were created, blessed, and commanded as a couple—and they were tempted and fell as a couple.

GET THE PICTURE

**William Blake, *Satan Watching the Caresses
of Adam and Eve* (1808)
Illustration for *Paradise Lost*
Museum of Fine Arts, Boston**
Visit familyproject.com to see this painting.

William Blake was one of the most noted illustrators
of Milton's *Paradise Lost*, from which this watercolor is
taken. Both a visual artist and poet, Blake had radical
ideas about religion and strongly rejected orthodox Christianity. But in this illustration he conveys something quite
orthodox, that it is Adam and Eve's physical intimacy and
love that draws Satan's attention, resulting in the temptation. Satan knows this love and intimacy uniquely and
powerfully presents something divine and holy. And he
will not have that.

This is what Satan is attacking, as illustrated in a remarkable
and curious painting William Blake did for a collection of illustra-
tions in Milton's *Paradise Lost*. Study *Satan Watching the Caresses of
Adam and Eve* and reflect on what you are seeing.

Satan is looking upon Adam and Eve, and as he gazes upon
this married, loving couple he knows precisely what he is looking
at. He gets the larger story and what each part of it means in God's
divine drama. He knows what this union represents without even
knowing the Word of God. Few people have to be told what Michelangelo's *Pietà* is made in the image of; anyone who knows the
Christian story knows what it represents. Satan cannot miss what

this couple is a physical, fleshly picture of. Adam and Eve, in their loving union, remind Satan of God! This obsesses Satan, who has a profound interest in destroying anything that represents and is dear to God. He knows that if he can destroy this couple, he is attacking something very significant and meaningful to God. Remember our illustration in Chapter 2 of what it would mean if we tore up the photograph of Professor Kass's daughter. It would be a great and dramatic affront to him. In fact, Satan knows that in a very real sense, he is attacking God Himself.[1]

The attack is planned, executed, and regrettably successful. The result?

Adam and Eve are no longer as God created them, living in the purity of their intimacy, fully knowing each other without limitation, hindrance, or shame. In a sense, they no longer image God as they once did for their perfect unity and intimacy is devastatingly diminished. The image is still there in a very meaningful way, but it is seriously marred. We know from our studies how fundamentally harmful the removal of intimacy is to a human. Satan knows this, too.

Adam and Eve become alienated not only from each other, but from God as well:

> And they heard the sound of the LORD God walking in the garden in the cool of the day, and the man and his wife hid themselves from the presence of the LORD God among the trees of the garden. But the LORD God called to the man and said to him, "Where are you?" And he said, "I heard the sound of you in the garden, and I was afraid, because I was naked, and I hid myself." (Genesis 3:8-10)

God asks a few searching questions of Adam, much as any parent would ask when he or she knows a child has done something

wrong. They are not really questions seeking unknown information. They are asked to reveal truth. Every parent has asked such
questions—and all children, in their ignorance, have had to answer
them.

> [God] said, "Who told you that you were naked? Have you
> eaten of the tree of which I commanded you not to eat?"
> (Verse 11)

God is telling Adam and Eve that awareness of their nakedness
was a knowledge or awareness that He never intended them to have;
it was a destructive missile aimed at the gift of being God's icons in
the world. It's a factor in their disobedience, and therefore a fundamental break in their intimacy with themselves, with each other,
and—most troubling—with God. For the first time, man is afraid
and insecure. He tries to protect himself—curiously not from the
Enemy who sought their destruction but from God Himself, who
gave them everything good. The first effect was this demolished
relationship and the shame that came to man.

Man must cover himself. He must hide. And we have been
hiding ourselves ever since. And this nakedness business is not just
about morality and clothes, for goodness' sake. It is about who we
were in our innocence and acceptance and then how we would
struggle with shame, alienation, and disintegration. God is the author and source of the former, Satan the originator and perpetrator
of the latter.

Pope John Paul II explores the significance of this part of the
story, explaining,

> This change [regarding Adam and Eve's nakedness] emerges
> from their consciousness as a fruit of the tree of the knowledge

of good and evil. . . . This change directly concerns the experience of the meaning of one's own body before the Creator and creatures. In particular, this change, which [Genesis 3:10] outlines in such a concise and dramatic way, concerns directly—perhaps in the most direct way possible—the relation between man and woman, between masculinity and femininity.[2]

It is indeed an attack on the man and woman as well as on human masculinity and femininity, because it is in these that the very image of God is revealed in the world. The destruction and perversion of their God-blessed union and communion have been a dramatic and very consequential part of the human drama ever since, have they not? Some have lightheartedly called it the "battle of the sexes." But in the beginning, it was not so. This change in the nature of their original state, their nakedness, is a huge human cancer that has eaten us alive ever since in the depths of our souls and psyche. The effects are impossible to overstate.

And Satan is cackling with delight! He knows exactly what he has done, as we will see in just a bit.

CONTENTION IN PARADISE

Now look what happens when God asks His questions about the first couple's wrongdoing. They immediately turn on each other:

The man said, "The woman whom you gave to be with me, she gave me fruit of the tree, and I ate." Then the LORD God said to the woman, "What is this that you have done?" The woman said, "The serpent deceived me, and I ate." (Genesis 3:12-13)

If you have children, have you seen this in them? You played the game when you were a child as well. And every generation before you has done so, going back to the beginning.

It's called, "But it wasn't my fault!" In adult language, it's "passing the buck." It's self-protection at another's expense. Not only did Adam not protect Eve from the temptation of the serpent, he actually threw her under the bus in order to protect himself. Not very manly. She didn't overpower the man and put the fruit in his mouth.

Is Adam making a good point here? Universally, both men and women know that Adam is being a snake himself, not "manning up."

And who else does Adam blame? It seems he wants us to know it was God's fault because He was "foolish" enough to put Adam there with that woman. Everyone's guilty but Adam. Self-protection at the expense of others was not part of man's original state. It is a product of selfishness, which comes straight from Satan. God is about others. Satan is about self.

But the knowledge of their nakedness is not just uncomfortable or inconvenient, as if they'd simply been caught in the rain without an umbrella. It brings them utter shame. They are driven to hide their most remarkable and unique distinctions as human beings from one another.

No one told them they should be ashamed because they ate the fruit. It was a "natural" consequence, as when one drops a precious vase and then it breaks. One just follows from the other. Our euphorically happy couple is no longer naked and not ashamed as God describes them in the last verse of Genesis 2.

The result of the Fall? Sin brought alienation. As we know, God's nature is community, togetherness, and intimacy. Satan lives in and brings isolation, alienation from what God has created us *for* and what He has created us *as*.

These are really the two options of life and reality as we know it: God, the originator and lover of all His creations; and Satan, who perverts and despises those creations because they come from God. As Bob Dylan told us so plainly, it might be the devil or it might be the Lord, but we're "gonna have to serve somebody."

• One is eternal and authentic; the other is limited and false.
• One is original; the other only counterfeits.
• One brings goodness; the other only corrupts.
• One brings light; the other brings darkness.
• One brings communion and acceptance; the other brings alienation and rejection.
• One brings grace; the other brings shame.
• One brings love; the other, hate.
• One brings life; the other glories in death.

You can tell who is behind anything by asking which of these qualities are present.

INTEGRATION AND DISINTEGRATION

Under God's creation, we were integrated. That means being put together properly and living consistently in that design. It is where our word "integrity" comes from, of course. And it doesn't just mean doing what is right—for example, being honest. It is deeper than this. Those with integrity do what is right and are honest because they are properly connected with God, themselves, and others. God is all about integration—bringing things together as they should be.

Apart from God, we become dis-integrated: disintegrated from ourselves, from others, from God. Most of us know and understand the word "disintegrated" in terms of sci-fi weapons that totally wipe something out, making it non-existent. There is something meaningful in this understanding. Satan wants us to be non-existent, to be obliterated because of who and what we are. Disintegrated. But as we will see, he has more than that in his crosshairs. Let us pick the story back up in Genesis 3.

It is here that God gives us our Third Definitive Statement, marking this dramatic and profoundly consequential point in the story. We find it in Genesis 3:22:

> Then the LORD God said, "Behold, the man has become
> like one of us in knowing good and evil."

This is too much knowledge for us because we have overstepped our boundaries. We are no longer as God had intended or created us to be. And there is a very dramatic consequence of this, which we find out about in the following verse:

> Therefore the LORD God sent him out from the garden
> of Eden to work the ground from which he was taken.
> (Verse 23)

We are not only alienated from God, ourselves, and each other. We are alienated from the land God gave us—driven out, exiled. This is the Fall, the third part of our fuller Christian worldview, following pre-creation and creation.

This is not just a picking up and moving on, as difficult as that can be. This is something much more devastating. *Adam and Eve Banished from Paradise*, a fresco by Tommaso Masaccio found in a Florentine church, dramatically communicates the nature of this expulsion from God's original home for them. Adam and Eve are not walking together as a couple, hand in hand, arm in arm, but as individuals. They do not have their belongings packed up and slung over their shoulders.

GET THE PICTURE

Tommaso Masaccio, *Adam and Eve Banished from Paradise* (1427)
Brancacci Chapel, Florence, Italy
Visit familyproject.com to see this painting.

An early Italian Renaissance artist, Masaccio lived a very short 27 years—but affected the art community significantly in that time, serving as a major influence on Michelangelo. This dramatic painting is a fresco from a column in the Brancacci Chapel in Florence, powerfully highlighting the utter shame and agony experienced by Adam and Eve in their banishment from the habitat God created for them. Adam hides his face while Eve hides the femininity of her body. It is perhaps the piece of art that reveals this most truly.

Masaccio knew his theology. Eve's face conveys soul-wrenching shame and agony. She is undone, her eyes dark, hollow, and lifeless. She covers the God-blessed and powerful femininity of her being. Why does she do this? Because she is ashamed of herself or because she feels vulnerable now to her husband's gaze? Or God's? We do not know. It is most likely all of these, and a deep, disintegrating shame is at its core.

Masaccio's Adam covers his face—the primary expression of his emotions and himself—in absolute shame. Isn't this what criminals often do in the "perp-walk" as they are being transported between the courthouse and jail? Adam is demonstrating for us what will become a universal human and recognizable reaction to wrongdoing. Shame is the moral equivalent of isolation, isn't it? Man cannot brush it off. We will go so far as to kill ourselves to try to escape its evil grasp.

The couple's togetherness is no consolation, as if they could say, "Well, at least we're in this mess together!" They are suffering a number of deaths and doing it individually.

FOUR DEATHS

Francis Schaeffer explains in his book *Genesis in Space and Time* that four kinds of death were introduced into creation at the Fall. As a result, we all face and are crippled by them:

1. *Death between man and God.* Man and God are no longer intimate. This alienation is what the rest of God's story is about—the consequences of it and God's seemingly unending work to make things right, to make a way for us back to Him.

2. *Death between man and himself.* We all have fear. We are insecure. We doubt ourselves and feel shame about who we are and what we do. We often don't think we are worth loving, either by ourselves or by others. Much of the psychosis that humans suffer is due to their inability to come to terms with and live with themselves. The Fall has created a great chasm there. In fact, the great Christian thinker Blaise Pascal said the primary trouble with man is that he cannot live quietly within himself.[3] He is not comfortable there. He seeks to avoid this with busyness and diversion of every kind.

3. *Death with others.* Schaeffer calls this the "sociological separation." We do not relate with others as we were intended to. We mistrust, we are shy, we use others. These

are things the virtuous person must always be mindful of, for they are more natural to us than their opposites.

4. *Death between man and the earth.* Being banished from the garden, man's relationship with the earth and nature now shows the signs of decay. We must struggle with and against it to get what we need and what had originally been designed to come naturally. We harvest by the sweat of our brows and ache in our shoulders, arms, and backs. Our relationship to God's physical creation is deeply marred.

Schaeffer beautifully states, "The simple fact is that in wanting to be what man as a creature could not be, man lost what he could be."[4]

THE CURSES

In Genesis 3 we learn that because of Adam and Eve's disobedience to God, they face dramatic consequences. These affect their relationships with each other and their work:

> To the woman [God] said, "I will surely multiply your pain in childbearing; in pain you shall bring forth children. Your desire shall be for your husband, and he shall rule over you." (Verse 16)

It is curious that her consequences have to do with her work as a mother and wife; for Adam, his struggles will come as the provider for his family.

> And to Adam [God] said, . . ."Cursed is the ground because of you; in pain you shall eat of it all the days of your life; thorns and thistles it shall bring forth for you; and you shall

eat the plants of the field. By the sweat of your face you shall
eat bread, till you return to the ground, for out of it you
were taken; for you are dust, and to dust you shall return."
(Verses 17-19)

Adam and Eve are now cursed in important parts of their work,
and in their family and social relationships.

This is the life they have to work out now—this life of enmity,
mistrust, and friction outside the Garden. The same is true for each
of us as the children of Adam and Eve. Our disobedience brings
broken relationships, which is contrary to what we are created and
intended for.

It is the deep, staggering tragedy of our tale. And this very dark,
story-changing turn happened to a husband and wife in the drama
of a marriage.

If you're married, what are the seemingly insurmountable struggles and life-cursing mistakes you have made in your relationship?
Have they brought the curse of the Fall upon all humanity? No?
Then regardless of what they might be, they are less dramatic and
destructive than those of God's original couple. Take heart. God is
not shocked by the troubles, darkness, or sin in your family. Certainly not to you, but to God it's small potatoes. It is no challenge
for Him to heal them.

Both parts of the story—the good part about what we are made
for, and the bad part of what our first forebears ruined in their
disobedience—form an answer to Gauguin's question, "Who are
we?" We must understand this tragic part of the story in order to
understand who we are. In fact, the Fall is the great equalizer of all
humans. We are all fallen, no one more or less than another.

We are glorious, even divine, in our creation as God-imagers.
But we are also utterly lost and hopeless in our rebellion and

disobedience to God. This is the enigma of man. Both parts are true. Our sin reminds us we are not "all that," yet our divine image-bearing lets us know we are not nothing. But of course this is not what God intended or wants for us.

Is there anything He can do, or is willing to do, to rescue us from this tragic dilemma?

OUR HOPE IN THE SECOND ADAM

Therefore, just as sin came into the world through one man, and death through sin, and so death spread to all men because all sinned. . . . If, because of one man's trespass, death reigned through that one man, much more will those who receive the abundance of grace and the free gift of righteousness reign in life through the one man Jesus Christ. (Romans 5:12, 17)

As the story turns bad, it doesn't stay bad. Scripture tells us that sin and death came into the world by the disobedience of one man, Adam. But the good news is that our hope and salvation from sin and death come through God's own Son, whom Christians from the beginning have referred to as the second or last Adam (1 Corinthians 15:45-49). The first brought death; the last brings life.

This Savior is the Christ, the eternal and beloved Son of God who is spoken of through the prophets and the apostles and most dramatically in John 1:

In the beginning was the Word, and the Word was with God, and the Word was God. He was in the beginning with God. All things were made through him, and without him was not any thing made that was made. In him was life, and

the life was the light of men. The light shines in the darkness, and the darkness has not overcome it. (Verses 1-5)

And then in verse 14, we read something very profound:

And the Word became flesh and dwelt among us, and we
have seen his glory, glory as of the only Son from the Father,
full of grace and truth.

How did this second Adam come? He left His heavenly place,
where He dwelt in the bosom of His Father, and while remaining
fully God—as the second Person of the Trinity—He became fully
man, fully flesh, and lived among us. This understanding of the
first Adam and the coming of the second Adam is told visually in a
stunning painting by Fra Angelico, a friar. He combines these two
stories, that of the first Adam and the coming of the second in one
image, reminding the viewer how they are connected in the story
of our redemption.

But *how* He came to dwell among us is no small matter. It has
a vast story to tell us.

A Savior is born . . .

Have you ever considered why Jesus came as He did? Why was
He born as a lowly child to an unknown couple in a backwater place?

Wouldn't it have been so much more efficient—given the importance of His saving mission—for Him to simply appear out of
nowhere, fully grown on the outskirts of Jerusalem? He could have
walked into town, turned Himself over to the authorities, and proclaimed, "Hi, My name's Jesus, God's Son. You've read about Me
in the Scriptures. You've turned away from the Father in sin. I'm
here to redeem all of mankind. So let's get this started. Where's the
nearest cross?"

GET THE PICTURE

Fra Angelico, *The Annunciation* (1427)
Museo del Prado, Madrid
Visit familyproject.com to see this painting.

Fra Angelico, a remarkably talented painter of the early Italian Renaissance, created nearly exclusively biblical scenes for cathedrals. This wonderful piece brings two very important events together, one bringing the need for the other. Here we see Adam and Eve being expelled from the Garden after their disobedience. Then we have God sending Christ to Mary's womb as the Savior of the world. Whereas Adam and Eve were disobedient to God and brought death, Mary obeys God and brings life through the divine child that grows within her.

Angelico created this painting as a sermon about the natural state of man and the supernatural way that God provided for our salvation. And a very powerful and dramatic sermon it is.

It seems sacrilegious to even imagine such a scene. But do we really understand why that approach to our redemption would have been inconsistent with God's character? Why did His divine plan unfold the way it did?

The biggest day on most of the world's calendars is the day we celebrate the coming of the Son of God in the form of a newborn baby. He was born to a Middle Eastern couple lacking any stature or influence, too poor to secure a proper place to give birth. No one would even take them in, despite their dramatic need. The humble husband had to give his wife the unfortunate news that the best he could do was a dirty stable where animals made their beds.

Consider that family drama on this silent night. Heaven touches earth most dramatically; the Son becomes one of us, a human, in what theologians call the incarnation, the fourth essential part of our fuller Christian worldview. It is profound, what C. S. Lewis called the "grand miracle," explaining "It was the central event in the history of the earth—the very thing that the whole story has been about."[5] This is the very center of the Christian story; without it, nothing else is possible. The Slovenian composer Jacobus Gallus so beautifully explains the nature of this history-changing event:

A wondrous mystery has been proclaimed today; all natures are renewed:
God has become human: He remained what he was, and what he was not, he became, suffering neither confusion nor division.[6]

The incarnation would make our salvation and freedom possible, breaking down the divide between the spiritual and the physical, bringing these two worlds together in the Person of Christ.

It is important for all believers to know that this does away forever with the first heresy to invade the church, that of gnosticism—which held that the spirit was real and desirable, while the flesh was only apparent and should be avoided and overcome. The incarnation obliterates such a view and brings all of reality—the spiritual and the physical—together in absolute harmony. Thus there is no sacred and secular. The baby is the Christ who is Lord of *all* creation; there is no division.

We cannot ignore that this grand miracle happened. God has placed it before each of us to decide for ourselves whether it actually did, and if so, what we will do with that knowledge. Nor can we ignore *how* it happened, for the *how* is just as important as the *that*. The way God did it cannot be separated from the doing; it all goes together.

AS THE FIRST ADAM CAME IN FAMILY, SO DID THE LAST

No Christian should fail to appreciate the immense significance that this grand miracle, the dramatic center of God's story, happened by His choice in a real family in an actual place in a genuine human drama much like the one in your family. A young, poor couple travels back home after going to a distant city to pay taxes. At this very time, God decides to reveal His God-become-flesh beloved Son to the world. Of all the options—and with the benefit of being God come unlimited options—He wanted to do things this way, in a lowly and very real family. It is a deeply dramatic and profound statement about the esteem God has for family.

The first Adam cannot be understood without understanding his place in family. The last Adam cannot be understood without understanding His place in family.

Jesus was very much part of a family from infancy until His death on the cross, day in and day out. His mother was there when He entered the world, and she may have been among the last ones to hold Him before His ascension to the Father. She was there at His first recorded miracle and at His crucifixion. It is no small thing that Jesus thought of His mother as He was dying that humiliating and excruciating death, instructing the apostle John to care for her in His absence. Even in His execution, He was a son watching out for His mother. We cannot miss the dramatic implications this has for a Christian theology of family.

The early church understood and referred to Mary as the "second Eve." Like Eve, she had a choice presented to her. Unlike Eve, she decided to obey and cooperate with God's plan. And as Eve's choice brought death to the earth, Mary's obedience brought—and still brings—life!

Also, consider that Jesus didn't start His public ministry until He was about 30 years of age—a bit of a late bloomer, it would seem. But it was God's will that Jesus spend the first three decades of His life in a very particular way. We know of His birth, His dedication in the temple. We know how He grew in stature and wisdom, and that He lingered in the temple for three days, giving his parents a terrible fright. Then we have a remarkably long radio silence until we get to His baptism, which tradition tells us was probably at age 30 or so. So what was Christ the Savior doing these many years between His birth and His baptism?

Have you ever thought about this part of our Lord's life? Why is there no record of these years in either the sacred or secular texts? Is it possible that there wasn't much worth recording? This silence in itself says a great deal.

Consider any possible given day of our Lord's young life as He grew into a man. It is not far-fetched to imagine that "Today Jesus of Nazareth got up at 5:30 a.m. and spent some time alone in prayer, reflecting on passages from the *Ketuvim*. He then fetched the day's water for His mother, found out the pot had a hole in it, and had to get the bigger one for today and put this one aside for repair. Jesus and Mary prepared and ate breakfast, then cleaned up, chatting a bit about their neighbors who seemed to be up all night again, quarrelling. Mary reminded Jesus He had promised to help her friend Miriam move her extra table to her son's house this afternoon. Jesus asked what was wrong with Miriam's son's back as Mary gave Him that look that mothers give, implying her request was not really a request at all and that good Jewish boys don't question their mothers. But His playfulness made her smile. He went to work for about five hours in the shop, building two doors out of cedar for Cephas's new house. Mary wondered why, since Cephas hasn't paid for the hutch Jesus delivered two weeks ago. After finishing His work, Jesus headed down to the lake with Andrew, as He often has, to enjoy the cool breezes before going to move that table and walk home to help with dinner."

It is not difficult to imagine that this is close to how God incarnate spent most days over these 30 years. Nothing significant.

Christ, the God-man, for the majority of His earthly life was a growing, maturing boy living a pretty ho-hum routine in a humble family. He worked hard, studied well, played with His friends, and was obedient to His parents.

GET THE PICTURE

John Rogers Herbert, *Our Savior Subject to His Parents at Nazareth* (1847) Guildhall Art Gallery, London
Visit familyproject.com to see this painting.

Herbert was an English mid-Victorian painter who believed his purpose as an artist was to communicate God's truths. This is a rare work in that it doesn't portray Christ in a known biblical setting, but simply living His life as a dutiful son of His parents—doing the everyday chores every member of a family is expected to do. Consider that Jesus—God Himself—did such things for decades, before and after He started His public ministry. This is a statement of the divine nature of such seemingly humdrum work; if God is content to do it, it is holy.

And so it went, year after year. The sovereign, eternal God of the universe was content to become one of us, to linger in a normal, workaday human life much like yours—and to do so for three decades. He didn't seem to be in a hurry to get on to the really important work of saving mankind. That would come in its own time.

This fact sanctifies the mundane and everyday, for what God does is profoundly sacred and holy, is it not? Even if it's taking out the trash when your mother asks you to, or making sure there's enough wine to last until the wedding party is over. Jesus, the Christ and the Savior, was a family man. He started out that way on Christmas day and remained that way until Good Friday.

So it was through family that the Son became flesh and dwelt among us in order to free us from the curse and consequences of our original parents' sin. Those born of Adam—which is all of us—are condemned in our sin, separated from God as Adam and Eve were. But there is great hope:

> But to all who did receive him, who believed in his name, he gave the right to become children of God. (John 1:12)

The first Adam brought death—in the context of family.

The last Adam brought life—through the context of family.

And we can accept this new life from God in the context of being welcomed into His family as His very children.

In this chapter we've learned about the tragic turn in the story of God's children. It touches all of creation and every part of our humanity. But God does not leave us in our despair and alienation. He sends us a Savior and does so in a dramatic way—through a family.

Just as all other stories have an antagonist and protagonist, God's story has both—the original versions of both, in fact. And just as in all good stories, one is victorious and the other is vanquished when the crisis is resolved. But the truth, danger, victory, and restoration found in God's story make it the greatest one of all.

THE BIG STATEMENT FOR REFLECTION

Because of the free will that God gave man, which authentic love requires, God's despiser targeted what he knew was the image of God in creation. His deception and Adam and Eve's disobedience sabotaged each important relationship. But there was a second Adam—the Son of the Father—who brought new life to all of us, and He did so in and through a family.

QUESTIONS FOR CONSIDERATION

1. Later on in God's story, He gives humanity 10 commandments. Jesus summed these up in two great commands. But God originally gave Adam and Eve one simple rule. What does this say about the nature of rules and obedience?
2. Based on what happened in the Fall, how might Satan attack a married couple today? What might he tempt them to do? What might cause them to yield? How might they resist?
3. Adam and Eve's disobedience led to alienation, separation, and blaming each other. Are these things every married couple has experienced? Is it worth trying to overcome them? Why or why not?
4. Why does it matter that Jesus came through a family? How does it elevate your family's significance? How could your family participate in God's plan to redeem the world?

Part III

YOUR FAMILY PROJECT

Now, a change in course.

Up to now, we have been looking at the overarching view of family—what it is in light of who God is, what He created us to be and do, and how family reflects God's image and plays a central role in fulfilling His purposes in the world.

This theological and philosophical look at family is essential to all Christians because of the central role it plays in understanding God and what He is doing with humanity in the world. But from here on we begin a different route in our journey.

Beginning in the next chapter, we start to examine what we call "the particulars" of family, building on the foundation of what we have learned so far, what family *really* is in the here and now. It's about what *your* family and the families around you mean and do, and who the greatest enemies of your family really are.

WHAT GOD HAS
JOINED TOGETHER

Anyone paying the slightest bit of attention to the noise in the public square over the past 40 years knows that there has been a very robust public debate about the nature and importance of family in society. Many have referred to it as the "culture war"—caricaturing it as a battle in which moralistic, conservative Christians have sought to require the world to live by their standards of what family should be. On the other side, it is said, are the cultural elites—media, Hollywood, and academia—who have mostly advocated for greater family diversity and experimentation.

Ask any journalist, scholar, or political pundit when the culture war over the family started and who started it, and he or she will answer you quickly and assuredly along these lines: "It started in the United States in the late 1970s and into the Reagan era, begun and driven by religious conservative leaders like Anita Bryant, Jerry Falwell, Phyllis Schlafly, Dr. James Dobson, Pat Robertson, and D. James Kennedy."

Many would not think to question this answer, because we've heard it over and over. But it is not true.

The beginning of the modern "culture war" on family actually had a slightly earlier and more interesting start. It was not busybody "Bible thumpers" who started it, nor was it a Republican presidential administration that exploited it. It started more than a decade earlier in a completely different way.

In March 1965, a mid-level member of President Lyndon Johnson's administration, Daniel Patrick Moynihan, released a powerful and groundbreaking report from the White House that immediately became politically infamous. *The Negro Family: The Case for National Action* was both a family and civil rights manifesto. It warned that while the newly passed Civil Rights Act of 1964 could do much to rightfully lift the fortunes of black Americans, these gains would most likely be undercut by another important social factor: the crumbling black family. The husband and father was the critical weak link. The strength and health of the family was a social justice issue of great concern to Moynihan and his boss. He opened this pioneering report with these stark words:

> The United States is approaching a new crisis in race relations. . . . The fundamental problem, in which this is most clearly the case, is that of family structure. The evidence—while not final, but powerfully persuasive—is that the Negro family in the urban ghettos is crumbling. So long as this situation persists, the cycle of poverty and disadvantage will continue to repeat itself.[1]

These are powerful words, and were wholly new to the public political debate on social well-being. Moynihan, with great passion, warned that the fact that far too many black children reached adulthood having lived apart from their fathers at some time in their childhoods was a situation so serious it demanded what he called "national action" to correct it.

It may seem obvious that for all races, adults who are socially, educationally, and financially successful more likely came from stable, intact families. But criticism of the Moynihan Report (as it became known) and its author was fierce, immediate, unanticipated, and highly personal. What audacity, some said, for a white academic to blame the plight of black Americans on their difficulty in holding their families together! This is not what Moynihan was saying, but it was echoed repeatedly until it became a manufactured "truth." Writing to a friend months after the report's release, Moynihan lamented, "If my head were sticking on a pike at the South West Gate to the White House grounds the impression [of disdain toward me] would hardly be greater."[2] This, and a speech that President Johnson gave later that summer at Howard University on the topic of the report, were the first major shots in the modern culture war on the family.

Today, however, opinion about the Moynihan Report has changed dramatically. Sociologist and professor James Q. Wilson explains that at the time of its release, the report was "denounced left and right by academics . . . [but] now it is generally regarded to be right on the mark."[3]

Given our study of the family in this book, we must discover why the public and political discussion of the family's importance and well-being causes such fireworks in the culture. Many answers to this question have been tossed around; one is that people are uncomfortable talking in the public square about something as personal as family. It seems to be meddling in people's private lives, doesn't it?

But this widely held belief spawns another question: Are marriage, parenthood, and family private or public institutions? This gets at the very nature of family itself: What is it, what does it do, and why is it necessary?

We will answer these important questions by looking at four different sources—Scripture, sociology, anthropology, and political philosophy.

FAMILY: PUBLIC OR PRIVATE?

As we have seen in previous chapters, the first institution God established was a family. It was not a government, a business, or an institution of learning. It is not even His body, the church. Not yet.

> So God created man in his own image, in the image of God
> he created him; male and female he created them. God
> blessed them. And God said to them, "Be fruitful and mul-
> tiply and fill the earth and subdue it, and have dominion
> over the fish of the sea and over the birds of the heavens and
> over every living thing that moves on the earth." And God
> said, "Behold, I have given you every plant yielding seed
> that is on the face of all the earth, and every tree with seed
> in its fruit. You shall have them for food. And to every beast
> of the earth and to every bird of the heavens and to every-
> thing that creeps on the earth, everything that has the breath
> of life, I have given every green plant for food." And it was
> so. And God saw everything that he had made, and behold,
> it was very good. (Genesis 1:27-31)

So God creates humanity in two similar but very different forms: male and female. And God immediately blessed them and commanded them to get busy doing things. This part of God's Word is what is called the "cultural mandate," the explanation of what God has given the first two humans to do, what their existence and work are to be about.

What is first? They are to get busy being fruitful and reproducing after their own kind, to start a family from their union as man and wife. And God's order is to have this family produce other families, and so on, to fill the earth. It's a domino effect, except in a good way.

And what comes next? This first family and those after are called to subdue the earth, to manage it, to make it useful and productive, their home. They are to oversee the living creatures and plants, to care for them, to multiply and harvest them ("for you may eat from any of the trees . . .") for the good of these God-imaging humans. Starting with family, the first community, they are to build a society.

The first act of family—the marital embrace between husband and wife to bring forth new life—is the most private of all acts. This is true in all cultures. Parenting these new God-imaging creatures called children is also a private act, for it is the role and responsibility of parents to train up their children in the way they should go. But it is not wholly private, is it? Others participate at the parents' invitation and request. Typically this involves members of the extended family helping to protect, prepare, raise, and educate the children. Eve could not call on her mother for help, encouragement, or advice in caring for her new baby. Other mothers will naturally do so if their mothers are available and capable. As the child grows, others in the community will join this important process—be they doctors, educators, babysitters, religious leaders, or older women who share their experience. Parenting is not a completely private activity.

More publicly, community institutions—business, industry, government, law enforcement, churches, schools, even one's neighbors—expect parents to work hard raising well-educated, honest, hard-working, innovative, relatively selfless young adults who will help any of these institutions do what they are commissioned to do by the larger society. All societies have a deeply practical need for the men and women of today to give birth to and raise the men and women of tomorrow. Each generation needs a new one to come along, for these become the healthcare workers, business owners, educators, inventors, political and military leaders, police officers, and taxpayers who pay to maintain the community infrastructure— and the previous generation's retirement benefits.

Children grow to be what no society can do without: contributors and consumers. But it's happening less and less today, and not without serious consequences. A 2012 article in the *Atlantic* entitled "Europe's Real Crisis" explains that a nation's economic fortunes "are as much demographic as they are financial." People who create wealth, jobs, and tax payments do so through earning, investment, creating, employing, and consuming. And of course, you have to be born to do this. A nation that doesn't replace itself and more can't survive from generation to generation. The *Atlantic* explains how stark the shrinking birth trend is in much of the world:

> The United Nations estimates that by 2030, the number of people older than 60 will be growing more than three times as fast as the general population. By 2050, one in every five people will be over 60. In the developed world, the proportion will be more like one in three. Europe (along with Japan) is the forefront of an unprecedented shift.[4]

This article explains that the economic growth of a nation cannot be ordered pronto like a pizza, but requires a long time in the baking. It's dependent on two essential ingredients: a growing population of workers and higher worker productivity. In fact, a recent report by Morgan Stanley explains that a country's larger proportion of older citizens relative to its shrinking proportion of younger citizens may now be a more important indicator of its likelihood to default on its debt payments than the actual size of the debt itself.

Consider this in terms of a household budget. A home has $25,000 of credit card debt and only one employed person who earns $40,000 annually. Not a good debt risk. But what if this home carrying that much debt had six people each earning only $20,000 to $30,000 annually? Which home would you want owing you money? Apply that same dynamic to a nation's debt. New people matter.

This requires having babies and raising them to apply themselves to a task and see it through; procreation and good parenting are really what drive a nation's economy as much as anything else, if not more. Since these two things work best when they take place under the protection of a marriage, it's a serious social problem that most nations in the world are seeing less of both. Politicians are taking anxious notice. Many European nations are giving men and women strong financial incentives to have children, and not because babies make these officials feel all warm inside. It's because of the socially pragmatic role babies play in the future and vibrancy of every single community, and they are seeing less and less of it.[5]

This is how all societies, without exception, begin, grow, and maintain themselves. And it starts with

- a public ceremony of marriage
- a private act of physical marital union
- the relatively private act of childbirth, usually facilitated by a midwife or doctor and perhaps a grandmother

- the private and public act of parenting, which happens in the community and with the help of segments of the community
- ultimately, the sending of the matured child from his or her family of origin into the public world—to begin contributing and most likely starting a new family

This is primarily the way family works in all cultures, and has since the first two human beings appeared. And this serves an irreplaceable public good. This is both a biblical truth and an anthropological reality.

So, is family a private or public institution? We can conclude that family is much more public than it is private. And it starts with marriage, which does four essential things that all societies need:

1. *Marriage socializes men.* Anthropologists tell us that a society's most serious problem is the unattached male. Apart from the family, they don't tend to be very pro-social creatures. They don't tend to settle down. Marriage is the answer. Natural marriage socializes men by channeling male sexuality and aggression in socially productive ways. And it is women who do this through marriage. Marriage is meant to ensure that the man protects, provides for, and cares for the mother and their common children. The social requirement and expectation of this are what settles men down and requires them to focus on building a home and family.

Gail Collins of the *New York Times* wrote a book titled *America's Women,* which examines the role of women in American culture. In a 2003 interview on National Public Radio, Collins said, "The most important implicit role women play in society is to make men behave."[6] Other scholars have recognized the same thing.[7]

2. *Marriage regulates sexuality.* Marriage establishes sexual guardrails, a requirement for successful societies. We cannot survive with everybody doing whatever they want sexually. Every so-

ciety must have socially held and enforced boundaries, mores, and standards about sexual behavior; marriage is how societies manage human sexuality.

3. *Monogamous marriage protects women from exploitive males.* When we do not have a social norm of monogamy, women become commodities—things to be collected, used, and discarded. Marriage helps protect women by regulating sex. When women socialize men through marriage and parenthood, men are more likely to care for and respect their wives and other women. When fewer men are married to women, fewer men care for and respect them.[8]

Matrimony is all about a man caring for, protecting, and providing for his child and that child's mother. Marriage is what attaches this man to that woman in a permanent, exclusive relationship that allows the woman to make demands upon and have expectations of the man.

4. *Marriage provides mothers and fathers for children.* Healthy children define a growing society. And marriage is the way we ensure that the next generation grows up with the irreplaceable benefit of being raised by their mothers and fathers. No society since the beginning of time has found a better way of doing this, and it is very unlikely one ever will.

WHAT DO THE SOCIAL SCIENCES SAY?

Ask any mayor, governor, police officer, prison warden, teacher, school principal, social welfare professional, pediatrician, or psychologist whether family strength and cohesion matter for the public life of a community. They'll tell you, "Of course." The more marriages and married parenting we have in any community, the easier and more successful any of these professionals' work becomes. Mountains of sociological research over the last four to five decades have convincingly and consistently shown that intact marriages and families increase the physical and mental health of their members, as well as giving them a longer, happier life. They dramatically increase their likelihood of educational success, their likelihood of being employed long-term, their earning and savings ability, their sexual satisfaction, and their helpful involvement in and contribution to the larger community and its safety.

Marriage produces these benefits; cohabitation doesn't come close. In fact, living together doesn't elevate any of these factors over those who are not in a domestic relationship. It can tend to lower them below those of true singles, however.

Living in an intact family with married parents also significantly reduces the likelihood of being a victim of domestic and sexual abuse, being involved in criminal activity, being incarcerated, suffering from substance abuse, living in either moderate or severe poverty, having generally unhealthy behaviors—and the list goes on. This is true for men, women, and children. These findings are a sociological truism; the social science research on this topic proves it time and time again, regardless of how the research is done.[9]

William J. Goode, one of the early deans of the academy of social scientists, explains the social universality of marriage and family:

> The intense emotional meaning of family relations for almost all members of society has been observable throughout man's history. . . . The family is the only social institution other than religion which is formally developed in all societies. . . . Each person is kinsman to many.

He goes on to describe the unique and necessary job the family accomplishes:

The family is the only social institution charged with transforming a biological organism into a human being. By the time other institutions begin to shape the individual in important ways, his family has already accomplished much of this transformation, having taught him to speak and to play out many social roles.

Goode continues,

Almost no family role responsibilities can be delegated to others, as more specialized obligations can be in a work situation. . . . The family is the fundamental *instrumental* foundation of the larger social structure, in that all other institutions depend on its contributions. . . . In all these ways, the family is an instrument or agent of the larger society; its failure to perform adequately means that the goals of the larger society may not be attained effectively.[10]

Simply put, any society can only be as healthy and vibrant as its families are strong. These two are intrinsically linked; caring for family is caring for the larger community and human thriving. The job the family does in creating healthy, happy, productive human beings is irreplaceable. No other social institution—government, education, healthcare, business, or even the church—can accomplish this essential task.

WHAT DOES ANTHROPOLOGY SAY?

Let us see how this is true and why by looking at an important field of study: anthropology. Anthropology is the study of man and how he lives his life in a particular time and place. It observes, records, and analyzes human behavior, social life, and community structures. Anthropologists have long been interested in the role marriage and family play in how humans live in different cultures, places, and times.

Anthropology as a discipline doesn't make value or ethical judgments per se, but rather observes what is there in any given culture. As we consider what anthropologists through the ages have learned and said about marriage, parenting, and sexuality, we must appreciate that they are not explaining what they think is bad or good about a culture and its needs. They don't concern themselves with what *should* happen to make things better. They leave that to others. Their role is to observe, record, and analyze.

As such, anthropologists can help us a great deal in our understanding of the relationship of marriage and family to the human culture throughout history and across different parts of the world. It helps us learn what the family is—if it can even be understood as one thing—in human experience and history.

First, Professor Donald Brown, whom we mentioned earlier regarding human universals, explains how marriage and family are themselves universals rather than mere social constructs particular to certain cultures at certain times:

> The universality of kinship terminologies provides a further case of cultural reflection or recognition of physical fact. A kinship terminology is that linguistic domain (discrete set of terms) found among every people, in which . . . all terms are translatable by the terms required for sexual reproduction, or combinations of them: father, mother, son, daughter. . . . Marriage—which is distinct from procreation, per se—so regularly impinges on kinship

terminologies that it is usually counted as one of the two fundamental building blocks of kinship. Accordingly, the father and mother of an individual are normally husband and wife.[11]

Simply put, it is universally true that kinship—family ties, relationships, and responsibilities—is founded upon the sexual, procreative union between a man and woman who are, by social expectation and encouragement, husband and wife. The extended family is a collection—a social molecular structure—of this basic triad of mother, father, and child. This transcends a culture's religion, law, politics, and economics. It applies to all human societies.

Likewise, in her book *Male and Female*, anthropologist Margaret Mead finds the same thing:

> When we survey all known human societies, we find everywhere some form of the family, some set of permanent arrangements by which males assist females in caring for children while they are young. . . . In every known human society, everywhere in the world, the young male learns that when he grows up, one of the things he must do in order to be a full member of society is to provide food for some female and her young. . . . Every known human society rests firmly on the learned nurturing behavior of men.[12]

She is explaining that family requires the male to settle down and contribute his time, energy, and resources to the care of his wife and their common children. It is what turns men and their male energy into productive, safe citizens.

Bronislaw Malinowski, in his groundbreaking book *Sex, Culture, and Myth*, observes,

In human societies, however, there are added to the sexual and parental sides of marriage other elements: marriage is given the hall-mark of social approval. . . . It defines the relations between husband and wife and between parents and child, as well as the status of the latter; it imposes duties of economic co-operation. . . . Marriage again is in no human culture a matter of an entirely free choice.[13]

There are social expectations and requirements of who marries whom. Parents, siblings, and extended family have long disapproved or favored certain engagements, and they typically do so with significant influence.

Noted Yale anthropologist George Peter Murdock offers this definition and explanation of marriage and family across cultures in his landmark book *Social Structure*:

Three distinct types of family organization emerge from our survey of 250 representative human societies. The first and most basic, called herewith the nuclear family, consists typically of a married man and woman and their offspring, although in individual cases one or more additional persons may reside with them. . . . Among the majority of peoples of the earth . . . nuclear families are combined like atoms in a molecule. . . . A polygamous family consists of two or more nuclear families. . . . An extended family consists of two or more nuclear families affiliated through an extension of the parent-child relationship rather than the husband-wife relationship . . .[14]

So Professor Murdock explains that the term "nuclear family" is not a moral, traditionalist, or even Western cultural term, but a universal, anthropological one describing the fundamental and most irreducible building block of any society.

More recently, a Dutch anthropologist working from an evolutionary point of view wrote,

> All known human societies recognize the existence of the sexual pair-bond and give it formal sanction in the form of marriage. With only a handful of exceptions presently to be examined, married pairs are not only expected to copulate with each other, but to cooperate in the raising of offspring and to extend to each other material help. . . . Marriage is nevertheless the cultural codification of a biological program. Marriage is the socially sanctioned pair-bond for the avowed social purpose of procreation.[15]

Don't tell him, but this is precisely what the Scriptures say about how humans from the beginning have constructed their lives together, isn't it?

FAMILY: A SOCIAL CONSTRUCTION?

As we have stated earlier, the primary and undergirding orthodoxy on nearly every mainstream university campus today is that family is a "social construction." In this view, the family is the way it is because religious or political forces of a culture demand that it be that way. There is nothing "natural" about the family. It is established, crafted, and molded according to what a particular society believes or wants. We encounter and are challenged by this view of marriage, family, and gender when we speak on this topic at secular universities, being lectured (often scolded and demeaned) on how we are naïve to not understand such a basic fact.

We counter our challengers with this question: "What are these dramatically, monolithically powerful religious and political forces that have imposed marriage and family as it universally exists in all cultures at all times, as these leading anthropologists have told us is the case?"

They don't have an answer for this. They must reject the conclusions of the brightest stars in the field of family anthropology in order to maintain their wholly ideological position. But *something* has imposed a universal view of marriage, family, and sexuality on all cultures at all times. For the non-believer, the answer to that question would be nature. For the believer, that answer would be nature's God. Christianity has its answer, and it is true to what anthropologists have observed throughout decades of work.

DOES ANTHROPOLOGY EXPLAIN
WHEN MARRIAGE STARTED?

So if we find marriage in all human cultures, at all times, what does anthropology tell us about when it started?

In terms of biblical history, we know marriage began with the creation of humanity. Curiously, anthropologists give us a somewhat similar answer. Edward Westermarck, in his three-volume *The History of Human Marriage*, explains:

> Marriage is generally used as a term for a social institution. . . .
> Marriage always implies the right to sexual intercourse: society holds such intercourse allowable in the case of husband and wife. . . . At the same time, marriage is something more than a regulated sexual relation. . . . It is the husband's duty . . . to support his wife and children. . . . That the functions of the husband and father in the family are not

merely of the sexual and procreative kind, but involve the duty of protecting the wife and children, is testified by an array of facts relating to peoples in all quarters of the world and in all stages of civilization.

. . . As for the origin of the institution of marriage, I consider it probable that it has developed out of primeval habit.[16]

In other words, it seems marriage has always just *been*. Kathleen Gough, another leading light in this field, published a celebrated article in 1971 titled "The Origins of Family." The first line of her article admits with academic humility, "The trouble with the origin of the family is that no one really knows." Gough continues, "It is not known *when* the family originated, although it was probably between two million and 100,000 years ago."[17] In other words, it has been around longer than anyone can tell. There is not a point in human experience or history where scholars can tell us that marriage started, as they can with humanity's use of specific tools, modes of farming, commerce, and the development of various religious practices. It is almost as if it were there since . . . in the beginning.

Family, Society, and Political Philosophy

Political philosophy explains man's ideas, debates, and differences on how society should construct itself as an ideal community. What does it have to say about family?

Unlike anthropology and sociology, which seek to merely observe and report on human behavior, politics is more ideological and idealistic. It imagines what is best for a people and their government and seeks to realize that. Let's begin with the ancient Greek philosopher Plato and his unique take on the relationship between the family and the state.

PLATO

Plato, the most important student of Socrates, in his *Republic* presents his thoughts on how a human society functions in the ideal. The place of the family here is quite radical. In Plato's vision, the main drivers and builders of society—the Guardians—would have no family as it is typically considered. He explains,

> No one man and one woman are to set up house together privately: wives are to be held in common by all: so too are the children, and no parent is to know his own child, nor any child his parent.

Plato believes that this conception of family is somehow self-evident in terms of desirability by all, but questionable in terms of functionality:

> I imagine no one would deny the immense advantage of wives and children being held in common, provided it can be done. I should expect dispute to arise chiefly over the question whether it is possible.

The unions formed among the Guardians would not be directed by love, interest, or desire of the individuals, but merely driven ultimately by the good of the state. His is a very early eugenics idea in which the healthy, beautiful, and intelligent are intentionally created, while the sick, uncomely, and dull are intentionally weeded out.

> If we are to keep our flock at the highest pitch of excellence, there should be as many unions of the best of both

sexes, and as few of the inferior, as possible, and that only
the off-spring of the better unions should be kept.

This approach takes a very utilitarian view of family and the
life it produces:

> And the brides and grooms in service to the state will be
> brought together for procreative purposes at select times of
> the years. And pregnancies shall commence at this time of
> Festival and only as many as the state requires with the . . .
> aim at keeping the number of citizens as constant as possible,
> having regard to losses caused by war, epidemics and so on:
> and they must do their best to see that our state does not
> become either too great or too small.[18]

For Plato, the family exists exclusively for the good of the state.
The basic functions of the family—marriage, procreation, and parenting—are defined solely by the apparent needs of the state.

Can you count the cultures we have seen throughout history
that have functioned for any considerable time under such a definition of family? If this were *Jeopardy*, the correct answer would be,
"Alex, what is zero?"

Precisely, and it's not for want of trying.

UTOPIAN SOCIETIES

There have been many attempts to create a society where family was
intentionally redefined. Many have sought to realize Plato's basic plan.
These utopian communities, as they've become known, tried to establish a social and family system contrary to the universal norm. They
are important to study and didn't start with the hippies of the 1960s.

The Israeli *kibbutzim* were a utopian idea born in the early years of the twentieth century, based largely on a new way to do agriculture and economics in a communal setting. In time, participants started raising their children collectively, with select caregivers assigned to care for all the children together in the common "children's houses." It was their declared goal to prove the nuclear family deficient, as these parents had only the weakest of connections with their children. One child who grew to adulthood in a kibbutz in the 1960s wistfully recalled,

> We would visit our parents every afternoon between 4 p.m. and 8 p.m., then they would return us to the children's house to sleep. Our . . . mothers never cooked us a meal, never washed our clothes or sang us a lullaby. The kibbutz system sought to limit private intimacies in case they diverted member's energies from the communal project.

These memories were not shared as warm remembrances. After a time, the kibbutz faced serious problems. The communal sleeping arrangements of children were gradually abandoned, "in large part driven by women who grew up in the children's house and, having become mothers, refused to let their children experience that same system" of alienation, emotional coldness, and prison-like living arrangements. Children of this system explained, "We learned to numb ourselves. I haven't cried since I was 10. I'd like to but I can't."[19] Children were taught that emotional expression and personal attachment were weak and self-indulgent.

The Oneida Community was another example of a utopian arrangement. Established in 1848 by John Humphrey Noyes in upstate New York, it was a cultish sect that practiced what it called "complex marriage." This was a program established by Noyes in which all men and women would have sexual access to all others, the only guiding principle being consent. Developing love relationships was not allowed, as all adults were to be free for anyone else.

As in Plato's *Republic*, only certain desirable members of the community were allowed to procreate. A committee was required to assess a couple and approve its worthiness to bear children for the community. All others practiced a sexual technique developed by Noyes that was designed to prevent pregnancy. The children born to the community, as in the kibbutz, were raised collectively in the "children's wing" of the community mansion. Parents could visit their children, but were strictly prohibited from developing an emotional bond with them.

But all was not ideal, as anyone could guess. Soon a heated debate developed among the men in the community regarding the young women. Dare to guess what that might be about?

At what age would the community introduce its young girls to sexual activity, and who would take responsibility for this initiation? It was obviously a very contentious topic, given that the age of initiation was getting younger and younger. Noyes himself believed it was God's will that he do the bulk of the initiating. The other men had their doubts about Noyes's calling. A warrant for his arrest for statutory rape was rumored to be forthcoming, so Noyes felt it time to visit Canada. The community's familial ideals fell into disarray. It didn't even last through Noyes's lifetime.

Complex marriage was soon abandoned due to jealous conflicts. Most of the young adults, having been raised in this family experiment, desired to return to the exclusive nuclear family form for their own well-being and that of their children. Nature has a way of righting itself after a time, primarily because of the stubborn way nature works. The Oneida Community as it was founded broke up, but some of its members founded a company based on the production talent created in the community. This new company eventually became the Oneida Limited Corporation, a major manufacturer of silverware that you might ironically give as a wedding present or bring out in your own home at Thanksgiving and Christmas.[20]

People have had big ideas of how they could refashion the family and develop a better, more just society. But for some reason those ideas never really work. We are seeing the same thing today with vast family redefinition—resulting in widespread divorce, cohabitation, and unmarried childbearing. Each of these has been well documented to lower the well-being of men, women, children, and the larger community. Most recently, gender-less marriage and parenting have been championed by cultural elites as yet another family form that could improve upon the nuclear family. It was hubris 100 years ago, and it is hubris today. You might think we would learn that a working replacement for the mother-and-father-married-for-life family is not likely. Its architect and designer knew what He was doing.

Other political philosophers largely recognized this, whether they realized it or not. One of them was Aristotle, Plato's student and Alexander the Great's teacher.

ARISTOTLE

Aristotle, in the first book of his *Politics*—his explanation of how the good and virtuous social life is achieved—takes up the question of the place of family in the community. Considering how the city or *polis* (where we get our words like "politics," "metropolis," and "police") developed, Aristotle explains that the "noblest view" would be that which showed us "how such things develop[ed] naturally from the beginning." He continues, almost as if he might have Genesis 2:18 on his mind:

First, then, it is necessary that those who cannot exist without each other couple together, as male and female . . . for the sake of generation (and this not from deliberate choice, but because, like other animals and plants, they have a natural desire to leave behind something else like themselves).

From such beginnings society develops, because,

the household first came to be, so Hesiod spoke correctly when he composed the line: "first a house, a wife and ox for ploughing," because as far as the poor are concerned, the ox takes the place of a slave. The household, then, is by nature a community set up for the needs of everyday, whose members Charondas calls, "fellows of the same bread" and Epimenides the Cretan "fellows of the same manger."

For Aristotle, the family precedes society, law, and the state. But it is not an end in itself:

But as soon as several households have come together in a community for other than the needs of the day, then there is a village. By nature, in fact, the village seems to be principally an offshoot of the household, namely the children and the children of children, those whom some call "fellows of the same milk." . . . And when the community made up of several villages is complete, it is then a city . . . and though it exists for the sake of staying alive, it exists for the sake of living well. Consequently, every city exists by nature.[21]

For Aristotle, unlike Plato, the mighty river of human society does not exist for itself. It is made up of countless drops of water that join together to make something much larger and more powerful; it would be nothing if not for each drop coming together to make a whole. This is exactly what the nuclear family is to society. Aristotle saw it clearly long before 1950s suburban America, when many of our elite today mistakenly think the nuclear family got its start as an ideal. It is old and central to human society.

So, according to Aristotle and the various anthropologists we have heard from, the family is not a creation of the state. Instead, the state is a creation contingent on many families coming together. And healthy, intact families at that.

ABRAHAM KUYPER

We have seen secular, social-science, and classical-philosophical views of the family as a social institution. Are there any Christians who have developed a strong social view of and case for the family based on orthodox, biblical understanding? Indeed—and one of the most solid understandings of the family's relation to the state comes from Abraham Kuyper, an influential Dutch prime minister, journalist, statesman, and theologian of the last century.

In his celebrated Stone Lectures of 1898 delivered at Princeton University, Kuyper endeavored to apply the theological thinking of Calvin to various areas of public life. The third of his six lectures on Calvinism—titled "Calvinism and Politics"—discusses the primary parts or spheres of the human community, their relation to one another, and their relation to God. These are the Sovereignty of the State, the Sovereignty of Society, and the Sovereignty of the Church. The word "sovereignty" in this context means that each of these has unique and determined roles or domains that the others may not tread beyond or upon.

But each realm is checked in its power by subordination to

a greater authority. This is so, according to Kuyper, because the spheres "eradiate" from the primordial "Sovereignty of the Triune God over the whole Cosmos, in all its spheres and kingdoms, visible and invisible."[22]

Kuyper agrees with Aristotle that man is a political animal, one who needs an order and structure to his personal and public life— what he calls in Dutch a *zoon politikon*. This recognizes God's Second Definitive Statement, in that humans are fundamentally social creatures and must develop and live in a communal life together. They need to and must learn to live together in harmony and cooperation requiring rules and rulers. This gives rise to a political life of the community. But our original sin creates another need as well. Kuyper explains in poetic fashion,

> For indeed without sin, there would have been neither magistrate nor state-order; political life, in its entirety, would have evolved itself, after a patriarchal fashion, from the life of the family. Neither bar of justice, nor police, nor army, nor navy is conceivable in a world without sin. . . . Who binds up, where nothing is broken? Who uses crutches, where the limbs are sound?[23]

But with or without sin's effect on the world, we would have a political life because it was given to humanity to subdue and rule the creation. We would require a way to have a multitude of families—and the individuals in those families—work together cooperatively. The Fall did not initiate the question of whether we would have a government, but instead, what kind and to what end it would be needed. Whereas Plato and Aristotle saw the state as deeply primary, to differing degrees, Kuyper takes another view altogether. He would have us understand, as of "highest importance," the difference in the organic life of society (of which family is the primary component) and the mechanical character of the government in a fallen world. Kuyper explains the organic life of society and from where it arises:

> Whatever among men originates directly from creation
> is possessed of all the data for its development, in human
> nature as such. You see this at once in the family and in the
> connection of blood relations and other ties. From the dual-
> ity of man and woman, marriage arises. From the original
> existence of *one* man and *one* woman monogamy comes
> forth. The children exist by reason of the innate power
> of reproduction; naturally the children are connected as
> brother and sister. And by and by these children, in their
> turn, marry again, as a matter of course all those connec-
> tions originate from blood-relationships and other ties,
> which dominate the whole family-life. In all this, there is
> nothing mechanical. . . . For the vast majority of our race,
> marriage remains the foundation of human society and
> the family retains its position as the primordial sphere of
> sociology.[24]

The family is fundamentally organic. It springs up naturally among men. This is precisely what secular anthropologist Edward Westermarck explained—as we've already seen. Marriage and family are basic parts of creation and human experience; as such, they are the most basic part of human culture, existing before the Fall, straight from the mouth and absolute delight of God.

"But the case is wholly different," according to Kuyper, "with the assertion of the powers of government." He explains how the state has a God-ordained but mechanical origin, as found in the building of Babel's tower and the development of the nations:

> These people formed States. And over these States God appointed *governments*. And thus, if I may be allowed the expression, it is not a natural head, which organically grew from the body of the people, but a *mechanical* head, which from without has been placed upon the trunk of the nation. A mere remedy, therefore, for a wrong condition supervening. A stick placed beside the plant to hold it up, since without it, by reason of its inherent weakness, it would fall to the ground.[25]

The state therefore, is God-ordained—but as a mechanical device "according to apostolic testimony" to bear the sword. That role is three-fold:

1. To bear the sword of *justice* among and for its citizens.
2. To bear the sword of *war* as protection against its enemies.
3. To bear the sword of *order* to protect its citizens against civil rebellion.

Thus, given the organic nature of the family and the mechanical nature of the state, the family cannot be coerced to change according to the purpose and will of the government as Plato proposed.

Why? Because the organic cannot be directed by the mechanical. The latter exists, as God's servant, to protect and nurture the organic—as a stick placed by the gardener beside the trunk of a plant to hold it up. "The State may never become an octopus, which stifles the whole of life," Kuyper warns.[26]

But, as Kuyper informs us, this does not mean the organic spheres are wholly autonomous from the state. The state must intervene in family matters, but only in the following cases:

1. The social spheres, such as family, art, science, agriculture, industry, or commerce transgress their own boundary lines and infringe upon the others;

2. To defend the weak ones in these spheres against the abuse of power by the strong, as in the case of domestic violence or child labor abuses; and

3. To encourage all to collectively bear the personal and financial burdens for the maintenance of the natural unity of the state.[27]

This is the importance and wisdom of what has become known as Kuyper's "sphere sovereignty." Each territory of society has its role, and no sphere is to encroach upon another. Yet all affect one another.

As Kuyper explains, "The sphere of the State is not profane," because it does have a necessary, albeit mechanical function.[28] It exists to serve and protect the sovereignty of the other organic spheres, including and especially the family. Curiously, this is precisely what Scripture, anthropologists, and sociologists explain—the first by divine revelation and the other two by honest observation of universal human culture and experience the ingredients of well-being and happiness: natural revelation.

COMMUNITY SERVICE

This is what your family is and does. It is not just a private institution, having no effect outside its own walls. When we see what families do in and for a community, we cannot escape the truth that families, while largely private in their functioning, are quite public in their consequences and effect. Each of our families has great influence and impact beyond the walls of our homes, both for ill and for good. Much of that depends on the health of the relationships within our walls and around our tables.

As Daniel Patrick Moynihan and his boss found out, talking about how we should do family can have explosive consequences. But avoiding that discussion is not an option if we want our society to be healthy, safe, productive, educated, and fully human. The family is irreplaceable, both personally and publicly.

What kind of contribution are your marriage and family making to your community? Are you raising the kind of young people who are likely to be responsible, sacrificial, serving, well-educated providers for the needs of society? Is your marriage, in all its struggles and imperfections, a message of hope to your community?

Your neighbors and community leaders certainly hope so. Every family, after all, is very much a public good and trust.

The Big Statement for Reflection

Family is much more than a private, sentimental home-and-hearth institution. It's the first factory that builds healthy humanity, with no close competitor. All communities need as many families as possible in which husbands and wives, mothers and fathers are raising their children together with dedication, care, and intentionality. This is the first sociological truth of any community.

Questions for Consideration

1. Sociologists tell us that birth rates have declined for decades because children are more of an "economic burden" to parents today. But we are learning that a lack of children in a nation is a devastating economic burden. Is this a good

reason to value children? Why or why not? What are some additional reasons?

2. Recall the ways in which marriage changes men. Have you seen this in your own experience? Do you think marriage changes women? If so, how?

3. Why do you think utopian communities are attractive to some people, but have never worked past one generation? What does man's divine image-bearing nature have to do with this?

4. How does the influence family can have on community, city, state, and nation change how you see your own family's influence on your world? How can you make sure that your family exerts more influence on the culture than the culture does on your family?

MOTHERS AS
IMAGE-BEARERS

Which day is more celebrated in our homes, our churches, and our culture: Mother's Day or Father's Day? Intuitively, that's not a hard question to answer. Mothers are a consistently powerful and meaningful force in the lives of their children.

The answer is not a statement on the effectiveness of the greeting card companies' marketing, or that a mother is more important than a father in a child's life. It's practical and real that our hearts tend to warm a bit more for our moms, and most dads wouldn't have it any other way.

Reuters reported a study a few years ago that Mother's Day creates the highest volume of phone calls around the world than any other day of the year.[1] Conversely, *Bloomberg Businessweek* revealed a few years earlier that Father's Day had the highest volume of collect calls—back when collect calls were common![2] We wanted to honor Dad, but were glad to let him pay for it.

Who doesn't like moms? Insult someone's mother and you most likely just bought yourself a boatload of trouble. Even the most soulless, conscienceless people feel a strong sense of righteous indignation if you speak ill of their mothers. And they will act on that indignation, which won't work out well for the mother-insulter. This is largely true for all peoples at all times to varying degrees. Why is this? It's because mothers have a very special standing in our lives. Mothers were, and often remain, our primary source of warmth, belonging, and care to us, don't they? That's what mothers do. Motherhood is literally the womb of humanity, its gatekeeper. If you can't find a mother to let you into this world, you ain't gettin' in.

The power of motherhood is profound. Motherhood is central to both humanity and to the Christian story. Consider the two most significant women in history; the Old and New Testaments begin with them. They launch the beginning of two of the most important stories ever told. One starts in a bad way, the other in a very good one.

Eve, designed to be the mother of humanity, was created by God—as is every mother after her. She, with her husband, brought sin into the world.

The other mother is Mary. As the mother of our Lord, she brought the Savior of the world into the world. It was the Father's delight to send His Son into our realm through the womanhood of a young, materially poor Middle Eastern girl from the nowhere town of Nazareth. Motherhood is where the earthly life of our Savior begins.

If some Catholics can be accused of sometimes making too much of Mary, Protestants are guilty of steering clear of her. We tend to shy away from saintly talk of her, lest we be accused of sounding "too Catholic." But doesn't Christian discipleship call us to love what Christ loved? Jesus loved His mom with a very special love; so did God the Father, choosing her to bear His Son to the world. Why shouldn't we love Mary with a special love as well, just as we would Paul, Moses, or Stephen, the church's first martyr . . . or even Billy Graham?

Mary was the first to boldly proclaim who Jesus was in her great song of praise, which we know as the Magnificat (Luke 1:46-55). She did so before John the Baptist did.

On my (Glenn's) first trip to Rome, I set a whole day aside to visit the art museum at the Vatican, one of the greatest collections on Earth of extremely important works of the Christian faith. When I got to the Sistine Chapel I just stood there for perhaps two hours—they don't let you sit down in there—taking in all the amazing work around me and the way it tells God's story from beginning to end, all in glorious pictures.

The last piece Michelangelo painted, nearly three decades after his famous ceiling, is the massive work that covers the entire wall of the chapel behind the altar. Called *The Last Judgment*, it is a very busy work—lots going on in every part of it, nearly too much to really take in. Your eyes are first drawn to the center, where Christ, bathed in a distinct light, is summoning the faithful to eternity with Him, and the faithless to damnation. But as I looked at Christ, something really disturbed me. As He sits upon His throne, Michelangelo has Mary sitting right next to Him.

Okay, I thought, *That's going a wee bit too far. Mary sitting on the throne with Jesus at the final judgment?* The words "crazy heretical" popped into my mind. It bothered me for a long time.

But many years later I was blessed to be able to visit the Sistine Chapel again. What had bothered me the first time made sense to me this time. If one studies the piece carefully, Mary is not sitting with Christ on His judgment seat, co-ruling with Him. She is sitting by the side, clearly lower than He is, with a look of seeming reservation, fear, and wonderment. She is not in control of these events, but is nestled and protected at Christ's side, gazing at those who are condemned. She is along for the ride while her Son takes care of His final business, as it were. She was there at the beginning and is portrayed as being there at the end. Michelangelo is portraying, in some sense, homage to the powerful role of a real mother in God's incarnation and the redemptive story of man. In this great and majestic moment of the Final Judgment, we are being reminded of where Christ came from as the God-man. And just as we recognized earlier, mothers hold a special place in our lives. It is the same for our Lord. And so, where does Mary sit? Simply anywhere her Son wants her to. This should not seem too unorthodox to us. Let us not give Mary more honor than is proper, but we should not give her less. How do we feel when someone honors our mother?

GET THE PICTURE

Michelangelo, *The Last Judgment* (1541)
Sistine Chapel, the Vatican
Visit familyproject.com to see this painting.

This remarkable work fills the entire wall behind the altar of the Sistine Chapel. It was painted 25 years after the artist completed the chapel's ceiling. The painting is a very large work with much going on—primarily Christ on His throne, judging all of humanity, bidding the righteous to spend eternity with Him in heaven and condemning those who have rejected the Savior.

How God Got Here

When Mary received the announcement from the angel Gabriel that she would bear God in the flesh, she made haste to visit her relative in a town in Judah—with trepidation and joy, no doubt. Elizabeth, John the Baptist's mother, who bore him miraculously in her barrenness and old age, greeted Mary as follows:

> [Elizabeth] exclaimed with a loud cry, "Blessed are you among women, and blessed is the fruit of your womb! And why is this granted to me that the mother of my Lord should come to me?" (Luke 1:42-43)

Our Lord, the King of Creation, came to us through a very real and humble woman at an actual place in time. God entered the world through a fallopian tube, growing in a womb—then, nine months later, through a cervix and beyond. This was God's intention. It was quite a statement about motherhood.

Mothers matter in no small way in God's story. God the Son had a Father, but He was also given a mother. Jesus' story is profoundly a family story. His mother is no mere conduit for God's entrance; after the birth, she's not dismissed from the action. She remains one of the key parts of His life as He grows, matures, starts and works His ministry, and faces His death and resurrection.

A Model for Motherhood

As we saw earlier, Mary was there when the young Jesus was discovered teaching the elders in the temple. These learned men were astounded at His great wisdom—and she was terrified as a mom, searching frantically for her lost Son for more than three days.

GET THE PICTURE

Henry Ossawa Tanner (1859–1937),
The Annunciation **(1898)**
Philadelphia Museum of Art

The Visitation **(1910)**
Kalamazoo Institute of Arts
Visit familyproject.com to see these paintings.

Tanner was one of the first widely noted and celebrated black painters in the United States as well as internationally. Growing up and studying art in Philadelphia and then abroad, he was noted for his beautiful treatments of biblical scenes. In the first, we find the young Mary visited by the angel Gabriel, her face aglow in his glorious light as he announces the coming of her Son, the Messiah. Her youth, innocence, and prayerful submission are dramatically portrayed by Tanner in a very humble human setting.

The second is a presentation of Elizabeth's joyful surprise as her relative Mary comes to visit and share the joy of their unique pregnancies. Tanner portrays Elizabeth sitting at her table, perhaps having a snack as this wonderful biblical scene unfolds. Elizabeth's delight and surprise are beautifully evident in her face and body language.

Mary was there as Jesus performed His first recorded miracle at the wedding in Cana:

> On the third day there was a wedding at Cana in Galilee, and the mother of Jesus was there. Jesus also was invited

to the wedding with his disciples. When the wine ran out, the mother of Jesus said to him, "They have no wine." And Jesus said to her, "Woman, what does this have to do with me? My hour has not yet come." His mother said to the servants, "Do whatever he tells you." (John 2:1-5)

This is a remarkable mother-to-adult-son exchange. Notice the typical communication that happens between two people who know each other all too well. Mary has not actually asked Jesus anything directly; she is just making an observation. It would have been rude of Him to respond to her, "Yeah, how about that? They should have planned better." Like any son, He knows Mom's statement is more than a mere observation. It's a request, even a command. He knows this and gently rebuffs her, with a tinge of frustration.

But look at her response. She pays no attention to her son's rebuff. Rather, she tells the wedding attendants to do what Jesus says—knowing He will follow the directions that she didn't even have to utter. Jesus knows that what Mom wants, she gets—if anyone is going to live peacefully. That is the power of motherhood, and the role of a good son.

It is interesting to note that Mary's last recorded words in Scripture are, "Do whatever he tells you." If our question is, "How should I respond to Jesus?" His mother's answer is always the right one: *Obey Him. Do what He tells you.*

Mary was also there at Jesus' crucifixion. A very important mother-son exchange happens that is little noticed by most of us. In John 19 we read,

Standing by the cross of Jesus were his mother and his mother's sister, Mary the wife of Clopas, and Mary Magdalene. When Jesus saw his mother and the disciple whom he loved standing nearby, he said to his mother, "Woman, behold, your son!" Then he said to the disciple, "Behold, your mother!" And from that hour the disciple took her to his own home. (Verses 25-27)

What was this about? At His death, while carrying the sin of all humanity upon His body and the separation from His Father that would come, God the Son was thinking of and caring for His mother. It is not sentimental or trite to say that the God-man, Jesus, was a good boy. Mary was so much more than the woman in the manger scene. And while Scripture doesn't record it, we can imagine that as in Michelangelo's *Pietà*, Mary despondently held the lifeless and tortured body of her boy. What mother would not take up her son's dead body in her arms and hug him one last time?

GET THE PICTURE

Peter Paul Rubens, *The Entombment* (1612)
Getty Museum, Los Angeles
Visit familyproject.com to see this painting.

In stark contrast to Michelangelo's famous *Pietà*, this work is dramatically human. The painting grabs the heart—not for its beauty, which is certainly there, but for the realism of our Savior's lifeless, pierced, bleeding body and the agony of a mother holding her boy who has been senselessly and humiliatingly murdered. Rubens has us look upon Mary not so much as a heroic biblical figure, but as a mother. Her eyes are deep red, worn out with suffering. Perhaps it is the apostle John supporting the

Savior's body, since he was asked by Christ to care for His mother. Take note of what Jesus' body is also supported by: a stone block, symbolic of the cornerstone, Christ, which the builders rejected. There is also the wheat straw, symbolizing the life His death brings us—as well the manger's hay that supported Him at His birth. And finally, like wheat, He is the Bread of Life.

This is a remarkable work, reminding us that Christ's life and death happened in the real world and the drama of an actual family, visited by all the joys and pains humans endure.

The pathos of this moment in the divine story is captured dramatically in a painting by Peter Paul Rubens that hangs in the Getty Museum in Los Angeles. This is not a heroic or beautiful representation. The mother who held her boy close to her heart with great joy on His first day now holds Him close with great pain on the day of His death. She held Him as He came to us from the Father in the incarnation; she holds Him before He returns to the Father as our Savior in the ascension.

The Father gives us the Son through a mother; now she gives Him back.

Rubens's painting shows us Mary's gaze. It is as if she is thinking two things at once. As any mother would, she struggles: *Why my son? Why now? Why in this way?* But she also knows her boy is no ordinary man. We can also imagine her saying, even with great anguish, precisely what she said to the angel Gabriel when he announced God's good news at the beginning of her son's life: "Behold, I am the servant of the Lord; let it be to me according to your word" (Luke 1:38).

She knows her Lord's purposes are much larger than her mother's heart. She is always oriented toward obedience to God, from the start of Jesus' earthly life to the very end.

The story of Jesus is intrinsically the story of a mother and her son. It is not meaningful only at Christmas. Can we gather how meaningful it is for motherhood? It means nothing less than that motherhood is a wholly divine activity and calling. Even the grinding mundaneness of a mother's work is something our Lord participated in. When God saw fit to demonstrate Himself in the world, He gave motherhood a crucial role.

Consider: What if God's Son had somehow come into our realm through a waterfall, a volcano, or a panda? Wouldn't waterfalls, volcanoes, or pandas be a sacred part of the Christian story and practice? Wouldn't we appreciate them as significant? This grand miracle happened in the life of a mother.

Finally, we read in the first chapter of Acts that just after Christ's ascension to the Father, Jesus' mother was with the disciples at this critical moment in the Christian church. They were praying for the fulfillment of Jesus' promise that the third Person of the Trinity would come upon them:

> "[Jesus said,] You will receive power when the Holy
> Spirit has come upon you, and you will be my wit-
> nesses in Jerusalem and in all Judea and Samaria, and
> to the end of the earth." And when he had said these
> things, as they were looking on, he was lifted up, and
> a cloud took him out of their sight. . . . All these with
> one accord were devoting themselves to prayer, together
> with the women and Mary the mother of Jesus, and his
> brothers. (Verses 8-9, 14)

She was not only a key part of our Savior's life, but remained involved in His ministry as His church was being established. And she was there as He returned to His Father's side in the ascension, the sixth key part of a fuller Christian worldview.

Motherhood matters because it is so central to human experience and to God's story. It is profound in both the human and Christian story, which are really one and the same. The Old Testament, the New Testament, our Savior's earthly life, and each of our lives begin in motherhood. Mothers, be encouraged.

Not Just a Hallmark Card

So what do these truths mean for you and your family? First, they won't allow any Christian to think in merely sentimental terms about motherhood. It's far more than a warm, comforting, protective part of human experience. It is profoundly divine and therefore eternal. Mary will always be Jesus' mother, for it was not temporary duty. Motherhood will always be significant, even into eternity.

In light of these truths, we must look at our faith anew and realize how . . .

- God the Father honored motherhood by sending His only begotten Son into the world through the full womanhood of a mother.
- God the Holy Spirit honored motherhood by bestowing it upon Mary, bringing both divine and human life to her virginal womb (Luke 1:34-35).
- God the Son honored motherhood by honoring His mother in loving ways every day of His earthly life.

When we understand these parts of the Christian story, our interaction with motherhood—whether as a child, a mother, or a father—can never be the same. Nor can we ever exhaust the meaning, power, and eternal significance of motherhood's holy calling.

This is one of the great wonders of the Christian story. No wonder very few people feel no warmth toward the idea of motherhood and their own mothers. This is wired into all of us because it is a central and intrinsic part of God's story.

Mothers. Given what we have learned here, will we ever be able to see Mother's Day as just a Hallmark card again? Children, when you celebrate your mother and motherhood, you are celebrating something massively significant, both human and divine.

THE BIG STATEMENT FOR REFLECTION

If mothers are not the most powerful people in the world, who are? Everyone starts with a mother in the most intimate way. And the Christian story starts at its two most critical points with two different mothers, one bringing life to the world's first child but death to all through the Fall. The other, sometimes referred to as the second Eve, brought life through her Son who is the Way, the Truth, and the Life (John 14:6). Mothers are powerful players who bring and nurture life.

QUESTIONS FOR CONSIDERATION

1. To you, what is the most meaningful part of the Jesus story where Mary plays a part? Why? What does it tell you about your view of motherhood?

2. How do you think Jesus felt about His mother, given what we are told in Scripture and what we know about His nature, love, and obedience? How does this compare with most people's feelings about their mothers? How well do you think most people express those feelings?

3. If some people are attacked by the Enemy because of their importance to God or role in His story, how do you see motherhood being attacked today? Do you think it needs to be defended? If so, how? If not, why not?

4. In ten words or less, what is the story of your mom and your relationship with her? How has it been meaningful, or perhaps less than meaningful? How has this shaped who you are?

FATHERS AS
IMAGE-BEARERS

One of many complaints we have with contemporary television and movies is this: There's a scarcity of regular dads who are mature, work hard, love their families, are respected, and teach their children well. They know what they're doing and are fun to watch while they're doing it. Whether you take in a TV show, a movie, or even a few advertisements, you'll see dads who, more often than not, are doltish, clueless, goofy, neurotic, and childish. You won't see many examples young men can look at and say, "Now, that's the kind of dad I want to be!" This is unfortunate.

Of course, television and movies are about entertainment. But dads can be intelligent, respectable, and funny all at the same time.

But what's most concerning is such portrayals' implication: Dads don't really matter. They even just seem to get in the way.

It seems that the media—and too often those in Christian circles—downplay or even deny the positive impact of fathers on families, culture, and community. The only problem with the assertion that dads don't make much difference in their families or communities is that it's flat-out false, for they do in so many important ways.

The reason dads matter is more than merely moral, traditional, or sociological. Dads matter because of who God is.

Consider this from C. S. Lewis about the man he says had more influence on him than anyone else:

> The most important thing we can know about George Mac-
> Donald is that . . . an almost perfect relationship with his
> father was the earthly root of all his wisdom. From his own
> father, he said, he first learned that Fatherhood must be the
> core of the universe. He was thus prepared in an unusual
> way to teach that religion in which the relation of Father
> and Son is of all relations the most central.[1]

"That religion in which the relation of Father and Son is of all relations the most central." In other words, Christianity depends upon and stems from a Father loving a Son. Period.

Fatherhood is absolutely central to the Christian story. According to George MacDonald's father, it is the core of the universe. If we want to know anything else about the Christian faith and the basic nature of all reality, it is built upon this fact.

Jesus often spoke of His Father—more than 170 times in the New Testament. In nearly every case He used the word *abba*, which is understood as a very personal reference to a father—as in "my father." Some have suggested it was a term like "daddy" or "papa," but many authorities on the language of the time disagree.[2]

We all understand the natural qualities of motherhood because moms have a unique and innate connection with their children. Who would argue with the statement that the most powerful emotional bond is the one between a mother and her child? This is humanly universal. "Mother-abandonment" and "motherlessness" are not phrases we use because, fortunately, these are not common.

Fatherhood, though, is a different matter.

Sociologists and anthropologists tell us that every society's most fundamental social problem is the unattached male. All cultures must find ways to usher boys into healthy, productive manhood, because this process doesn't happen as naturally as it does for girls moving into healthy womanhood. It's not unreasonable to say that Cain and Abel's relationship ended the way it did partly because they were two young men.

Unless young men become attached to something meaningful, calling them to discipline, self-sacrifice, and the care and protection of others, it is unlikely they will turn out to benefit the community. Unattached males are more unpredictable, violent, risk-prone, and selfish than others. We don't find young married fathers absent from gangs just because gang bylaws forbid them to join. Likewise, William Golding's novel *Lord of the Flies* was not just about how human nature can turn evil if unchecked; it was about the unbridled male nature.

There are really only three forces that can serve to tame male tendencies: military service, the discipline of sports, and marriage and fatherhood. Marriage and fatherhood are much more effective than the other two, which is why all human cultures have worked to find a way to collectively encourage these roles for men. It turns them into different kinds of men, those that society can never get enough of. If it doesn't, their boys are unlikely to become good men. Gang life is a likely natural alternative. Let's look again at how anthropologist Margaret Mead explained this:

> When we survey all known human societies, we find every-
> where some form of the family, some set of permanent
> arrangements by which males assist females in caring for
> children while they are young. . . . In every known human

society, everywhere in the world, *the young male learns that when he grows up, one of the things he must do in order to be a full member of society is to provide food for some female and her young. Every known human society rests firmly on this learned nurturing behavior of men.*[3] (emphasis added)

This is because the mother and child need this, but so does the man as well as the community. Marriage and parenting tend to change men for the better. If you had to leave your child with a strange man for 20 minutes while you took care of an emergency, which would you choose: a 28-year-old married father and his young daughter, or a single 28-year-old man with no child? The answer is obvious for a reason.

Marriage is the way cultures around the world and throughout time have attached men to their offspring and to their babies' mothers. Few mothers need to be compelled to hang in there until their children reach adulthood. Men, in general, do. No other institution is able to do this for men, and as marriage weakens, so does fatherhood. It is a sociological reality. And as married fatherhood declines, so do the safety, productivity, and growth of a community. You will not find a culture that disproves this truism. The rise and fall of marriage and father-engagement go hand-in-hand. This is not merely a sociological coincidence. It has a very deep, organic, spiritual origin.

Christians need to understand that human fatherhood has to be defended and worked for because it is under constant attack. Why? Well, because of what it represents: the very core of the universe, the relationship between God the Father and God the Son. That is why the Enemy despises it so and attacks it so viciously. It is why every society must be so intentional about encouraging and protecting it.

Let's consider how this reality has played out in the Christian story, in the earthly life of God's own Son. It is largely a story of fatherhood.

JESUS AND FATHERHOOD

The offense that brought Jesus' sentence of capital punishment by crucifixion was not primarily His miracles, or even His teachings, per se. His crime was deeper.

The religious leaders of the day asked Jesus who He was, given His confident and wise teaching, His miracles, and the adoration of the masses. All this got Him in some very hot water with the powerful folks of the day. His answer had profound consequences, as we read in Matthew 26. The high priest asked Jesus,

> "I adjure you by the living God, tell us if you are the Christ, the Son of God."
>
> Jesus said to him, "You have said so. But I tell you, from now on you will see the Son of Man seated at the right hand of Power and coming on the clouds of heaven." (Verses 63-64)

Jesus knew exactly what He was saying. He knew His words were putting the flame to the fuse. And the response was immediate. The high priest tore his clothes, indicating clearly and dramatically that he was not missing an ounce of the full weight of Jesus' words and intention. It wasn't just that this was crazy talk of a man trying to start a religious movement. To the high priest's ears, there was nothing more blasphemous.

Jesus claimed to be the very Son of God, and therefore God Himself. His hearers well knew the radical implications of what Christ said about Himself. And so Jesus was condemned and sentenced to death for announcing His Sonship.

It was a crisis of fatherhood.

And what about the birth of Jesus? It, too, involved a crisis of fatherhood.

Mary, the mother of Jesus, was concerned when she learned she was to have a child. She wondered how this could be when she had never known a man. She was told by the angel not to fret, because the child within her was to be the result of a very intimate visit by God's Holy Spirit (Luke 1:35). Not yet married to Joseph, her betrothed, she may have taken little comfort at this news. What about her social reputation in the gossip mill that a small town always is? How could she explain her pregnancy? "Well, it's really quite a story. You see, an angel told me not to be alarmed, that the Holy Spirit made me this way." Who would reply, "Well, that's pretty exciting!"? She would be seen not just as a loose woman but as a desperate crackpot as well. Joseph himself was not convinced by this explanation and made plans to quietly break off his engagement. A crisis of fatherhood.

As Joseph was thinking of how he might extract himself from this embarrassing situation, an angel of the Lord appeared to him and told him the same thing Mary had been told—and that he should not hesitate to take her as his wife. He was assured that this thing was very much of God (Matthew 1:18-24).

God could have said that Joseph was not necessary to the situation. We might imagine Him saying to Joseph, "Don't worry about Mary or the child. I will make sure they're cared for and protected. After all, I'm the Creator of the universe. So you're free from this unusual and embarrassing obligation. Run along."

Instead, God endorsed the role Joseph would play in the life of His Son, Jesus. God essentially says, "Joseph, be there for Jesus; it will be all right, and I'll be with you through it all. He will need you."

God wanted His Son to have an earthly father there because He knew how much it matters. And so it was that Jesus had two fathers—a heavenly one and an earthly one.

There are literally countless paintings of the Madonna and Child, but very few of Joseph with his son. One of the few is Guido Reni's beautiful work of a relatively elderly Joseph tenderly holding his newborn son. It's clear how intimate they are, face-to-face, eyes-to-eyes. Joseph warmly and tenderly cradles the babe. Jesus, the Lord of the universe, gently plays at Joseph's beard, a symbol of loving affection in the paintings of that age.

As the boy Jesus grew under the care and wonderment of His parents, He no doubt maintained a healthy relationship with Joseph. We do not know the details. We do know, however, His first recorded words in Scripture.

GET THE PICTURE

Guido Reni, *St. Joseph with the Infant Jesus* (1620s) Hermitage, St. Petersburg
Visit familyproject.com to see this painting.

Reni, an Italian artist of the High Baroque School, created some of Christianity's most beautiful frescoes—such as *St. Dominic's Glory* in the Arca di San Domenico in Bologna. The tenderness and intimacy communicated in Reni's infant Jesus is singular, with the baby wrapped as in gold; the face of the God-child is warmly close to and set upon His earthly father, playfully and curiously touching his beard. Joseph looks upon the child both as a loving father and a worshiper of God.

They came from Jesus' mouth when He was 12. His parents had accidentally left Him behind in Jerusalem. After they discovered He was missing, a frantic three-day search ensued. They finally found Him in the temple and offered a stern rebuke for scaring the wits out of them. Jesus responded by asking,

> Why were you looking for me? Did you not know that I must be in my Father's house? (Luke 2:49)

Notice the calm obviousness in the boy Jesus' voice, as if to say, "Uh, where else would I be, Mom?"

GET THE PICTURE

William Holman Hunt, *Finding of the Savior in the Temple* (1860)
Birmingham Museum and Art Gallery
Visit familyproject.com to see this painting.

Hunt was one of the primary founders of the Pre-Raphaelite Brotherhood of England, formed in 1848 by painters and poets. This painting, selling for a large amount and later copied and distributed, established Hunt as an artist and secured his finances—allowing him to spend his life painting and to build a house in Jerusalem. This work is a rare reflection of the moment Christ's parents encounter Him after losing track of Him as they were headed home to Nazareth from Jerusalem. Hunt aims at realism rather than symbolism in his presentation of Jesus and His parents at this charged family moment.

As we just saw, Jesus was killed by the leaders of His day for say-ing He was the Son of the Father. He died a painful, cursed, utterly humiliating death because Satan was bent on attacking the eternal nature of God as a Father.

How do you wound a father more viciously than killing his only son?

This single event—the crucifixion of Jesus—is foundational to the Christian faith. It also demonstrates that fatherhood is deeply consequential in both the spiritual and natural realms.

THE CROSS

Jesus' violent death on the cross tells us a great deal about both motherhood and fatherhood. It is not only a Savior on the cross but a son. We are reminded of this as we read this part of God's story carefully.

We learn that at noon on the day of this terrible execution, the sky went dark and remained that way for three hours. What was happening?

The earth turned dark because the Father had turned His face away from the Son; the sin of all humanity that He willingly bore in His own body and soul on our behalf had come between them, as sin does. The Scriptures tell us that at this darkness, Jesus cried out in a terrible voice,

> My God, my God, why have you forsaken me?
> (Mark 15:34)

This is a remarkable thing, perhaps the turning point of all human history. But what does it mean?

For the first time—and the last—in all eternity, the intimacy between the Father and Son was disrupted. The communion of Father and Son was severed in a painful way. Jesus did not refer to His Father with the intimacy that He had before, but with the distance of calling Him God. For the first and only time, the Father had forsaken the Son—or at least the Son felt as if He had been forsaken.

It was a crisis of fatherhood.

And then the Son died.

THE AGONY OF SEPARATION

To understand how painful the rift between Son and Father was, let us notice something that had happened the evening before.

Luke reports that when Jesus stole away from the disciples to spend time with His Father, something very curious happened:

> And being in an agony he prayed more earnestly; and his sweat became like great drops of blood, falling down to the ground. (Luke 22:44)

Luke, Christ's disciple and a physician, refers to a documented physiological condition in which blood is excreted along with sweat from the pores of the human body at times of extreme anxiety. Called "hematidrosis," it was observed and described in medical texts as early as Aristotle, and later Leonardo Da Vinci.

What could have been the source of our Savior's deep anxiety that evening? Many would say it was the physical pain He would experience during His torturous death the following day. This is understandable, considering that although Jesus was God incarnate, He was also fully man with a real human body. That pain would affect His body as it would any of ours. This was the subject of a sermon the great Jonathan Edwards preached in 1739 titled "Christ's Agony," centering on this very scene in the Garden.

But would anticipating these sufferings have such an effect on Christ? Edwards, in this sermon, explains that many martyrs have been crucified, as Christ was; yet their souls have not been so overwhelmed. According to tradition, Bartholomew had his skin peeled from his body, and most of the disciples looked at their martyrdom with anticipation. Were they stronger than Jesus?

We would suggest that, at its heart, Christ's profound agony and anxiety were rooted in a more intense pain: His impending separation from the Father. This would be His deepest torment because of His eternal and unspeakably deep intimacy with His Father.

GET THE PICTURE

Rogier van der Weyden, *Crucifixion Triptych*
(central panel, 1445)
Museum of Fine Arts, Vienna
Visit familyproject.com to see this painting.

Van der Weyden is considered one of the great artists among the Flemish Primitives of the sixteenth century Northern Renaissance, along with Jan van Eyck. He was noted as the official painter of Brussels. This painting shows both the demonic and maternal presences attending Christ's death as the sky grows dark at the Father's forsaking. Mary's anguish is apparent as she tries to cling to her son. John is there to assume her care at Christ's request.

Christ's death would strike the very essence and nature of God the Father and God the Son by dividing them. In so doing, it would shake the very foundation of the universe, of all reality.

No human words can fully describe what this separation really meant. It would appear that Satan, the arch-enemy of God and all that represents Him in the world, was about to be victorious in driving a very real and consequential wedge between two Persons of the Trinity. Jesus' desperate cry on the cross was the sweetest music Satan's ears could ever hope to take in.

The cross was, at its core, the ultimate crisis of fatherhood.

GET THE PICTURE

**Matthias Grünewald, *Small Crucifixion*
(c. 1511–1520)
National Gallery of Art, Washington, D.C.**
Visit familyproject.com to see this painting.

A German artist, Grünewald portrays the grisly and grotesque suffering of Christ on the cross, rather than showing Him heroically. He accomplishes this uniquely. This smaller, lesser known painting is similar to his larger and more famous work, the Isenheim Altarpiece, a triptych created for the chapel of a monastery dedicated to treating patients with a painful skin disease known as St. Anthony's Fire (ergotism). The suffering of these patients was excruciating, and Grünewald wanted to portray Christ as one who identified with their great pain.

The Ecstasy of Reunion

But while this separation was very real, it was not permanent. Christ overcame His scandalous death in resurrection. Satan's egomaniacal obsession to destroy the relationship between Father and Son was permanently thwarted. Satan's triumphant cackle at Christ's death was turned into the wailing of ignominious defeat in a matter of days.

It is important to understand that this cosmic struggle—and sacred victory—centered on the integrity of a relationship between a Father and a Son.

And what happened shortly after Christ defeated sin, death, and hell in the resurrection? He was taken up bodily into heaven to sit, just as He'd promised the high priest He would, at His Father's right hand (Mark 16:19). In this part of God's redemptive story—the ascension—the Father and Son are united. Victory is won. This is why we include ascension as a central tenet of our fuller Christian worldview. It is no small part of the story, this reunion between Father and Son.

The crisis of divine fatherhood was real, but it also brought our salvation. Sin and death were swallowed up as Father and Son were united and restored.

Take faith and hope that Fatherhood is indeed the core of the universe.

But the fullness of our salvation has not yet come. We will learn more about that in Chapter 11. Theologians have a phrase for this part of God's story: "The already and the not yet." This means our salvation has been secured for all who repent of their sins and cast themselves on the hope of Christ—but our total release from the grip of sin and death is still to happen. Already. Not yet.

The Christian story explains the power of fatherhood, the consequences of its absence, and why the sting is so bitter when fathers and children find barriers between them. It explains why all cultures must find ways to continually encourage and strengthen the bond between fathers and their offspring. This is why it is no mere coincidence that the very last words in the Old Testament speak strongly to this topic:

> Behold, I will send you Elijah the prophet before the great
> and awesome day of the LORD comes. And he will turn the
> hearts of fathers to their children and the hearts of children
> to their fathers, lest I come and strike the land with a decree
> of utter destruction. (Malachi 4:5-6)

Whether or not a devastating curse comes upon the people is linked to whether or not the hearts of the fathers are toward their children and the children's to their fathers. Considering these last words of God's before a 400 year silence until the coming of the Messiah, we must note what an angel of the Lord announced at the beginning of the New Testament about what Christ's forerunner would faithfully proclaim:

> Your wife Elizabeth will bear you a son, and you shall call
> his name John. . . . And he will turn many of the children
> of Israel to the Lord their God, and he will go before [the
> Messiah] in the spirit and power of Elijah, to turn the hearts
> of the fathers to the children, and the disobedient to the
> wisdom of the just, to make ready for the Lord a people
> prepared. (Luke 1:13, 16-17)

Fatherhood is a deeply precious and meaningful thing, powerfully intrinsic to God's nature and thus His purposes and actions through history. It would be difficult to overstate this truth.

God the Father has promised He will never forsake or abandon us (Hebrews 13:5). We are also told,

> Sing to God, sing in praise of his name . . .
>> rejoice before him—his name is the LORD.
> A father to the fatherless. . . .
> God sets the lonely in families. (Psalm 68:4-6, NIV)

What a wonderful hope from a Father who cannot break His promises, nor would ever want to.

He is a very good and loving, forgiving Father. He gave His only beloved Son in order for us to be His very own adopted daughters and sons through His holy and everlasting love.

Thereby overcoming all fatherhood crises, forevermore.

GET THE PICTURE

Pieter van Aelst, *The Trinity* (1530)
Museo del Prado, Madrid
Visit familyproject.com to see this painting.

Van Aelst was a Flemish artist working from Brussels as a painter and tapestry maker. This picture is a portrayal of the bodily ascension to the Father of the crucified and resurrected Christ. The Holy Spirit is there as well, depicted as usual as a dove above the Father's and Son's heads. The empty cross presented by one of the angels reminds us of Satan's defeat in Christ's victory.

The Big Statement for Reflection

At the very center of the Christian story—as well as the core of the universe itself—is a relationship between a Father and a Son. A crisis of fatherhood is at the center of this story as well. Men have the honor and privilege of participating in fatherhood due to the natural biological and procreative process. God created males to have this possibility, to have a part in the divine through one of their most basic human drives. But Satan does and always has had it in his crosshairs because of what fatherhood is. We must be diligent to protect and honor it.

Questions for Consideration

1. Do you agree that major parts of Christ's story include "crises of fatherhood"? Why or why not? If so, how do you think it matters? What crises of fatherhood have been part of your life?

2. Jesus was the Son of God; we who are forgiven and brought into God's family by faith in Christ become God's sons and daughters, too. This makes Christianity unique among all other religions and philosophies. How could you explain this to someone who is not yet part of God's family?

3. If you're a father, how does this part of the Christian story challenge the way you think of fatherhood? How could it change the way you serve your family and community as a dad?

4. What about Joseph's role in the story of Jesus makes you appreciate the role of dads in families today? How might this element of the Christmas story help you appreciate the stepdad or father figure who enriches the lives of fatherless ones in our midst?

CHILDREN AS IMAGE-BEARERS

Death and taxes are not the only sure things in life. They are not even the *first* sure things. Long before you ever gave the slightest concern about either, there were two things absolutely sure about you and all who ever existed.

Each person who has ever appeared upon the earth is made in the image of two people (Genesis 4:1-2). When a child is born, Grandpa exclaims, "Look, she has your eyes and her daddy's nose." This is obvious enough, but it's one of the most basic things about being human. Every single one of these billions of new creatures comes into the world as a unique, mold-breaking baby boy or girl, each one issuing from the intimate union of a male and female. These three who are one flesh—father, mother, child—are the presentation of a new family into the world.

Yet each of these new humans is the image-bearer not just of a particular mother and father but, as we have learned, of God Himself. Beyond the wonder of a new child, this is pretty great news for and about each of us.

Every child is a statement of God's delight in creation. Every child is a bold proclamation from God that He still wants to uniquely reveal Himself to the world through each of us. Every child is a powerful, magnificent, and deeply divine statement. *Every* child! This is why Christians in the early days and ever since have been the primary ones to rescue babies that have been abandoned by their parents. Their belief about every human life didn't leave them any choice.

Each mother and father, since the first two started it all, has partnered with God in creating the world's next human. That's pretty significant work. This divine partnership is explained to us by Eve as the first in a long, long line of mothers. As her first child came into the world, she exulted in this miracle: "I have gotten a man with the help of the LORD" (Genesis 4:1). This was the first God-human cooperation, and its most significant. The result is precisely what God is seeking: godly offspring (Malachi 2:15).

Ideally, every husband and wife, every father and mother, gets to participate in this service to God. As anyone who has gone through the painful turmoil of infertility or other problems that prevent having children knows, the inability to participate in this glorious experience is exceedingly heart-wrenching. Many couples face it, but all feel it as deeply as if they were the only ones. This is the nature of great pain.

WHAT IS A CHILD?

Children are the everyday beginning of the world, coming to us freshly born each day by the hundreds of thousands. Each— whether the parents appreciate it or not—is a gift to us and to the world from the love of the Trinity, given through the iconic love of a man and woman in their marital union.[1] This mystery is wonderfully shown in a fifteenth-century book illustration, a remarkable image we studied earlier that tells us the first word in our Christian understanding of marriage, sexuality, and the family.

Called *A Married Couple Receiving a Child from the Holy Trinity*, it is the opening illustration for a chapter in a book that has quite a long title, as many books did in those days: *The Book Which Among Other Matters Deals with the Birth of Our Lord Christ, His Life, His Passion*. We studied the piece back in Chapter 3, but it deserves examination and consideration here as well.

It tells us that each child is the result of two kinds of love, both human and divine. Knowing the birds-and-the-bees story, we know that something remarkable can happen when a husband and wife come together in the marital embrace. That loving, passionate, life-giving union can create something greater than anyone or anything else can create: a new human being with an eternal soul who will grow to shape the world and others in important ways, shifting the balance of the universe in a real sense. And it reveals to the world a very special part of who God is that no other baby has revealed or will reveal.

Yet as we learned from Eve, we don't do this alone but with the help of the Lord. Each child is not just a mechanical, biological fact, but a gift to us all from God. Most people—religious or not—accept this as true. Yet the Christian story goes a bit further. The love of man and wife participates with the love of the Trinity to bring forth each new God-imager who is made *from* love, *for* love, and will learn to love as every healthy human does.

We come from the intimacy of God, through the intimacy of our parents, into the intimacy of our families, for intimacy in our own lives and a relationship with God and man. It is a glorious thing to be human and to accept that gift as someone's child. It is true of all of us.

Given this, it could be said that there is no such thing as a true individual. Let us quote again theologian and author Michael Downey:

> The human person is not an individual, not a self-contained being who at some stage in life chooses or elects to be in relationship with another or others. From the very first moment of existence, the infant is toward the other, ordinarily the mother or father, who in turn is toward the infant. From our origin, we are related to others. We are from others, by others, toward others, for others, just as it is in God's nature to exist in the relations of interpersonal love.[2]

While each child in the world may not come from the pure love of a mother and father—for selfishness is too often at work in human relationships—every child does come from the purity of the Trinity's love, a great and true hope. That is where you came from regardless of your earthly parents; therefore, your destiny does not stem from how caring your parents were. Most of humanity, as God intended, seeks to replicate this godly love in marriage and family life, but sadly it does not always happen, even among the best of us.

Of course, an infinite difference exists between the eternal mystery of love and creativity among the Trinity and the one-flesh manner in which male and female generate new life. God is spirit, not flesh. And while God is passionately intimate, more than we can fathom, He is not sexual. His humans are.

Nevertheless, in the biblical vision, human sexuality is intended to reflect something of the eternal exchange of life-giving love found in the Trinity. This is what our *A Married Couple Receiving Child from the Trinity* illustration is all about.

And it is why a seemingly simple painting like Vincent van Gogh's *First Steps* can be especially appreciated by Christians. It speaks to this truth when it appears, at first glance, to be merely a nice picture of a mother, father, and child.

GET THE PICTURE

**Vincent van Gogh (1853–1890), *First Steps,*
After Millet (1890)
Oil on canvas; Metropolitan Museum of Art,
New York City**
Visit familyproject.com to see this painting.

In Van Gogh's beautiful work, we see a mother and father taking time from their labors—his gardening and her hanging wash over the fence to dry—so they can encourage their child to take his first steps. They are an earthly trinity, enjoying each other's company—thrilling to and marveling at each other's existence, both simple and profound.

This painting is a human reflection of the Trinity that is ultimately behind, under, over, and in the universe. That is what family is, and what family echoes for those who have eyes to see and ears to hear. The child completes this human trinity.

As Pope John Paul II explained to Mexican believers at Puebla in 1979,

It has been said beautifully and profoundly, that our God in his most inner mystery is not solitude, but a family. For internally God bears fatherhood, sonship and the essence of family, which is love. This love, in the divine family is the Holy Spirit.[3]

Children and the Future of Nations

Carl Sandburg was not speaking as a theologian but as a poet when he said,

A baby is God's opinion that the world should go on. . . . Never will a time come when the most marvelous recent invention is as marvelous as a newborn baby. . . . A baby is very modern. Yet it is also the oldest of the ancients. A baby doesn't know he is a hoary and venerable antique—but he is. Before man learned how to make an alphabet, how to make a wheel, how to make a fire, he knew how to make a baby— with the great help of woman and His God and maker.[4]

Indeed, God is quite big on offspring:

Behold, children are a heritage from the LORD, the fruit of the womb a reward. Like arrows in the hand of a warrior are the children of one's youth. Blessed is the man who fills his quiver with them! (Psalm 127:3-5)

Children are more than sweet bundles of soft hair, smooth skin, infectious giggles, and entrancing smiles. As we've already established, they are among God's image-bearers. But there's something more: Raising healthy, thriving, loving, intelligent, diligent children is something we must do because the next generation is our tomorrow.

Consider that in more than 75 countries—nearly all the developed nations of the world—the fertility rate is well below that needed to simply replace ourselves (2.1 children per woman) and to maintain a nation's workforce and social structure at current levels. The average woman living in a developed nation will give birth to

1.66 children in her lifetime, 21 percent below the level needed to sustain a current population over time. There are 60.6 million fewer children in the developed world today than there were in 1965.

You might ask, "Couldn't we live with a bit fewer folks in the world?"

Well, the United Nations predicts that over the next 40 years, 53 percent of the world's population growth will come from increases in people over 60; only 7 percent will come from people under 30.[5] The growing percentage of older folks, ballooned by the shrinking number of younger ones, translates into a severe shortage of taxpayers and social providers to care for the elderly. When young, we have to rely on the older ones; when old, we have to rely on the younger ones. When either of these is out of balance, people suffer.

Not having babies is like digging the earth out from under your chair. You'll soon find out those babies you didn't have could have been quite helpful as well as fulfilling. It's not just personal, but will have drastic public consequences: In 20 years or so, there will be a troubling shortage of business owners, teachers, healthcare providers, police officers, inventors, medical researchers, taxpayers, artists, community leaders, farmers, repairmen, clergy, common laborers—and on it goes. Those who didn't have babies in the last two to three decades will realize dramatically that the helpers they need today and in the coming years are the babies they didn't have then. This public purpose of procreation is seen in the fact that many European nations—by public policy—are paying couples handsomely to bear children. It is simple economics.

God's first command to humanity, "Be fruitful and multiply" (Genesis 1:22) is not just a quaint religious sentiment. Among many things, it's the first statement of societal economics and community support. Children matter because people matter, and no society can sustain itself without new generations.

Children and the Evil One

As we've seen before, that which represents God and His nature in the world tends to be assaulted by the Enemy in his bitter hatred of God. This is why children have been such victims of brutal and senseless violence throughout history. They represent the goodness of God, His life-giving nature. It is startling to realize how regularly children have been exploited in so many cultures. They have been slaves—sexual, laboring, and otherwise. Extinguished by abortion. They have been abused in the most unconscionable ways, often by family members. They have been neglected, sent off to war, denied the innocence and happiness of their own childhoods, used selfishly as objects. The evil one knows exactly what he is accomplishing with each one.

Get the Picture

Giotto, *Massacre of the Innocents* (c. 1305)
Scrovegni Chapel, Padua
Visit familyproject.com to see this painting.

Giotto, a famed painter from Florence at the end of the Middle Ages, created this tragic scene in his most ambitious and noted project, the decoration of the interior of the Scrovegni Chapel. He provided this scene to remind us how important Christ's birth and life were and how God saw to it that the coming of our Savior would not be thwarted even by such a demonic holocaust. Here we see Herod overseeing the great massacre while mothers helplessly try to save their babies, and some turn their backs on the evil that is taking place.

A biblical example: What happened on the darker side of the Christmas story? Herod, who dubbed himself king of the Jews, was furious because he had been tricked by the wise men, who did not report back to him about the whereabouts of the newborn King (Matthew 2:16-18). They suspected Herod's intentions were evil. They were indeed; he wanted this newborn King eliminated because he was jealous of his own power. Not knowing the baby's exact whereabouts, Herod ordered all male children in the land two years of age and under to be slaughtered. He was willing to destroy them all, just to get the one—if it would preserve his own kingship.[6]

Today we know this ghastly event as "the slaughter of the innocents." It continues through political and ideological and ethnic holocausts around the world—as well as in the tragedy of abortion when mothers are compelled, usually through the encouragement or abandonment of their child's father, to cease being protective life-givers and become life-takers. It is contrary to a woman's nature. All these atrocities happen ultimately because of what children are and their divine nature.

All God's Children

How does God feel about children? What can families learn from the answer to that question?

We know that they are vital to His story. As Malachi 2:15 tells us, God is seeking "godly offspring"—children He can love and care for, and who will bring Him glory. And not all of them are young.

Ephesians 5:1 calls us to "be imitators of God, as beloved children." Just as children tend to copy their parents, we are to imitate God's goodness, gentleness, and holiness. And we're invited to do so as His beloved children.

Repeat to yourself, out loud, "I am a beloved child of God our

Father." It is a smart thing to repeat to yourself every day. No statement we can utter about ourselves is more dependable than this, simply because the God of the universe stands behind that promise. And no other part of His glorious creation can claim that position as beloved child of God.

As if that weren't enough good news, we discover more about this relationship in Romans 8:

> For all who are led by the Spirit of God are sons of
> God. For you did not receive the spirit of slavery to fall
> back into fear, but you have received the Spirit of adop-
> tion as sons, by whom we cry, "Abba! Father!" The Spirit
> himself bears witness with our spirit that we are children
> of God, and if children, then heirs—heirs of God and
> fellow heirs with Christ, provided we suffer with him
> in order that we may also be glorified with him. (Verses
> 14-17)

We are not just God's children, but His adopted children, having "received the Spirit of adoption" as His very sons and daughters. That's not just warm, sentimental wording—it's legal language, if you will. The point is driven home again, just to make sure we don't miss it, in Ephesians 1:3-6:

> Blessed be the God and Father of our Lord Jesus Christ,
> who has blessed us in Christ with every spiritual blessing
> in the heavenly places, even as he chose us in him before
> the foundation of the world, that we should be holy and
> blameless before him. In love he predestined us for adop-
> tion as sons through Jesus Christ, according to the purpose

of his will, to the praise of his glorious grace, with which he
has blessed us in the Beloved.

This verse tells us that not only are we the adopted children of
the Father, but He chose us as His beloved children before the foundation of the world—in pre-creation. When all that existed in all
of eternity was a Father loving a Son and a Son loving a Father, evidenced by their Spirit, we were in their minds and on their hearts.

> Behold what manner of love the Father has bestowed on
> us, that we should be called children of God! Therefore the
> world does not know us, because it did not know Him. Be-
> loved, now we are children of God; and it has not yet been
> revealed what we shall be, but we know that when He is
> revealed, we shall be like Him, for we shall see Him as He
> is. And everyone who has this hope in Him purifies himself,
> just as He is pure. (1 John 3:1-3, NKJV)

God also tells us, as we saw in the previous chapter, He is a
Father to the fatherless and "settles the solitary in a home" (Psalm
68:5-6).

God graciously accepts those who have no one, or who sense
they have been abandoned. The Father's desire, and the work of
the Spirit and the Son, is to bring us into their family as beloved
children through adoption. We all have a home.

And there is no better, more loving, more reliable family.

This invitation is extended to each of us. It is ours to accept or
reject. God does not force anyone to be His child. What have you
done with this invitation? And what kind of invitation can you offer
to those who need family?

Wait No More:
God Wants to Adopt You

Adoption is a gift to the orphan. It is not an "If you do this for us, we'll do this for you" contract. Proper performance is not required to keep the offer of sonship in place. It is sheer grace, based on the parents' desire to give love and care to a child who doesn't have those necessities.

This is God's deep and passionate heart for you—to adopt you into His own home and family through the salvation Christ bought for each of us in His death and resurrection. Sons and daughters are also heirs of the riches and goodness of the Father, as is any earthly child who has a father with any kind of heart.

Like any adopted child, we don't need to do anything to make this happen. We simply need to trust Him, giving our whole lives and security to Him, to receive this gift freely. We take Him at His word and live with the confidence that He is our "Abba, Father." Does an adopted child demand to see the official adoption forms before he is convinced he is a member of his new family? Does he need to go back and check it time and again, just to be sure? No, he takes his parents' word for it in trusting confidence.

Much more sure and dependable is the word of our heavenly Father, who tells us that believing in His Son makes us His children. Being adopted, through faith, is how all of us orphans can be part of His magnificent family. Will you accept this gift?

A Son's Story

You might wonder, as many of us do, "How could God accept me, much less invite me to be His child? I'm so unworthy." Jesus told a story to help us understand how. We know it as the story of the prodigal son, but it could be called the story of the forgiving father (Luke 15:11-32).

A son asks his wealthy father for his share of the inheritance because he wants to escape the farm and experience the excitement of the world. He leaves home and has a big time with lots of wine, women, and song. His money runs out sooner than he expected, and so do his so-called friends. He has no one, and the only job he can get is feeding pigs, remembering that even his father's servants have better things to eat than he does.

At the end of himself, he decides to go back home to his father, ask for forgiveness, and hope to be taken on as a hired hand. He heads home, not knowing how or whether he will be received:

> And he arose and came to his father. But while he
> was still a long way off, his father saw him and felt
> compassion, and ran and embraced him and kissed
> him. And the son said to him, "Father, I have sinned
> against heaven and before you. I am no longer worthy
> to be called your son." But the father said to his ser-
> vants, "Bring quickly the best robe, and put it on him,
> and put a ring on his hand, and shoes on his feet. And
> bring the fattened calf and kill it, and let us eat and
> celebrate. For this my son was dead, and is alive again;
> he was lost, and is found." And they began to celebrate.
> (Luke 15:20-24)

GET THE PICTURE

Rembrandt, *The Return of the Prodigal Son* (1662)
Hermitage, St. Petersburg
Visit familyproject.com to see these paintings.

Rembrandt, famous for his dark and beautiful paintings of biblical scenes, portrays tenderly the son's shame and desperation and the father's unconditional grace and joy. This work is widely celebrated and contemplated for what it communicates about the deeply accepting heart of God.

Bartolomé Estaban Murillo, *The Return of the Prodigal Son* (1667)
National Gallery of Art, Washington, D.C.

Murillo was one of the important participants in the Spanish Baroque school. His prodigal, much less celebrated than Rembrandt's, is every bit as moving and passionate. While father and son are central, looking deeply and gratefully into each other's eyes, this painting has more surrounding activity; servants bring the fatted calf and the new clothes of blessing, while even the playful family dog is excited to see this return.

Two wonderful paintings, both known as *The Return of the Prodigal Son*, tell the story as well (see "Get the Picture"). They communicate to us that the father did not condemn his wayward son. He probably looked for the young man daily on the horizon, to see if today might be the day he would come home. When the father's wish comes true, he runs toward his beloved son and welcomes him in the most comforting embrace. The father offers grace, acceptance, and boundless forgiveness. Our heavenly Father calls us to offer the same in our families, especially to our children.

The Big Statement for Reflection

Children are the way God continues to show forth new and unique parts of His image and likeness in the world, and it happens hundreds of thousands of times a day around the globe. Christ, the second Person of the Trinity, began His earthly life as a child. Children are not just cute, cuddly, and fun creatures; they carry great meaning within them and bring it to the world. And in our redemption, we become the passionately loved and welcomed children of God.

Questions for Consideration

1. Does it seem irreverent or even blasphemous to say that mothers and fathers participate with God in creating new life? Why or why not?

2. How are you an image and representation to the world of your parents' love? If you're a parent, how do your children represent you? Which of your traits would you like them to display, and which would you like them to ignore?

3. We can know more about the Father by understanding the parable of the prodigal son. What do you learn about the Father from this story? Which of His qualities do you most need to develop as you interact with your family?

4. How do you feel about being adopted as a child of God? How can you cultivate an "adoptive" attitude toward members of your family? If you haven't been adopted by God yet, what is holding you back?

THE ENEMY

If you think the family is under attack today, you're not alone. An Internet search for the phrase "attack on the family" yields over 20 million results. It's a hot topic, one on many people's minds and of deep concern in their souls as well.

The specifics of that attack, though, are a little fuzzy. Can you think of a particular family that is "under attack," perhaps one burdened by circumstances and pressures that seem insurmountable? They are all around us, perhaps even living at our address. How would you describe the "enemies" of that family? Who do you think "has it in" for that household? Or do you believe the target is the family itself as an idea or institution?

Perhaps the first question we should ask is this: When did this assault on families begin? The fact is that the family was under attack long before the 1960s. In this chapter we take a closer look at the enemies of the family, both familiar and forgotten, that have faced us for eons.

Pop quiz: When did history's first and most vicious attack on the family occur?

Hint: It successfully ambushed a particular rural, farming,

married couple minding their own business. The husband and wife were simple, innocent folks, unaware of the ways of the world. You know what it is.

This inaugural attack had them bringing a little thing called the Fall to the rest of humanity. Among other things, it led to one of their sons killing the other. Family dysfunction is old.

Things haven't changed much since those days—the days of Adam and Eve—whose story we've already examined.

Ask many people who was behind that attack, and they would pin it on the devil. They would be right. But why him? What's his beef with the family? Doesn't he just despise God and those who seek to obey Him?

As we've already seen, Satan had his heart set against the family from the beginning because he well knew what it uniquely represents. In a sense, he's a brilliant theologian—just a very self-absorbed, bitter, God-hating one. But he does understand God's story better than any of us.

Many sophisticated people have no problem respecting Jesus. But they have no patience for seemingly antiquated ideas like the existence of a real Satan or a literal hell. Read the words of Christ in the four Gospels, however, and you'll find that He spent a great deal of time talking about the wicked schemes and work of Satan—how he binds people up in sin, sickness, and death. He knew they were real.

Jesus often engaged Satan and his minions with great authority and condemnation. Some say this was simply because Jesus was a product of His pre-scientific age, as if the incarnate and eternally existent God of the universe was unable to see beyond the times. But Christ's talk of, interaction with, and victory over Satan are not allegory, allusion, or symbolism. The serious reader of the Gospels can come to no other conclusion than that Jesus knew the dark side of the story to be true and profoundly consequential.

Speaking to the religious leaders, Jesus made His perspective clear:

> You are of your father the devil, and your will is to do your father's desires. He was a murderer from the beginning, and does not stand in the truth, because there is no truth in him. When he lies, he speaks out of his own character, for he is a liar and the father of lies. But because I tell the truth, you do not believe me. (John 8:44-45)

That is serious talk, and Jesus was serious about it. So should we be.

THE SATAN FILES

In some ways, Satan is easy to figure out. In his all-consuming jealousy, he hates God and everything that God loves. We must know that:

- Where God loves, Satan hates.
- Where God gives life, Satan brings death.
- Where God brings truth, Satan brings lies.
- Where God brings trust and faith, Satan brings uncertainty and doubt.
- Where God brings conviction, Satan brings accusation.
- Where God brings forgiveness, Satan brings condemnation.
- Where God gives grace, Satan gives shame.
- Where God brings beauty, Satan brings hideousness.
- Where God brings acceptance, Satan brings alienation.

- Where God brings community, Satan brings self-centeredness.
- Where God brings peace, Satan brings discord.
- Where God brings selflessness and service, Satan brings selfishness and slavery.

Because families are such a key part of God's story, Satan detests them—God's family, your family, and ours.

One of the greatest mistakes Christians make is to see Satan as merely a mischief-maker, playing tricks to trip us up in our pilgrim's journey with God. But Satan is not just about sabotage; he goes for the throat. His mission is about life and death, and he plays for keeps. There is no neutral ground this side of heaven, and Satan is after it all. Your family is very much in his crosshairs.

He despises family because family—intimate, permanent, self-giving, procreative union—is God's very nature reflected in the world.

- Satan despises God by saying that humanity, made in His image, is not special or valuable.
- Satan despises God by saying that male and female are meaningless, each of which uniquely shows forth a part of God's image that the other cannot.
- Satan despises God by saying that marriage is optional or merely a private relationship between people who want the relationship to meet their own needs.
- Satan despises God by saying there is nothing special, sacred, or worth protecting and celebrating in our sexuality.
- Satan despises God by saying our procreation is to be limited because it's harmful.
- Satan despises God by destroying fatherhood, turning the hearts of the fathers *from* their own children.

- Satan despises God by unnaturally dividing mother and child through neglect, abuse, and the tragedy of abortion.
- Satan despises God by destroying the innocence of childhood through an increasingly harsh and toxic culture that cares only about the fulfillment of adult appetites and the bottom line.
- Satan despises God by destroying the sacred communion of each family with discord, bitterness, hurt, shame, busyness, and distraction.

SATAN'S ATTACKS ON THE FAMILY OF LATE

Every age seems to bring new assaults on the family, and ours certainly has. Many concern the way we understand families, what they're for, and how we form them.

One question we hear often is, "What difference does it really make what forms families take, as long as they're based on love?" Well, Satan knows why. It's because these new forms don't image what God had and has in mind for family. Satan also knows that when we stray from God's design and intention, very important things start to suffer and fail. If there's anything Satan is dead set against, it's human well-being. And he knows that family health is the primary determinant of both community and personal well-being for children, women, and men.

Because of this inherent design, as we've seen, particular family forms and values are essential for all cultures to recognize and esteem. Transcending the pressures of politics, law, religion, and economics, societies typically follow these forms to varying degrees because they work. They work because they align with the image in which we are all created, and this is true whether we realize the connection or not.

God's Ideals

Let's look at the godly ideals that all families and communities should be mindful of and practice in order to be healthy and enduring. These are qualities Satan is trying to deface and draw us away from.

1. *Self-giving love.* Opponents of the natural family often tell us, "Love makes a family." This is true, but not the whole truth. It's like saying, "Flour makes a loaf of bread." Love is the most fundamental component of a healthy family, as flour is the primary component of a good loaf of bread. But a family and a loaf of bread obviously require more in order to be what they are supposed to be.

Familial love is more than mere feelings of closeness, romanticism, and even commitment among various people. Familial love is based on relationships that flow from marital love—that of a man and woman in an exclusive, all-giving, sacrificial, lifelong bond from which children usually can originate. This love, in its ideal, is not a *taking* kind of love, but *giving* of oneself to the other. This is true of marriage as well as parenting.

Every family should seek to emulate the love, intimacy, and service of the Trinity. A family may appear idyllic even though its members are selfish and narcissistic. But such a family is unhealthy and cannot flourish. It is a community that is not fulfilling the role of family.

2. *Importance of male and female.* Both male and female are necessary for the family because the trinity of family requires that these two distinct parts of humanity love each other, complement one another, and cooperate in the creation and growth of the family. A family that says it has no need of either male or female is not healthy because it rejects one half of humanity. Each gender, being unique, represents a part of the image of God that the other cannot. That is why it is not good for man to be alone, and why all cultures

throughout time have centered family around the coming together of the two halves of humanity.

Some families are missing either male or female due to death, desertion, or divorce. Few in such families would contend that this is the ideal situation. They know and feel this deeply. Families that intentionally reject either male or female by design—such as same-sex homes or single adults who intentionally achieve single parenthood through artificial reproduction—fail to recognize the importance of each gender. They fail to recognize the fullness of humanity as expressed in the nature of God.

3. *Marriage.* The first command God gave Adam and Eve was to join together as one flesh. The first human institution is marriage; it has existed since the dawn of civilization, and every culture has some set of laws, rituals, or community-held mores about the expectation of marriage for adult men and women. Most cultures also have maintained—until very recently in the West—taboos against children being born outside of marriage. Anthropologists tell us that marriage benefits men, women, and society as a whole because it curtails the enticing of men to become sexual predators and consumers and the enticing of women to become items to be collected and used.[1]

Marriage is the foundation of the family because it is the relationship where man and woman give themselves totally and exclusively to one another. They give to their spouse the trinity of their own being: body, mind, and spirit. This is offered in the marriage ceremony, a public pledge of total self exclusively to another. Sex outside of marriage lacks any true, lasting commitment to such giving.

4. *Sexuality.* The sexual embrace is the most intimate of all human communions, so much so that it is God's symbolism of the two becoming one flesh. Most cultures—Christian and otherwise—recognize that a marriage is not fully finalized until it has been

consummated and the man and woman have become one. This is the only human relationship that brings such a unity.

Sex is a gift we receive from God at His delight and that we give to another by surrendering ourselves totally, completely, and exclusively in this embrace. We offer ourselves, not just physically but also emotionally and spiritually, as an expression of love to our one-flesh spouse.

5. *Parenthood*. As we have learned, parenthood is where every human—either as a parent or as someone's child—enters the communion, wonder, and mystery of the human trinity. The love of a husband and wife, bound to each other for life, should flow into the creation of new life in the family via procreation or adoption—just as God's trinitarian love is life-giving. The three Persons do not keep love to themselves, but share it with their offspring. So should we.

Parents bring new life into the world through love and passionate intimacy and, ideally, welcome children with great anticipation, warmth, provision, and protection. While conception can be the result of cold and impersonal copulation, few desire such a union as the source of their lives. We would all like to have proceeded from and been raised in the love and intimacy of a mother and father. Mental health professionals explain that an individual's deep emotional struggles often arise from the absence of this warmth and love from a child's earliest years. Parents are the first and best providers of this love, warmth, and protection. Their role is irreplaceable.

6. *Extended family and kinship*. The nuclear family, as anthropologists refer to it (father, mother, and child), explains the starting point of family, not the end. This basic human nucleus, noted by thinkers like Aristotle and before, exists in all human generations. It both results *from* and *in* an extended family of grandparents, aunts, uncles, and cousins—our kin who connect us with the story of who we are. These people are most likely to help nurture and protect the

formation and healthy growth of the essential nuclear unit. Some extended families live in the same home; others live apart. Regardless, this larger kinship matters in many important ways.

SATAN'S DECEPTIONS

In contrast, the following are some of the beachheads on which Satan has established particular control in the last 50 or 60 years. The first has been the most destructive and dangerous.

1. *Individualism and selfishness.* Self-denial and service to others are not widely practiced values today. This erodes the heart and spirit of family; it fails to model the love of the Trinity, whose members serve one another with joy. Following their example, we first learn to live for others in the context of a family. Selfishness and the fight for our individual interests is the primary enemy of the family.

2. *Anti-natalism.* There is a troubling trend away from married couples bearing and raising children. The National Marriage Project in the United States has warned that "demographically, socially and culturally, the nation is shifting from a society of child-rearing families to a society of child-free adults."[2] Journalist Jonathan Last describes our increasingly intentional child-free culture in fine detail in his book *What to Expect When No One's Expecting.*[3] Demographer Phillip Longman warns, "No industrialized nation still produces enough children to sustain its population over time, or to prevent rapid population aging."[4]

Raising healthy, thriving, loving, intelligent, and diligent children is something we must do with great sacrifice and effort. This is the most important task of families and society as a whole. Children are a blessing, not a curse or nuisance.

3. *Divorce.* God is very clear when He says, "I hate divorce" (Malachi 2:16, NIV). He hates it because it tears apart those who

have become one flesh—as well as the children of that union. It is a vivisection, not just of a family, but of every person in that family.

We might even say that divorce rips apart a specific revelation of God, the image-bearing family that was intended to tell us about who He is, what He's done, and why that matters. This explains what novelist Charles Williams meant when he said, "Divorce is not bad morals; it is bad metaphysics."[5]

Mountains of research stemming from the West's 40-year experiment with no-fault divorce show it to be harmful for men, women, and children in far deeper ways than even the most conservative critics ever imagined.[6]

4. *Polygamy and multi-partner marriage.* As God declared, it is not good for man to be alone. What He provided as a solution was woman—one woman. This "Other" is God's dramatic demonstration of what man and woman both need, explaining why women tend to be treated with more dignity and respect in monogamous cultures.[7] In polygamous cultures women tend to become objects to be collected and used in sex, childbearing, and domestic labor. This is true in typical and serial polygamous cultures, where men either have many wives at one time or a number of wives, one at a time, over a lifetime.

Yes, polygamous marriage is mentioned in biblical history. But these texts are descriptive, not prescriptive. Being mentioned in the Bible doesn't necessarily make something "biblical." God does not condone polygamy, judging from His design for marriage clearly stated in the first chapter of Genesis, Christ's affirmation of the Genesis model in Matthew 19:4-6, and the last chapters of Revelation in which Christ takes one beloved bride for Himself, the church.

5. *Premarital and extramarital sex.* Any sexual activity outside the protective and covenantal bonds of male-female marriage is

harmful to individuals and entire societies—because it joins two people physically without also uniting them mentally and spiritually. In marriage, a man and woman publicly commit themselves wholly to each other. Non-marital sex, on the other hand, says, "I only want part of you, not all of you." Marital union is a lifelong, complete relationship; non-marital sex is isolated, limited, and transient. It is not true intimacy because it holds back important things.

6. *Cohabitation.* Yet another refusal to give all of oneself to another is evident in cohabitation, the world's fastest growing family form. This living arrangement is functionally much different from, and less healthy than, marriage. Cohabitating relationships are consistently less durable and more volatile, experiencing significantly higher rates of domestic violence and keeping individuals more isolated from family and friends. Cohabiters encounter higher levels of infidelity, depression, and drug use and do not fare as well financially as their married peers. In fact, there is no significant well-being measure that cohabitation provides over marriage. Many sociologists believe this is because cohabitation tends to promote more individualistic attitudes and confused expectations among couples regarding the future of the relationship. And it tends to harm women more deeply than it harms men.[8]

7. *Artificial reproductive technology.* This relatively new development concerns the ability to produce human life outside the intimacy of a mother and father. Artificial reproductive technology (ART) can help facilitate conception for married couples facing infertility. While there are conflicting views in the Christian community regarding the moral and spiritual implications of ART, some of the moral objections to the use of this technology are diminished if the couple does not go outside the relationship to obtain egg, sperm, or womb—or fertilize more eggs than will be carried and delivered by the wife. These two cases are outside the limits of what

happens between a man and woman in their natural, human reproductive union.

Although some aspects of ART can be useful in helping infertile couples conceive, it is not appropriate when employed by intentionally single people and same-sex couples. Such individuals and couples come to see the other sex merely as a source of sperm or egg, for that is the only thing they seek from the donor. This is a tragic reductionism of what male and female and the procreative union are. Here, reproductive materials do not meet in the beautiful warmth, intimacy, and love of an exclusive and fully committed marriage, but rather in a medical laboratory following the foreplay of a business contract. Surrogacy—having another woman carry the fertilized ovum of another man and woman to term for an agreed-upon fee—is also ethically outside the bounds of the marital union.

It is important to note that artificial reproduction is different from adoption. Adopted children are not intentionally conceived in separation from their biological kin. Adoption is a compassionate, even heroic, way to meet the needs of children who have lost parents or who cannot be raised by their biological parents or extended family. Adoption is deeply child-centered; artificial reproduction technology is primarily adult-centered. This is true even in cases of embryo adoption; in this process an embryo that was conceived by ART but cryogenically stored with no plans for implantation is adopted, with permission, by another couple. The embryo is then implanted in the mother's womb for gestation. The adoption and implantation of these embryos is distinct from the ART that gave rise to them.

8. *Same-sex marriage and families.* Since both man and woman uniquely represent the image of God, a whole family demands the involvement of both sides of humanity. Same-sex couples, by design, reject the necessity of one side of humanity. Any family

that proclaims male or female optional and seeks to establish itself without the other is not a healthy family. Concerning parenting, a compassionate society never encourages the intentional creation of motherless or fatherless families. But this is what every same-sex couple does. All the love in the world cannot turn a man into a mother or a woman into a father—two things that a very convincing body of research says children need, as we've previously seen.

CULTURE

Is Satan the only enemy of family that we should be wary of? There are two other things we must be mindful of as Satan exploits them for his purposes.

The first enemy Satan exploits is a significant and easy target in Christian circles today: the Culture. Our culture is like the air around us. It is the nature of our nationality and common values. It's a very fluid thing, sometimes changing like the weather—but typically much slower. We must always be aware of the nature of our culture, and the impact it is having on the children and adults of the community. The art and entertainment we allow to be widely created and presented determine our cultural health.

Our interest in—or obsession with—money and material things also determines our cultural well-being. So does the way we regard others, the value we place upon them, community interaction, and service to others. What we collectively value about the gift of sexuality—protecting it or flaunting it—also determines a community's cultural health. So do habits of diet, physical exercise, education, work, and family life.

All these are of interest to Satan because they drive our values, attitudes, behaviors, and experiences. To grasp this, we only need consider what we think of when we appraise certain places for raising our children. Regardless of what your values might be, give your gut response to the question of which places on the following list you might choose for raising your children:

- a small town with lots of parks, community volunteerism, and good schools
- the French Quarter in New Orleans
- Kabul, Afghanistan
- Beverly Hills, California
- Zurich, Switzerland
- a sunny beach community in São Paulo, Brazil
- an apartment in downtown Las Vegas
- the sex tourism areas of Bangkok
- a small estate in the rolling landscape of Italy's Umbrian hill country
- the red-light district of Amsterdam
- a small goat farm on the outskirts of Sydney, Australia

The reactions you gave to each location are the judgments you made about its culture. Culture is a very important thing in the war Satan has waged. Where does your culture sit in this balance? How has your family influenced it for good or for bad?

The "culture wars" that some cling to and others bemoan are a direct result of the tension we feel in our awareness that things are not always as they ought to be, and that we live in a society that does not appreciate the answers our faith provides. We wrestle with how to live and work and coexist well together. This has been true of Christians in the world since the days our Savior walked the earth.

And the family is often in the bull's-eye of the debates and the consequences of our collective cultural decisions.

But is the Culture the biggest enemy of the family? Is it greater than Satan? Or is there yet another enemy more pernicious?

The Greatest Enemy

Now we get to the meat of things. The pull and lusts of *self*, of our own internal and fallen hearts, is really the greatest threat to the family that each of us faces.

What is the place of the self in the war against the family? It is the strategic bull's-eye Satan shoots for when he tempts each of us, getting us to hold what seems best for us over what is best for others. It is our most susceptible point when he wants us to move arrogantly away from God and what He has for us. This is precisely what he did with Adam and Eve, and he does it with us.

Why? Remember, the Persons of the Trinity do not live for themselves, but honor and love one another. Satan, in stark and diabolical contrast, is all about himself. Increasingly, so are we.

Self and *me* are the most strategic footholds Satan has in our lives and in the world. Take a moment to glance back through some of the attacks on the family discussed earlier in this chapter. Then ask yourself, "How do the pull and desire and gratification of self play a role in each of these attacks?"

Isn't it remarkable? Satan needs only to satisfy the desires of self to hide his landmines. The culture simply amplifies the voices of selfish desire in each of us.

The greatest enemy to the health, well-being, and effectiveness of every family in this world is the pull of self. And the battle against the self is universal. From his horrifying years in the Russian Gulag, the great Soviet novelist and Christian believer Aleksandr Solzhenitsyn reflects,

> Gradually it was disclosed to me that the line separating good and evil passes not through states, nor between classes,

nor between political parties either—but right through every human heart—and through all human hearts. . . . Even in hearts overwhelmed by evil, one small bridgehead of good is retained. And even in the best of all hearts, there remains . . . an uprooted small corner of evil.[9]

Consider how Paul's confession long before recognized this in his own heart:

I do not understand my own actions. For I do not do what I want, but I do the very thing I hate. Now if I do what I do not want, I agree with the law, that it is good. So now it is no longer I who do it, but sin that dwells within me. For I know that nothing good dwells in me, that is, in my flesh. For I have the desire to do what is right, but not the ability to carry it out. For I do not do the good I want, but the evil I do not want is what I keep on doing. Now if I do what I do not want, it is no longer I who do it, but sin that dwells within me.

So I find it to be a law that when I want to do right, evil lies close at hand. For I delight in the law of God, in my inner being, but I see in my members another law waging war against the law of my mind and making me captive to the law of sin that dwells in my members. Wretched man that I am! Who will deliver me from this body of death? Thanks be to God through Jesus Christ our Lord! So then, I myself serve the law of God with my mind, but with my flesh I serve the law of sin. (Romans 7:15-25)

If the apostle Paul had this struggle, why do we think we might avoid it? This should humble us.

We cannot, with Christian faith driving our worldview, simply point fingers at Satan and cultural influences to explain the precarious position of family today. We must recognize, as Paul did, that we are fighting a battle of our own making—between the flesh that spurs our insatiable appetites for ourselves and the Spirit of God that offers life, grace, and the sacrifice of self for God and our families.

THE FAMILY REMEDY

So what can we do? Fortunately, God graciously gives us two resources to help us live more selfless lives.

The first is the family itself. The family is where each of us first learns that we must deny and sacrifice ourselves for the good of others. When we are infants, it really is all about us; this is very natural. Our parents organize their whole lives around our needs and happiness. But as we grow, good parents start to limit this—making us learn to wait for what we want, to share toys, to not hit others, and to realize that we will not get whatever we want by crying like we did in our first months of life.

Ask anyone who is married if marriage forced him or her to be more considerate of others and more self-sacrificing. He or she probably will laugh. The answer is obvious, and a little embarrassing. Much marital conflict—early and later—occurs when one partner is unwilling or unable to change certain behaviors, values, and attitudes for the sake of his or her beloved, and something's got to give if harmony is to be maintained.

Parenting does the same thing, but in a more natural way. We sacrifice our time, energy, money, and sleep for the sake of our children—and may even delight in doing so. But there are still parts of our previous childless lives that we would like to hang on to—more than we are now able. Going to movies or concerts, playing golf, watching a complete football game, or just enjoying some quiet reading time become either rare or nonexistent luxuries. So we learn to wait, to tolerate, to go without. Family is the first and most efficient place to counteract the self.

The second institution God has given to temper our selfishness is His church—the encouraging, challenging, transforming Body of Christ. While family is central in this role, the church is the next concentric ring in that essential work. Most pastors and other clergy will tell you, though, that the church can only do so much if families fail to do their part.

God's people must recognize the connection between Satan's self-absorption and our own. The first is connected to and shapes the last. Family is God's first natural, everyday remedy to that. His other is His redemptive work through the church and the indwelling gift of His Holy Spirit. God has already secured our salvation through Christ's sacrifice, but we are to resist the schemes of Satan until he is ultimately defeated.

That will happen just before the final wedding feast of the Lamb of God. It is to this glorious part of the story that we turn in the next chapter. It is the most dramatic "family" part of what God has been doing through *His*tory.

THE BIG STATEMENT FOR REFLECTION

God has an enemy who is relentlessly seeking to dethrone Him, driven by an all-consuming jealousy and hatred. Because of what family represents in God's story—His person and character—Satan has been set on attacking the family from the day of its appearance. The greatest beachhead for this attack is self, in the heart of every person. The enemy is us as much as it is Satan. But God offers remedies: the refining power of the family itself, the church, and His gift of redemption, which is our true hope.

QUESTIONS FOR CONSIDERATION

1. Why is it hard to protect your family from Satan's attacks if you see him as a mischievous troublemaker, a being with a tail and pitchfork and pointy ears, an ever-present saboteur, or an all-powerful equal to God? Based on this chapter, how should we see him?

2. This chapter lists some of the areas in which Satan accomplishes his most strategic and devastating work against the family. Where do you think Ground Zero of this work is right now?

3. How does your own family work as a remedy for the cancer of selfishness and "me-ism"? If you're married, how might your spouse answer that question? If you're a parent, how might your oldest child respond?

4. What is the "self" component of the attacks you think are the greatest and most threatening to families today? How might this affect the advice you'd give someone who was getting married, having his or her first child, or considering a divorce?

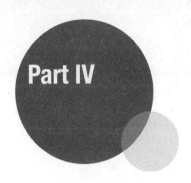

Part IV

OUR DESTINY AND DECISIONS

Our journey is nearing its end, or better yet, its culmination.

First, we will examine our destiny as believers in Christ, and the powerful and beautiful ways in which our family experience has been part picture and part reality of what is in store for each one of us.

Family communicates meaning, history, and the gospel itself. Family has been the story of God, the story of us, and is now the destiny that takes us far beyond the image-bearer status we have held throughout human history.

Finally, we'll close with some thoughts on what we can do today to embrace the honor of bearing God's image to this world through the beautiful but imperfect families we are in.

THE GREAT MYSTERY
AND DESTINY

*For this reason a man will leave his father and mother
and be joined to his wife, and the two will become
one flesh. This mystery is profound, but I am talking
about Christ and the church.*

—EPHESIANS 5:31-32, HCSB

What's the best part of a story?

It's the culmination, the event that the whole story has been driving toward, its climax. We want every story to lead us somewhere—to transport us to another place, a place better and more interesting than where we are now. Otherwise, what's the purpose, right?

Stories are something that all people in all places in the world enjoy because, as we saw in the first chapter, we are made both for story and out of story. This is because God, the master storyteller, has a story that leads us somewhere more glorious than we can imagine.

In any story where a nice young man and woman are interested in each other, we all hope their tale will end in their mutual happiness. We cheer for it; this hope is not just that they might be able to go out on a few satisfying dates together, but something more. In the movie *You've Got Mail*, everyone is excited to see the Tom Hanks and Meg Ryan characters get together at the end. And we all anticipate that the final "Don't cry, shop girl!" scene will lead to a walk down the aisle. How many would be satisfied to hear, "Oh, they dated for a few months, had a great time together, and then mutually decided to go their own ways," or "They moved in together, and for five years she's been waiting for him to pop the question"? No, we hope for more and will be disappointed with anything less. And this is where the movie leaves us, imagining how it will be that they live happily ever after. There is something very natural in this.

If we could have our way, the happy love stories would end with a wedding. So what about the happy ending to God's story that He has been telling us? It began with a wedding in the first chapter. It concludes with another wedding—but of a whole different sort.

This is like no other wedding ever performed, participated in, or witnessed. In the last book of God's story, on its final pages, we are told of a wedding in which Christ—the Lamb of God, the great and glorious Bridegroom—is finally united, after untold millennia of wooing and preparing, with His dearly beloved. This wedding is the culmination of time, the climax of God's story, His passionate pursuit of His beloved, the redeemed church.

Who are these beloved? They are those who trust in the Bridegroom's lovingkindness and forgiving grace, those who accept His divine proposal and commit themselves fully and faithfully—body, mind, and soul—to Him.

This is what the whole divine story has been about and is moving toward. We have beautiful hints of it throughout the Old and New Testaments, but we get our first big picture in the last four chapters of the Revelation of John the Apostle. This first picture is found in Revelation 19. As you read it, imagine the majesty of this extraordinary scene:

Then I heard what seemed to be the voice of a great multitude, like the roar of many waters and like the sound of mighty peals of thunder, crying out, "Hallelujah! For the Lord our God the Almighty reigns. Let us rejoice and exult and give him the glory, for the marriage of the Lamb has come, and his Bride has made herself ready; it was granted her to clothe herself with fine linen, bright and pure"—for the fine linen is the righteous deeds of the saints.

And the angel said to me, "Write this: Blessed are those who are invited to the marriage supper of the Lamb." And he said to me, "These are the true words of God." (Verses 6-9)

GET THE PICTURE

Jan van Eyck, the Ghent Altarpiece, *Adoration of the Mystic Lamb* (1432)
Cathedral of Saint Bavo, Ghent
Visit familyproject.com to see this work of art.

This wonderful piece is the large lower panel of a polyptych inviting us to imagine what the wedding feast of the Lamb might be like. It is a remarkably ambitious project by Jan van Eyck, working primarily in Belgium, with the whole piece being perhaps twice as tall as a man. The Holy Spirit, signified by the dove at the top center, illuminates and blesses the celebration. Streaming in endlessly from the four corners of the earth are the worshipers who are the bride of the Lamb, the redeemed of God who approach the Bridegroom, who is standing at the altar awaiting us. It is quite literally what *His*tory has been about.

The World's Most Stolen Piece of Art

The Ghent Altarpiece has many distinctions, one of which is that it's the most stolen piece in all of art history; interesting that its massive size and dramatic weight did not keep it in one place more often. It even spent some time during World War II stashed in a salt mine by Hitler's army, which was less than conducive to its preservation.

In this magnificent and ancient work completed in 1432 by the great Jan van Eyck and his older brother, Hubert, we become witnesses and participants in the adoration of the Lamb of God. Its structure is what's known as a polyptych, a multi-panel painting that can be folded and unfolded to explain important parts of the gospel depending on the worship and teaching needs of the cathedral in which it is housed.

It presents to us an upper and lower scene on its inner panels. Across the top, starting in the center, is God upon His eternal throne. Scholars continue to debate whether this is God the Father, Christ the Son, or a representation of the Trinity—distinguished by the triple-layered crown—which is a long and favored view. It is also possible that those seated next to Him indicate this is very likely Christ, ascended to His throne. The figure left of center is Christ's mother, Mary; His cousin and forerunner, John the Baptist, is on the left. To each of their sides are worshipers, probably angels, singing and playing instruments. On the outer flanks we see Adam and Eve, who have fallen into the snares of the evil one, reminding us of our desperate need for divine redemption. They are looking down on the final stage of this redemption in the lower center panel.

In the lower panels we have the culmination of this redemption, a panorama of a continual flow of the multitudes coming to this celebration of the purifying Lamb. The altar upon which the Lamb stands facing us is embossed with the scripture, "Behold the Lamb of God who takes away the sins of the world" (John 1:29) as well as "Jesus the Way" and "the Truth, the Life" (14:6). On the chest of the Lamb—who is Christ—there is a wound from which flows our Savior's life-giving blood, poured out for us in the chalice of communion from which we will all finally drink with the Bridegroom at the great and glorious wedding (Luke 22:18-20).

You can read all you need to know about this painting's history in Noah Charney's *Stealing the Mystic Lamb: The True Story of the World's Most Coveted Masterpiece* (Public Affairs, 2012).

We find here a great and mighty sound of praise, like that of thunder, from a vast multitude giving glory to God. The bride of the Lamb of God has come, having made herself ready. Those who are invited to this grand wedding and its feast are called blessed.

But before we consider this wedding, we must get the back story. Like most tales, this one gains significance when we venture back in its history to understand the foundation upon which it is all built.

THE BACK STORY

Our glorious Groom and His unrelenting passion for His radiant bride cannot be understood unless we go way, way back into the early years of their relationship. It is quite dramatic, and nothing close to easy sailing.

His heart has always been toward her, but hers has not. He has relentlessly and faithfully pursued His precious bride with complete abandon and without the slightest concern for His dignity. Any other man would have been quite happy to let this one get away—and no one would have faulted him for it. In fact, all would have encouraged it. But this is no common lover, and therefore no common love story. We know this story because the Groom's Father tells us the whole sordid tale in vivid detail, starting most dramatically in Ezekiel 16.

The story of this bride-to-be starts on the day of her birth. She was born to evil parents who immediately abhorred and cast her out, bloody and helpless into an open field to die. No one pitied her or had the slightest twinge of compassion for her. There she was, without hope, love, or the slightest bit of care.

But not for long.

This rejected child was discovered by the Groom's family, wallowing and crying in her own blood. They proclaimed the blessing of life upon this little one and took her to be their own. In their home, she thrived—majestic, beautiful, tall, and slender (Ezekiel 16:7, 13-14).

Being at the age for love, the Father's Son tenderly covered her with His own garments. He made a vow, a lifelong covenant with her, that she would become His bride, and He would become her Husband, Lover, Protector, and Provider. She was transformed from a rejected infant to a magnificent woman, decorated by her Beloved with fine ornaments of gold bracelets, elaborate silver necklaces, and much more. She was served the finest foods. Her Beloved describes her this way:

> You grew exceedingly beautiful and advanced to royalty.
> And your renown went forth among the nations because of
> your beauty, for it was perfect through the splendor that I
> had bestowed on you. (Verses 13-14)

He lavished her with His love and countless symbols of that affection. She was the envy of every other woman in the land, married or not.

But this is where the happy story ends.

"TRAMP" IS PUTTING IT NICELY

She did not return her Betrothed's love. In fact, that would be an understatement of ridiculous proportions. Nor did she simply throw her unfaithfulness in His face; she slapped Him with it, pummeled Him about the head and body, sending it painfully deep into His heart and soul.

This was not just a phase she went through, either. She practiced enough infidelity for many lifetimes. This is part of the biblical story they don't tell you on those little verse-of-the-day calendars. Your children don't bring crayon-colored pictures of it home from Sunday school. It is neither wholesome nor family friendly. The storytelling turns to judgment:

> But you trusted in your beauty and played the whore because of your renown and lavished your whorings on any passerby; your beauty became his. You took some of your garments and made for yourself colorful shrines, and on them played the whore. The like has never been, nor ever shall be. (Ezekiel 16:15-16)

She took all His gifts and used them in her championship infidelity. She even sacrificed the sons and daughters she and the Groom had created together (verses 20-21). All this time she gave no thought to the kindnesses done to her since her first day of life.

Her abominations reached world-class proportions. The Bible

tells us bluntly that she set herself up on elevated platforms in every square in the city, opening herself up physically and offering herself as a pornographic advertisement to everyone who passed by (verse 25). She multiplied her customer base to include men from surrounding countries, a very different kind of renown going forth among the nations (verses 26-29).

But while even a common prostitute will selectively refuse a patron on principle from time to time, she refused no one. She eagerly offered her services to all not only without fee, but *she* paid *them*:

> Men give gifts to all prostitutes, but you gave your gifts to
> all your lovers, bribing them to come to you from every
> side with your whorings. So you were different from other
> women in your whoring. No one solicited you to play the
> whore, and you gave payment, while no payment was given
> to you; therefore you were different. (Verses 33-34)

This lady was no mere tramp. There are not really words coarse enough.

Ezekiel is not the only place in which God tells us of the nature of His betrothed. In Jeremiah 2:20-25 and 3:1-10 God speaks of His beloved as one who has not seen a field or tree where she has not laid down, offering herself sexually to any and all takers, even "committing adultery with stone and tree" (3:9). He says her transgressions are so flagrant and vile that the strongest lye or the largest bars of soap cannot wash her clean (2:22).

But wait, there's more!

God tells the prophet Hosea that if he wants to know what His own marriage is like, he should find himself a common slut, marry her, give her children, and watch what happens. (Hosea 1:2). Hosea ends up with a faithless bride who practically waves a sign on busy street corners that says, "Will have sex for food!" (Hosea 2:5)

If you're married, think about this: What complaints do you have against your spouse? How has he or she hurt you? Have you been humiliated in crushing ways? Has he or she been unfaithful, even numerous times? Our Lord can so relate to your tremendous pain.

Pick the worst stories of marital betrayal that you have ever seen, even from the movies. Combine them all together and they cannot come close to rivaling the humiliation that God has suffered from His bride.

So at the height of her infidelity, what does He do?

The answer to this question is at the center of the Christian story.

HIS LOVE NEVER WANES

Who is this horrible, demeaning bride? She is God's chosen people. Us.

The Lord proclaims his angry judgment upon her—our—shamefulness, returning her deeds upon her own head as a reproof, declaring, "As I live, declares the Lord GOD, your sister Sodom and her daughters have not done as you and your daughters have done" (Ezekiel 16:48).

But this is not His last word on the matter. Given all the insult that has been His, He astonishingly concludes,

> I will not look on you in anger, for I am merciful, declares the LORD; I will not be angry forever. Only acknowledge your guilt, that you rebelled against the LORD your God. . . . Return, O faithless children, declares the LORD; for I am your master; I will take you . . . and I will bring you to Zion. (Jeremiah 3:12-14)

If we repent of our profound infidelity, He is willing to bring us back to His home to live with Him. God told the prophet Hosea how He would treat His bride with this good news:

> Therefore, behold, I will allure her, and bring her into the wilderness, and speak tenderly to her. . . . And there she shall answer as in the days of her youth. . . . And I will betroth you to me forever. I will betroth you to me in righteousness and in justice, in steadfast love and in mercy. I will betroth you to me in faithfulness. And you shall know the LORD. (Hosea 2:14-15, 19-20)

Finally, to Ezekiel and His people, God gives this great hope:

> Yet I will remember my covenant with you in the days of your youth, and I will establish for you an everlasting covenant. Then you will remember your ways and be ashamed. . . . I will establish my covenant with you, and you shall know that I am the LORD, that you may remember and be confounded, and never open your mouth again because of your shame, when I atone for you all that you have done, declares the Lord GOD. (Ezekiel 16:60-63).

Wow! As observers of—much less participants in—this story, what can we say to such patience, grace, and kindness? It is incomparable and unreasonable. But there it is.

OUR ATONEMENT: GOD'S WEDDING PROPOSAL

Because of our drastic infidelity to our God—seeking other "lovers" (money, fame, reputation, family, work, fashion, sports, impure sexuality, etc.)—we have earned guilt and shame. But as God had Ezekiel explain to His people, atonement for all our unfaithfulness is coming.

But how?

It comes in the form of a dramatic proposal.

Our atonement comes from Jesus, "the Lamb of God who takes away the sin of the world" (John 1:29). As Christ spoke to His disciples about and approached His sacrificial death, His terms would have been heard as betrothal and wedding language. To understand that, we need to look at how they saw marriage in their time and community.

In the days of Christ and before, the bride and groom would enter a betrothal period, similar to an engagement but much more serious and binding. Becoming betrothed was essentially the start of the marriage. The two were legally bound, but not quite husband and wife yet—so they could not yet know each other sexually or begin sharing a home together. But the betrothal was so legally binding that only a divorce could break the covenant it represented.

Betrothal initiated the time of preparation for the wedding and full entrance into the marriage. This time of preparation between betrothal, the wedding, and the marriage's physical consummation was typically up to a year in length, for there was much to do. One major task to be undertaken during this time would be for the groom to say goodbye to his betrothed and return to his father's house to build the necessary living quarters that he and the bride would need. He would not see her again until their new house was completed and approved as worthy for the new bride by the groom's father. At that point the groom would be sent by his father to go get his bride and bring her back to his father's home for the final wedding ceremony and celebration.

At the Passover meal Christ shared with His disciples on the evening before His crucifixion, also known as the Last Supper, Jesus spoke of having to go away. When Peter asked where He was going, Jesus answered, "Where I am going you cannot follow me now, but you will follow afterward" (John 13:36). His disciples found it a puzzling explanation until He finished it:

> Let not your hearts be troubled. . . . In my Father's house are
> many rooms. If it were not so, would I have told you that
> I go to prepare a place for you? And if I go and prepare a
> place for you, I will come again and will take you to myself,
> that where I am you may be also. (14:1-3)

Although not precisely sure what the Savior was getting at, the disciples would have recognized this as the point in a young man's life when he goes to his father's house to prepare a place for his bride and later returns to take her there. From our vantage point, we can see that Christ is speaking of Himself as the betrothed Groom who is leaving His beloved to go and prepare their future home in His Father's house. At a time known only by the Father, on His approval of the Son's preparations, the Son will joyfully return to take His bride to their new home, the one He began preparing when He left us and ascended to the Father. How beautiful is that to our ears?

In the wedding customs of Christ's day, the groom's father made the arrangements and the invitations. This could help to explain why Jesus said, "No one can come to me unless the Father who sent me draws him" (6:44). The Father alone invites us to the wedding feast of His Son because He set this grand event into motion.

At the betrothal ceremony, just after the establishment and signing of the marriage contract (the *ketubah*) and before the groom departs for his house-building mission, bride and groom drink from a common cup of wine. It symbolizes the new covenant made between them. This wine represents the blood of a sacrificial animal, marking the couple's submission to their new covenant. Sharing the cup seals the betrothal; the groom will not partake again until he can do so with his new bride at their glorious wedding celebration.

It is easy to see how similar much of this is to Christ's Last Supper with His disciples before He goes away to prepare a place for them. In the ordinance of communion, a cup symbolizing His blood is presented to us. We continue to drink of it in memory of His sacrifice and the betrothal promise of His return for us. Even the groom's abstinence from the wine until he is reunited with his bride echoes what Christ is referring to when He says,

> I tell you I will not drink again of this fruit of the vine until that day when I drink it new with you in my Father's kingdom. (Matthew 26:29)

While the groom goes off to his preparations, the bride prepares on her end. One important part is being bathed by her family and friends in anticipation of her groom's return, so that she can be found acceptable. The bride of Christ does the same, and has been doing the same since the Bridegroom departed, in the ceremony of baptism given to us by John the Baptist as purification in anticipation of that great day (Revelation 7:14). John the Baptist, Christ's cousin and forerunner, told us that he himself is the "friend of the bridegroom" and thus, at the bridegroom's betrothal visit, his joy is now complete (John 3:29).

Before the bridegroom leaves his bride after the betrothal, he gives her a gift as a promissory note, a seal for their union and his promise to return for her. The Father has given us, through His Son, the very seal of the Holy Spirit—the One Scripture calls "the guarantee of our inheritance until we acquire possession of it, to the praise of his glory" (Ephesians 1:14).

Finally, when the groom's father approves the new marital dwelling place, he directs his son that today is the day he has been waiting so long for. Now he can go get his beautiful bride and bring her home. In the case of Christ, only God the Father knows the hour when this will happen. Not even the Son knows (Matthew 24:36). Neither does His bride, who is waiting in great anticipation, keeping a watchful eye.

She must be prepared for that day and hour, for it could come at any time. This is what Jesus was referring to in His parable of the virgins who had to stay alert, keeping their lanterns ready as they awaited the return of the Bridegroom. Some of the virgins were not properly prepared and had to go buy more oil for their lamps—thus missing the Bridegroom's arrival. Jesus explains the story with a warning: "Watch therefore, for you know neither the day nor the hour" of the Groom's coming (Matthew 25:13).

When the bridegroom returns, his friends go before him, announcing his return with shouts of joy and the unmistakable trumpeting of the *shofar*. This is how Christ's return will be heralded, with the voice of an archangel and the great sound of the trumpet as explained in 1 Thessalonians 4:16.

Finally, as the bride of ancient Palestine wore a gown of radiant and extravagant fabric to her wedding, emphasizing her beauty and purity, so will Christ's bride be adorned with "fine linen, bright and pure" as described in Revelation 19:7-8.[1]

WHO ARE YOU?

We, the church, are the bride of Christ. We are the prostitute, record-shattering in our infidelity and dishonoring the One who rescued us and lavished every gift upon us. We cannot forget or ignore this.

But we are also someone else. We are the one our Beloved would not give up on, whose dramatic and insulting betrayals could not extinguish His great and undying love for us.

He is still coming for us, as He said. If any promise can be trusted, it is this one.

And what is that promise? We are told in beautiful detail:

> And I saw the holy city, new Jerusalem, coming down out
> of heaven from God, prepared as a bride adorned for her
> husband. And I heard a loud voice from the throne saying,
> "Behold, the dwelling place of God is with man. He will
> dwell with them, and they will be his people, and God him-
> self will be with them as their God. He will wipe away every
> tear from their eyes, and death shall be no more, neither
> shall there be mourning, nor crying, nor pain anymore, for
> the former things have passed away."
>
> And he who was seated on the throne said, "Behold,
> I am making all things new." Also he said, "Write this
> down, for these words are trustworthy and true." (Revela-
> tion 21:2-5)

This is the home, the dwelling place, Christ promised He would prepare for us. It brings us to God's Fourth Definitive Statement: "Behold, I am making all things new."

It reminds us of another, perhaps more familiar, story—the Brothers Grimm tale of Cinderella. A young girl lives in daily slavery to a very wicked stepmother and two daughters. She is covered with the soot of the cinders she must sweep from the hearth. She is not clean nor comely. All the young women of the kingdom are invited to a grand ball at the king's palace, but Cinderella is not allowed to attend. However, after the others have left for the event, her fairy godmother mysteriously provides all she will need, and off

Cinderella goes. At the ball she catches the attention and heart of the king's son. But she must leave the ball by midnight and rushes out without a word to anyone.

But the king's son will not forget this one who captured his heart, and he searches for her throughout the land. When he finds her, he sweeps her up to be his own, to live with him as his wife in the grand castle of his father. Her tears, pain, and shame are replaced with joy. The king's son made all things new for her.

This is what our King's Son has done for us—but in the real world, not fiction. Knowing what we once were, He longs to restore us to that prior glory when we were with Him at that garden party in Eden.

And as a bride does with her husband, we mysteriously become one with Him. Jesus tells us as much:

> Yet a little while and the world will see me no more, but you will see me. Because I live, you also will live. In that day you will know that I am in my Father, and you in me, and I in you. (John 14:19-20)

This is very provocative language, telling us that we will become one with Him, even as closely as He is with His Father. And we live happily ever after with and in Him.

This has never been truer or grander in any other story that ends with *happily ever after*. It is the story all others seek to imitate, each in its imperfect way. This is the final and everlasting scene in our fuller Christian worldview: consummation, the culmination of what God has been moving us toward and preparing us for all along. The full story of God and our life in Him cannot be told without this part.

Where Are You Going?

It is a remarkable story, beyond imagination—and true, every bit of it. We were created, we fell, and in the most glorious redemption story ever, we . . .

- Got back in good standing with God?
- Became "BFFs"?
- Moved in together for eternity?

There's far more to it than that. We, God's very image-bearers, receive far more than reconciliation with the Image Maker. We are invited into spousal union with Him. Read that over again a few times.

Wow.

That is far more than we could dare to dream, far more than we ought to expect, far more than we deserve, and far more than one might reasonably expect from God.

Remember Paul Gauguin's third question: *Where are we going?*

We're going to a wedding—one like none of us could ever imagine. It will be greater than anything that ever was, because He who has made the proposal is beyond comprehension.

Will you be part of this grand event?

Have you responded to the Groom's proposal? As with all other wedding proposals, there is only "yes" or "no." There is no "Let me get back to you on that," or simply ignoring the question. God is awaiting your reply today.

A friend or pastor from a Bible-teaching church can show you how to make sure you'll be part of this glorious celebration. Or contact Focus on the Family (1-800-A-FAMILY) for help. We pray that you won't miss this event. Our Bridegroom has long sought you, and given His very life on your behalf.

THE BIG STATEMENT FOR REFLECTION

God's story starts with a wedding and ends with a wedding. God will not give up on His beloved—His church. Those who respond to His marriage proposal with a "yes" will become one with Him as well as heirs to all He has and is. This is where we are going! It is where the whole story has been going from the first scene in John 1:1.

QUESTIONS FOR CONSIDERATION

1. Before reading this chapter, did you realize that the Scriptures start and end with two different kinds of weddings? Do you think this is a coincidence, or did God plan it that way for a reason? If the latter, what do you think that reason is?

2. How do you feel about the story from Ezekiel, Hosea, and Jeremiah? Most people tend to think of the Bible as a wholesome book, safe for the whole family; but there are sections that are very "adult." What does that tell you about God and His view of you?

3. Have you ever considered the Cross and the events leading up to it as a wedding proposal? How could this change your understanding of what the drama of the Cross is really about?

4. This chapter provides the answer to Gauguin's third question, *Where are we going?* Does anything about the answer surprise you? Concern you? Excite you? Why?

5. In light of what we've learned here, why do you think Jesus said we as individuals would neither be given or taken in marriage in heaven (Matthew 22:30)?

MY IMPERFECT FAMILY

One of the most perfect things in the world is imperfection. Study the following remarkable works and see what they have in common (to view them, visit familyproject.com). They are beautiful presentations of very plain, unremarkable people or settings. But the artist is showing us each is perfect in its imperfection:

- Dorothea Lange's *Migrant Mother* at the U.S. Library of Congress
- Michael Sweerts's *Head of a Woman* at the J. Paul Getty Museum
- Theodore Gericault's *Study of a Model* at the Getty Museum
- Henry Ossawa Tanner's *The Banjo Lesson* at the Hampton University Museum
- Vincent van Gogh's *Portrait of Artist's Mother* at the Norton Simon Museum of Art

Imperfection can be beautiful, and thank goodness it can. One way we can know this is by observing ourselves and our own families.

Throughout this book we have made a thorough study of what

family is in light of who God is, what He made humanity to be, and where God has been taking His story since the beginning. We have been looking at family as a very big idea from a very high view. But now we will end by considering your own family—what it's like, what it's for, and why God placed you in the one that He did.

The first thing we must realize about our families is simple: There is no perfect family. There is not even a close-to-perfect family. Anyone who says otherwise is delusional or just plain dishonest.

There, we've said it. Now we can all just relax, give up the pretense, let our hair down, and operate in reality.

As long as your family has at least one human being in it, it will be imperfect. We might not have too hard a time believing this about our own families, for we have a front-row seat to the drama. But we tend to think the grass is more perfect on the other side of the fence.

Guess what? Chances are that the family next door is more off-the-rails than yours—perhaps much more so.

Yes, there is a "keeping up with the Joneses" in the realm of family and spirituality, isn't there? But it's a trap based on fantasy. We all know that families can put on the face that says they're pretty much perfect—more spiritually together, better at parenting and educating their kids than you, enjoying a better marriage than you, getting life all together better than you. Often they are quite happy—and of course, proud—to tell you how you can have a perfect family like theirs.

Don't believe it for a moment. They would more likely be speaking truth if they said they have Bigfoot living in their basement rumpus room. These are people who sadly live in make-believe land, often tangled in spiritual pride, wanting you to play that game with them. Don't fall for it.

ROOM FOR IMPROVEMENT

Does this "no family is perfect" reality mean all is lost, that we should simply wallow in the mess that each of our families is? Can we ever hope to rise above the dysfunction we presently live in?

Of course, and that's the way all of life is. The absence of perfection doesn't mean we can't try to do better. The realization that we will never be perfect doesn't keep us from seeking to improve.

- Can you improve your diet to be healthier? Yes; even though you will never attain perfect health, you can do better than you're doing now and you should try.
- Can you improve your performance at school or work? Of course, and you can do so in very impressive ways even though you will never be flawless.
- Can you try to improve your relationships with others? Most certainly, and you should. But you will never be the perfect friend to everyone—or, for that matter, anyone.

You can pursue excellence in all these areas. In fact, a solid adequacy is nothing to be ashamed of; that's where most of us live. But chasing perfection is something quite different, and it's a recipe for (or the result of) delusional thinking. It is trying to create and live in a reality that doesn't exist.

DO YOU HAVE A BIBLICAL FAMILY?

Wouldn't everyone like to have a biblical family? Be careful how you answer; it's not what you might think.

As we read through Scripture, we find families from beginning to end. They are central in the story of God's work in and through history. But get this: There's not a perfect family in the bunch.

Most are spectacular messes to varying degrees. Many of them are world-class disasters.

Let's take a look at the major family stories featured in God's interaction with man.

1. *The first family.* In the early pages of Scripture, we read that Adam and Eve had perfect communion with God. Their wedding was actually officiated by Him. How cool is that? Off to a pretty great start, right? But it wasn't long before they ushered in that little problem called the Fall, alienating themselves from God, from each other, and from the rest of creation. Their "mistake" affected every human being to come afterward. A pretty big fail.

Then they had children. One of them ended up murdering the other. How do your kids act up?

2. *Clearing the deck.* The sinfulness of subsequent families gets so bad that God decides to destroy all of humanity through a global flood, regretting He has made man. But in His grace He chooses to restart humanity through one family: Noah's. After the flood, Noah creates a stir in his family with his love of wine and nudity. Read about it in Genesis 9:18-28. It's not a family-friendly story, and probably wasn't told time and again at the Noah family picnics.

3. *Helping God fulfill His covenant.* In Abram and Sarai's very advanced age, God promises that Abram will be the father of a great nation. His offspring will rival the stars of the sky and the sands of the beach in number. God apparently doesn't act fast enough; Abram and Sarai try to fulfill God's covenant through their own conniving. Sarai convinces her husband to give it a go with her maidservant to see if she might bring forth their first child. He obediently does. When the maidservant gets pregnant, guess what Sarai does? She's not delighted, and tells her husband so.

GET THE PICTURE

Matthais Stomer, *Sarah Leading Hagar to Abraham* (1637)
Gemäldegalerie, Berlin
Visit familyproject.com to see this painting.

You've got to love the look on both Sarah's and Abraham's faces. She is very matter-of-fact—even blank, perhaps—but clearly undoubting in her request as she gently takes the wrist and hand of Hagar and motions toward her elderly husband. Hagar has a slightly reticent but obedient gaze, matched by Abraham's awakened-from-his-sleep look of "What, seriously?" He stares into the eyes of his wife as if to discern whether she is serious, kidding, or just crazy. Stomer, born in the Netherlands, was most active in Italy, particularly in Rome. He was strongly of the Caravaggisti, the school of painters who studied and imitated the style and technique of the great Caravaggio.

---

4. *Pacifying the sex-crazed hordes.* Then comes Lot, Abraham's nephew. He's spending a quiet evening at home with some visiting angels who have come to his hometown of Sodom. Suddenly Lot hears a horrible racket at his door and finds every last man of the city there—demanding to have sex with Lot's guests. Committed to protecting the well-being of his guests—as any good host would—what does Lot do?

He presents the mob with another sexual opportunity. Offering his two virgin daughters to these sex-hungry men seems reasonable to Lot. Not exactly Father-of-the-Year material here, is it? It gets worse. In later years, these very daughters—not having yet become mothers—trick Lot into essentially fathering his own grandchildren with them. Is it an understatement to call this a sordid tale?

5. *Squabbling siblings.* In the tale of Jacob and Esau, one brother tries to cheat the other out of his birthright by deceiving their father—and it works. This family drama should put your children's fights in the backseat of the van in a new, less desperate perspective.

Jealousy runs in the family. Many years later, Jacob's sons take their youngest brother, Joseph—"Daddy's little favorite"—and conspire to kill him out of disdain for his favored place in the family. One brother has a bit of sense and recommends they not actually shed his blood, but simply toss him into a pit too deep to escape. That does seem kinder, as he'll just slowly starve to death there. Joseph's father is heartbroken at the apparent loss of his youngest, most cherished son. This is certainly more than a brotherly prank, nothing like your siblings have ever done.

6. *The man of God and the bathing beauty.* Next is King David. He has everything in the world. Along with endless riches, he has more wives than most men have acquaintances. But this is not enough. He wants one particular woman he sees out bathing one day. She is irresistible, even though she is the wife of one of his subjects. David steals her for his own and gets her pregnant. And he goes to the great length of arranging her husband's murder to cover up his sins. A man after God's own heart, we are told in Scripture—but far from perfect.

7. *Jesus' family tree.* Even Jesus' genealogy has some unsavory characters that never get mentioned at family reunions—prostitutes, deceivers, and such.

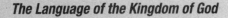

The Language of the Kingdom of God

Despite the fact that the Bible is not full of admirable family examples, the language God often uses expresses the place of family in His heart. Here are some family-related terms He uses to explain His kingdom:

- *Father and Son.* God's own presentation of Himself to us as Father is not merely for effect. It is precisely true to who He is. The second Person of the Trinity is the Son. It is an understatement to say that Father and Son are central to Christianity. As we've seen, they are central to all reality.

- *Birth.* To enter God's kingdom, the Son tells us, we must be born again (John 3:3). The family imagery of this is so dramatic that it caused one man to ask Jesus whether it is actually possible for a man to return to the womb of his mother.

- *Adopted sons and daughters; spiritual siblings.* Since the early days of the church, those who come into the family of God have been known to each other as brothers and sisters. We are also called the adopted children of God. Again, these words are not just imager, but actual and descriptive.

- *Betrothal.* As discussed in the previous chapter, Christ's heart for His church is that of a Groom for His bride. And a divine wedding awaits us.

The language of the kingdom of God is the language of family. And this is by divine design. It speaks truthfully to the nature and character of God, and the value He places on families.

Even His immediate family had its share of stunning drama. Mary and Joseph had to come to terms with apparent pre-marriage infidelity, explaining truthfully to their friends and family that the Holy Spirit brought this child to Mary's womb. This likely did little to tamp down the gossip. When the big day arrived, Joseph hadn't arranged precautionary pre-birth accommodations in advance of a family trip. Mary had to deliver their special Son in a stinky, exposed animal shed.

Years later their boy ran off without permission for more than three days, completely freaking them out with fear. They had to put up with His regular needling of His family's religious leaders. Finally there was His very public and humiliating execution by the Roman government. We have a fuller perspective on what that cross was about today, but at the time it was a profoundly confusing, tragic, and embarrassing event for family and friends.

Family brings hardship. But it also brings much joy. This is the irony of family. There does seem to be some biblical truth to the adage, "You can't live with 'em and you can't live without 'em."

There is a reason family can be so difficult. It's because it has a redeeming effect on us, and because it's constantly under attack for what it represents.

God well knows how gritty family life can get, and He's not shocked by it. But He has given everything to redeem it, which is a central theme of *The Family Project*.

Is There a Benefit in Being This Bad?

This brings us to why God has placed us in such families. Why didn't He make families so that everything would be happy and wholesome for us?

Our Lord is in the business of making all things new. He wants to change us into something we can never be without Him. He is all about transformation, moving us toward holiness. A perfect family cannot be a Christian family because a perfect family has no need of Christ and His redemptive work.

A Christian family is not just moral, though that matters. It's a family that has yielded itself to Christ and submits itself to His transformative work—making us something we are not yet. Our imperfect family is a major tool God uses to accomplish this miracle in our daily lives. G. K. Chesterton captured this beautifully in his typical viewing-things-from-an-upside-down sort of way:

> Of course, the family is a good institution because it is un-congenial. Aunt Elizabeth is unreasonable, like mankind. Papa is excitable, like mankind. Our youngest brother is mischievous, like mankind. Grandpa is [incoherent], like the world; he is old, like the world. Those who wish, rightly or wrongly, to step out of all this, do definitely wish to step into a narrower world. They are dismayed and terrified by the largeness and variety of family.[1]

In Christ's purification of us, Scripture says He uses affliction as a goldsmith or silversmith uses fire—to purify us.[2] Family is clearly one of those trying fires; it is here that each of us first experiences love and acceptance but also conflict, hurt, and the need for confession and forgiveness.

Family is the first place where we must learn to deny ourselves for the sake of others. And this does not just happen during our growing-up years, does it? Maybe it happened to you this week. You wanted to sit down and read a book quietly when someone asked you to take him to the mall or a friend's house. Or you were asked to help with the dishes when you wanted to watch television or play a game. Or your mother-in-law needed you to come over to change a few light bulbs for her, and it needed to be done *today*—even though you were already going to be there Tuesday. Family requires us to deny ourselves.

The behaviors, attitudes, and values a person has today were probably gained in his or her family of origin. Family is the factory of humankind; like any factory, it can put out quality or junk. It usually does either of these things through some kind of friction, stemming from its members' reactions to relational and emotional heat and stress. How we learn to deal with that at home is how we will deal with it in the world.

This is one of the most important abilities and purposes of family. We should be thankful for the bumpy ride family can be, knowing that we bring our own refining fire to our loved ones' lives through our personal imperfections and quirks—and they to ours.

GRACE AND TRUTH

Family friction does not automatically lead to growth, of course. Out of control, fire fails to refine; it can turn precious things to ashes.

What makes the difference? Learning the balance between two important spiritual concepts: *grace* and *truth*.

As Christ came into our imperfect world, He brought these qualities with him:

And the Word became flesh and dwelt among us, and we
have seen his glory, glory as of the only Son from the Father,
full of grace and truth. (John 1:14)

We are reminded in Ephesians 4:15 how important "speaking the truth in love" is. Truth without love—or grace—can be cold, harsh, unforgiving. Love—or grace—without truth can lead to enabling destructive or self-destructive behavior.

We and our families need always to seek to walk in the balance of grace and truth. Both are vital because of the imperfection of our families. Grace brings forgiveness. Truth can bring growth.[3]

Consider how this demonstrates itself in everyday family situations:

- When one spouse is quick to point out the shortcomings of the other (truth) while lacking love or patience or forgiveness (grace), how does that turn out?
- When one spouse is quick to overlook an offense (grace) by the other, but never speaks honestly to the heart of the issue (truth), how often does the problem get resolved and allow resentment to build up?
- When a child is in need of discipline and a parent lectures her about the situation (with lots of truth), but fails to show love or kindness (grace), what is the child really learning?
- When a child is in need of discipline and a parent offers only a permissive love and kindness (grace) without any consequence based on an understanding of the offense (truth), what are the chances that the child will recognize the battle of self described in Romans 7?

When husbands and wives, parents and children, and sisters and brothers seek to bring grace and truth together in their dealings with each other, more of Christ can be seen. The image-bearers can more accurately reflect and reveal the Image Maker.

STRIVE FOR HEALTH, NOT PERFECTION

If perfection is unrealistic this side of heaven, what should families be working toward? This is an important question, which is why we conducted some important research a few years ago on the qualities and characteristics that distinguish healthy families.

The good news is that applying this research in your family doesn't require a degree in rocket science. It doesn't depend on which school your kids attend, what neighborhood you live in, or the size of your bank account. These are relatively simple things everyone can do. The most difficult part is developing the habit of doing them and not giving up.

The health of your family does not depend on doing each of these perfectly or consistently, either. The key is trying to have more of them in your family life from week to week as much as possible. If you make an honest attempt to incorporate as many of these as you can, you're likely to greatly improve the strength of your family, your marriage, and the well-being of your kids (or as many of those as apply to you).

We've examined the best available research and come up with a list of qualities that tend to characterize successful families. Most of the studies we used were not conducted by Christian scholars, nor did they seek to determine what makes a healthy Christian family. Instead, these findings come from sociologists and psychologists who have observed smoothly functioning marriages and families in a variety of cultural settings around the world—and "just happen" to include many biblical principles.[4]

Here are seven of the most important general, overarching qualities of healthy families the research identified:

1. *Big-picture thinking.* Scholars say successful families realize that the meaning of family is bigger than themselves. We, of course, believe the family exists because of God and for God as well as the larger community. This helps us see our families and those around us from the larger perspective. God wants His Word and Spirit to go into all the world,

and we need such a global view. Families are the first place we should learn how to do this and why it matters.

2. *Commitment.* Thriving families are committed to the long haul in marriage and parenting, and to each other. They make family a top priority, putting it above their personal wants. They know that love is more than just an emotion but a decision to look out for the interests of others.

3. *High regard.* A healthy family demonstrates mutual respect, honor, care, and concern for all family members. It emphasizes affirmation and encouragement and downplays criticism.

4. *Flexibility and grace.* No family can survive if its members are not willing to bend and flex with one another. Grace, forgiveness, and a sense of safety are essential to smoothly functioning family relationships.

5. *Balance.* Balanced parents expect obedience from their children, but also encourage individuality. They realize that love, not just adherence to rules, is the key to healthy human development.

6. *Joy and humor.* Thriving families intentionally create an atmosphere of joy. They laugh together, play together, and delight in one another. But they avoid making jokes at anyone's expense.

7. *A service mindset.* Happy, balanced families care about the community around them. They take seriously the idea that their part of the world will be a poorer place if they don't do their part to serve others.

No family embodies these qualities perfectly. Family life, like spiritual life, is not about perfection, but health and transformation. These two are the goals and purposes of strong families.

ESSENTIAL BEHAVIORS FOR PARENTS AND KIDS

Are some families just destined to exhibit these seven qualities while others are not? Is family success a matter of luck? Or are there certain things you and your family can do to foster growth in these key areas?

We believe there are. Here's a list of a dozen practical behaviors that, when pursued, will get you moving in the right direction. They are as powerful as they are simple.

1. *Pray together.* A high regard for prayer should begin with Mom and Dad. Couples who pray together *do* stay together, which research demonstrates. Parents who pray also show their kids by example what it means to rely on God for all of life's daily concerns.

2. *Participate in a local church together.* Couples strengthen their commitment to one another—and families grow in a sense of unity—when they get involved each week with members of God's larger family in worship and hearing His Word proclaimed. There are no lone-ranger or free-agent Christians. Each of us belongs to the body and therefore should be involved in a local church.

3. *Perform daily acts of kindness.* Small, sacrificial deeds and thoughtful words draw family members closer together and create a positive environment for the growth of healthy, balanced kids.

4. *Learn your spouse's and children's love languages.* If you're married, ask your spouse from time to time, "How can I love you better this week?" Show your love in ways that he or she—and each of your children—will understand. For example, one child may appreciate a living-room wrestling match more than a candy bar; another might respond

better to a coupon for a free room-cleaning than to a gift card.

5. *Eat dinner together.* Do this at least four nights a week, but try for more than that. Research strongly shows that the family that shares meals not only stays together but actually enjoys it. And it improves the behavior of your children. Don't allow anything—phone, television, or text messages—to interrupt these times of family communion.

6. *Be actively involved in your children's education.* Join in their school activities. Know their teachers and the subjects they're studying. Checking their homework every night makes a big difference. Beyond boosting academic achievement, this encourages parent-child interaction. It also tells your child that learning and school assignments are important—and that he or she is worth your time.

7. *Know your kids' friends and where they are.* Accountability is essential for healthy families. Insist that your children let you know where they are, whom they're with, and what they're doing. This will show them you love them and care about them.

8. *Get inside their world.* Make a point of reading the books your kids are reading, listening to their favorite music, and watching movies or television programs with them. You'll be in a much better position to exert a positive influence over their cultural tastes and to discuss with them intelligently the pros and cons of the entertainment choices they're making.

9. *Give the benefit of the doubt.* As in any relationship, positive sentiments should always override the negative. Whether in parenting or in your marital relationship, never choose to think the worst of the other person when something goes

wrong. No relationship can stand on such a foundation. Expect the best, and be willing to overlook mistakes and faults sometimes as an expression of love and grace.

10. *Play together.* Something wonderful happens when children and parents get down on the floor to play together, when they enjoy board games or outdoor activities as a family, or when they learn to make music together. Don't miss these opportunities to strengthen family ties.

11. *Give praise and show love.* Husbands need respect. Wives long to know they are loved. Children need the security that can only be provided by caring, involved moms and dads. Create a home where these needs are met and you will have a healthy, thriving family.

12. *Build lasting faith.* Some of the best research shows that ensuring our children enter their adult years with a vibrant, enduring faith is not as complex as we might think.[5] The biggest factor is making sure they live in a family that practices its faith regularly and seriously. You don't have to be perfect disciples of Jesus—just diligent ones. Children who learn that Bible reading, prayer, and regular worship are important and practice these are very likely to continue to do so in their later years. Having other adults around them who take their faith seriously—extended family, teachers, coaches, family friends—has a strong impact as well. Children who have these resources are likely to keep a lifelong, growing faith. In one leading study of kids who left the faith in young adulthood, only 11 percent came from families where a vibrant faith was taught and practiced.[6] Kids typically hang on to what they are taught by their parents. They cannot hang on to what they were never given.

These behaviors aren't difficult to understand and they're available to everyone. Practicing them consistently will not necessarily solve all your family's problems, but they'll put you far ahead of the crowd—helping your family grow in grace, love, happiness, health, and relational durability.

WHAT IS YOUR FAMILY'S CALLING?

As we learned in Chapter 1, each of us needs a sense of purpose and significance. The same is true of families. Does your family have a mission? Is there a reason it exists in the community where you live? You might start to find your family's mission with the question, "What is my family here for, anyway?"

Some Christians might offer a functional answer:

- to fill and subdue the earth
- to provide a nurturing environment for raising the next generation
- to create boundaries for fallen humans who tend to self-destruct
- to carry the family's name, wealth, and possessions
- to protect family members
- to learn to get along with people

Some might even offer more philosophical answers:

- to be a carrier of curses and pains
- to organize society into units of similar-looking people
- to provide love to children
- to develop a sense of identity

The highly self-aware, "messy" family might offer a more cynical answer:

- to drive people crazy until they go off and start their own families to drive a whole new set of people crazy

But we hope that through this journey we've taken together, we're beginning to grasp answers that demonstrate an understanding of God's story intertwining with our own:

- to reflect the nature and character of God
- to demonstrate what the gospel is
- to make an impact on this world

Still, how do we do that? What's a way for our imperfect families and yours to reflect the nature and character of God and make a difference in the world?

After all we've considered—especially the attacks on the family described in Chapter 10—it might be tempting to pull your family together in your home, lock the door, and just be safe and strong together. But is the best way to be a good, solid Christian family to be an isolated one? Is it a biblical view of the calling God places on the family?

As we have examined repeatedly in this book, God created us for relationship. He wants us to be involved in the lives of others. He wants us to show the world Himself.

There are plenty of examples of individuals to whom God gave a special calling for a specific task. And throughout Scripture and history we see God moving through family. He uses family to achieve goals that are not easily accomplished individually.

Consider Noah. We often picture him as a loner who faithfully built an ark when there was no sign of rain, ignoring the ridicule of others, smiling on the ark with happy animals surrounding him, ending up with a rainbow over his head. But Noah's story is about the call on a family, not just an individual. When God wanted to hit "reset" on His creation, He found a faithful man and a willing *family* to preserve humanity—to once again be fruitful and multiply and fill the earth.

What if it had been Noah alone? No wife, no sons and their wives. What a lonely and sad ending to that story we would have. Well, actually, we would not be around to *know* the story, would we?

God used family to save humanity, and He can do it again.

So how can you understand and carry out God's calling for your family? Here are a few suggestions to get you started:

1. *Support the calling of a family member.* Perhaps Dad or Mom has a burden for a particular type of ministry in the church or community. Your sister wants to make weekly visits to the nursing home near the church to just sit and talk with the old folks there. Has the family prayerfully asked God how family members can help each other achieve these goals?

2. *Serve a bigger purpose.* Pray together about finding an existing mission or organization to support with your time and resources.

3. *Share lessons learned in family life.* What has your family discovered through experience that might help others? When we see our interactions, even the messy ones, as opportunities to practice humility and learn repentance and forgiveness and love, we create stories we can share.

4. *Show the power of family, foibles and all.* We can embrace the calling of demonstration, showing the world not perfection but redemption in the way we live. The world is watching; what will we let it see about God's role in our family life?

5. *Invite someone into your family.* Is God calling your family to throw open the door to a visitor, an outcast, a foster child, an orphan, a widow, a family new to town, a single person? Who might find a much-needed sense of "family" in your home?

6. *Seek to inspire and encourage reconciliation.* Paul says in 2 Corinthians 5:20 that Christians are "ambassadors for Christ" with a charge to plead with others to be reconciled to God. Consider for a moment how this call to stand for healing and reconciliation concerns families today. How might we lovingly come alongside others to encourage, plead, even beg them to embrace the healing and reconciliation that God offers in their own families? And what more effective testimony of God's power in this world can we offer in the church than for families and marriages seemingly torn apart and irreparable to find repentance, forgiveness, and love once again? It's worth our prayers, pleadings, and demonstrations of patient love.

This is not an exhaustive list, but we hope it encourages and inspires you to get on your knees as a family. When you do, ask God to give you a clear sense of calling: "Father, what is it that You would have for us to do together for You and Your world far better than any one of us could do alone?"

A healthy family is not about perfection, but redemption.

THE BIG STATEMENT FOR REFLECTION

In the kingdom of God, as in the world, imperfection has its own kind of beauty. The idea of the perfect family is sheer myth. But the idea of a healthy family can certainly be a reality. This pursuit will always take place in the arena of imperfection. In the struggle, tension, love, and grace of family we first learn how to be better human beings—more honest, patient, forgiving, giving, and less selfish and inconsiderate. Balancing truth and grace makes family a safe place to work on our inevitable flaws and become the people God created us to be.

QUESTIONS FOR CONSIDERATION

1. Do you think most people would agree that there is no
   such thing as a perfect family? Do you think many people
   pretend to have one? Do you think most people are fooled
   by that effort?
2. Why do you suppose most families in the Bible are train
   wrecks in many ways? If the Bible were being written
   today, featuring today's families, do you think that would
   change? Why or why not?
3. Consider this statement: "Family is the factory of
   humankind." Does that sound like a good or bad thing?
   Why? Is there any institution that could replace family
   in this role? How is your family like a factory? How is it
   different?
4. The lists of qualities and behaviors in this chapter are
   meant to be simple and easy to apply to everyday family
   life. If you had to choose just one from each list to work
   on this year, what would it be? How would you want your
   family to be different at the end of that year?

Conclusion

Are you worn out? It's fine to admit it if you are, because you should be.

We've traveled from the days of pre-creation to the crowning event of eternity, the grand and glorious wedding feast of the Lamb. How many have traveled that far in such a short time? It's quite a trip, but we made it and we hope it was worth the effort.

We learned some very big and glorious things about family, not by studying the family itself, but by looking at who God is in His biggest essence and then who we are as His creations. It is only in understanding these two things that we can really understand what family is about, what it represents, what it does in our lives, and why it really matters.

Christianity, as a profound faith, has great and important things to tell us in this regard. It answers so beautifully, and tells us clearly who our God is and why He fashioned us and the rest of humanity as He did. It tells us who we are, what we are, where we came from, and where we're going. It tells us both the good and the bad news about ourselves and explains why these are as they are. But as we have seen, it doesn't leave us in the bad news. God's is a story of great hope because He will not give up on us, despite our terrible unfaithfulness to Him, even going to great pains and sacrifice to make the things right that our disobedience so tragically messed up.

And as we have seen, family plays such a central part in all of this, from where the story started, its grand ups and downs, and where it ultimately is going. Family is so much more than a group of people who love one another or a moral or political issue in the culture war or a social grouping to be studied by social scientists. It is a divine institution that represents the fuller, truer nature of God in creation, and God has made each of us in such a way that we cannot live without it. In fact, "that way" is being created in His image, the image of a God who is a beautiful and eternal choreography of a Father, a Son, and their Spirit perfectly in tune with each other—three, but so close and lovingly intimate they are One.

Family is a great wonder. This is precisely because He who created it did so for us who are His children. He did this from His own delight because He is *the* wonder and reason for who we are and what we are, where we came from, and where we're going.

We came from love, through love, to live in love, to give love, and to go toward the greatest Love that will finally be manifest at the culmination of God's great story. And this is not a story that He is merely telling, but that He *is*. Each of us is warmly and graciously invited by the Lord of the universe and the center of all reality to come into it as His bride and His child. It is an invitation that cannot be lightly ignored.

There is a Groom, a Father, a family, and a home waiting for you.

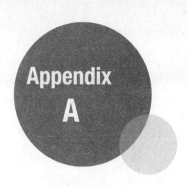

"IT IS NOT GOOD . . .": THE SCIENTIFIC SUPPORT

God's statement in Genesis 2:18 is more than a nice Sunday school Bible lesson. It is a profoundly rich statement about the most fundamental nature of being human, the consequences of which are so much deeper than most Christians come close to appreciating. The world of science has been affirming this statement in unbelievable and unexpected ways.

Some of the most cutting-edge science supports and proclaims this biblical anthropology more clearly and passionately than the most fervent, pulpit-pounding preacher. Some of the most exciting research on what it really means to be human is some of the most recent and sophisticated. It explains in great detail and complexity that it is not good for man to be alone. It is surprising how much science and theology are in sync here. Powerfully so!

Where to start? Let's begin with the most important human objective: survival.

What does a human being need to survive? Obviously food, water, and protection from the elements. They are basic. But there is something else one needs, actually more important than the others: love and physical intimacy. This is precisely what science is proving to us.

Medical doctor Dean Ornish, world famous for his research, writing, and lectures on how to increase our physical and emotional well-being through relatively simple lifestyle choices, says that love and intimacy are the top contributors to increased health, overall happiness, and longevity. In his book *Love and Survival*, Ornish makes a very bold claim based on his extensive research and interviews with leading medical professionals and researchers. When it comes to the health benefits of loving relationships, he explains,

> I am not aware of any other factor in medicine—not diet, not smoking, not exercise, not stress, not genetics, not drugs, not surgery—that has a greater impact on our quality of life, incidences of illness and premature death from all causes.

He continues,

> In short, anything that promotes a sense of isolation often leads to illness and suffering. Anything that promotes a sense of love and intimacy, connection and community is healing.

It is not good for man to be alone. To highlight just one reliable body of research that Ornish cites, eight large-scale studies examining diverse international communities from California and Georgia to Finland and Sweden measured the impact of social isolation on physical health. The studies found exceptionally parallel results: Those who had a strong community of friends and loved ones had a much lower risk of premature death from any cause compared to those who were socially isolated. The difference in measurements between the two groups ranged from two to five times greater benefit for the connected participants.[1]

Another noted medical researcher to examine the connection between overall physical health and relationship is longtime Johns Hopkins professor James J. Lynch, the first to document the dramatic medical and psychological implications of loneliness. He explains in his book *A Cry Unheard: New Insights into the Medical Consequences of Loneliness* that over the past few decades, a substantial body of medical research on all the important measures of human well-being have led us to "one inescapable conclusion: Dialogue is the elixir of life and chronic loneliness its lethal poison."[2]

Meaningful dialogue, relationships built through long-term, person-to-person chit-chat, has a profound influence for the good on the pumping of our hearts and the development of our immune systems and everything in between. The lack of even the most basic forms of intimacy contributes to mental illness, disease, and premature death. This reality has led Dr. Lynch to conclude that our bodies either thrive or suffer in two different important states of being, what he calls the "physiology of inclusion" or the "physiology of exclusion."[3] Intimacy is an elixir. Isolation is a toxin.

In fact, the *Atlantic* magazine featured a cover story in 2009 on a very sophisticated 72-year-long study conducted at Harvard on what really makes human beings happy. The study's longtime director, George Vaillant, when asked what has been learned, answered pointedly, "That the only thing that really matters in life are your relationships to other people."[4]

In the last two decades, this age when we were supposed to have jetpacks blasting us here and there, scientists have discovered— through incredibly high-tech investigations—fascinating facts about the human brain. They've discovered our brains are not so much intellectual organs as they are something else.

Daniel Goleman, a reporter on brain and behavioral sciences for more than a decade at the *New York Times* and holds a Ph.D.

from Harvard, explains in his book *Social Intelligence* what the emerging science of neurobiology is revealing:

> The most fundamental revelation of this new discipline: we are wired to connect. Neuroscience has discovered that our brain's very design makes it sociable, inexorably drawn into an intimate brain-to-brain linkup whenever we engage with another person.

This cutting-edge science is revealing that the human brain is fundamentally and essentially a relational organ. It can only really work in relationship with other brains. Every interaction we have with someone is not just an opportunity to gather facts and information for our brains, but for our brains to be influenced, both for good and for bad, by these connections with other people. We affect the brains and thus the bodies of everyone we interact with because there is a neural bridge or connection created between brains when we relate with others. Goleman explains,

> That neural bridge lets us affect the brain—and so the body—of everyone we interact with, just as they do us. . . . The more strongly connected we are with someone emotionally, the greater the mutual force.[5]

And the stronger the connection our brains have with someone—through regular day-in, day-out, emotionally vibrant interactions—the more our brains are affected and affect others. This brain-to-brain influence runs down into the deepest parts of our bodies, influencing our most vital bodily functions from heart health to immune, intestinal, and respiratory systems to emotional health and the general vitality of our bodies.

Allan Schore, professor of psychiatry and behavioral science at UCLA, is the world's leading scholar on the pathologies that develop neurologically from early failures to make important relational connections. His work allows him to . . .

> cite an extremely large body of interdisciplinary data which suggests that the self-organization [or formatting] of the developing brain occurs in the context of a relationship with another self, another brain. This [early] relational context can be growth facilitating or growth inhibiting and so it imprints into the early developing right brain either resilience against or a vulnerability to forming psychiatric disorders.

Professor Schore explains that this relational transmission of brain to brain happens dramatically through the eyes, which science is showing are indeed the windows to the mind. To gaze into and receive the gaze of another person is dramatic and essential to our mental and physical development.

> In particular, the mother's emotionally expressive face is, by far, the most potent visual stimulus in the infant's environment, and the child's intense interest in her face, especially in her eyes. . . . The infant's gaze, in turn, reliably evokes the mother's gaze, and this dyadic [back and forth exchange] system forms an efficient interpersonal channel for transmission of reciprocal mutual influences.[6]

This is Schore's academic way of saying that both mother and child are affected in the deepest parts of their neural wiring by their experience of gazing meaningfully into each other's eyes. It is so much more than emotional; it is deeply psychological and physiological. It makes both of them more healthy, stronger in mind and body. This is true of all close relationships.

Daniel Siegel, another world leader in this area of study, introduces his important book *The Developing Mind* with the question of why the brain is so affected by intimacy, which he's spent much of his career exploring:

> What are the mechanisms by which human relationships shape brain structure and function? How is it possible for interpersonal experience—the interactions between two people—to affect something so inherently different as the activity of neurons?[7]

Louis Cozolino, a colleague of Schore's and Siegel's in this cutting-edge work, explains that as a mouse's brain is shaped by its access to food—restructuring neurons and neuron connections relative to its changing means and sources of foraging and retrieving food—so is the human infant's brain relative to its higher-order need of intimacy. Hence, he explains that the health and development of what these scholars call the "social brain" of the human "is shaped as a reflection of an interlocking system of children, caregivers, and the community at large."

He continues,

> Each brain is dependent on interactions with others for its survival. Each brain is dependent on the scaffolding of the caretakers and loved ones for its survival, growth and well-being. . . . There are no single brains.[8]

And Sue Gerhardt, a British psychotherapist and co-founder of the Oxford Parent Infant Project explains in her book *Why Love Matters: How Affection Shapes a Baby's Brain,*

> The brain itself is a "social organ." . . . Both our physi-
> ological systems and our mental systems are developed in
> relationship with other people—and this happens most
> intensely in and leaves its biggest mark in infancy. . . . Our
> minds emerge and our emotions become organized through
> engagement with other minds, not in isolation.[9]

There is another bodily organ that plays a major role in intimacy and has a profound effect on the brain as well as the rest of a
person's well-being. If this organ is not engaged in relationship with
another's same organ at early ages and beyond, death can ensue.
This organ is the largest in the human body: the epidermis.

Our relationship with others is not just brain-to-brain, but also
must be tactile, physical. We need to be touched and to touch.
Something dramatic and necessary happens when one person connects skin-to-skin with another. What happens when you are on
a bus or subway and gently move your bare arm so that it cames
in contact with another's bare arm? You know what—and this is
true in nearly all cultures. Touching skin to skin is an intimacy
that strangers feel uncomfortable with. But when someone we
like and feel comfortable with touches us, that's a pleasant—even
assuring—experience.

Just as Dr. Schore tells us that our brains connect with other
brains through the eyes, we also connect with other brains through
our skin. Scholars refer to this important experience as "cutaneous
stimulation." (Don't you love how academics talk? "Okay, kids! No
cutaneous stimulation!")

Anthropologist Ashley Montagu wrote an exceptionally interesting book on this essential organ and its significance to human
development. Among the many angles he addresses is the process of
childbirth. Montagu spends considerable time looking at the general

health of children who are birthed naturally compared to those delivered by caesarian section. There is a notable difference here, specifically related to gastrointestinal and respiratory functions—although not enough to be of significant concern to mothers who have delivered or will deliver that way. It is more of a very interesting curiosity. Montagu explains that during childbirth,

> Contractions of the uterus upon the body of the fetus stimulates the peripheral sensory nerves in the skin. The nervous impulses thus initiated are conducted to the central nervous system where, at the proper levels, they are mediated through the nervous system to the various organs which they innervate [stimulate to action].

He continues,

> The short, intermittent stimulation of the skin over a prolonged period of time that are produced by the contractions of the uterus upon the body of the fetus thus appear to be perfectly designed to prepare it for postnatal functioning.

Montagu notes that during natural childbirth, with the newborn facedown during delivery, her nose, lips, and remainder of the head make intense contact with the mother in a very intimate way for both. The child's mouth—being stimulated in this way, and at nursing—is connected as the primary passageway to both the gastrointestinal and respiratory systems. The stimulation to one eventually stimulates the other. For the mother, her own skin-to-skin contact with her baby stimulates her uterus to contract after birth. Montagu explains how the pre-birth physical stimulation leads to the post-birth stimulation that is needed:

The uterine contractions of labor constitute the beginning of caressing of the baby in the right way—caressing that should be continued in very special ways in the period immediately following the birth and for a considerable time thereafter.[10]

All of this is the sophisticated, scientific explanation of something psychologists and psychiatrists experienced decades ago to their absolute horror. John Bowlby is the father of the psychology of attachment, studying how infant and parent interact and how the nature of this interaction affects child development. He explains in his landmark work *Attachment* that a young child's hunger for his mother is as great as his hunger for food. As we know through too many experiences through history, children living in orphanages and foundling homes who are well fed, changed regularly, kept physically safe, and have a comfortable, clean crib can still do very poorly. If not interacted with in intimate ways, making meaningful and regular, warm contact of skin-to-skin and eyes-to-eyes with an adult caregiver, they fail to develop and eventually die far too young.

This was first dramatically revealed to the medical world at large in 1947 when René Spitz showed a very startling, crude 16mm film of flickering black-and-white images to a conference of medical professionals in New York City. The silent film, *Grief: A Peril in Infancy*, told the story of babies who lived in such isolation, having their basic needs met but without any meaningful physical contact. In that film, and since, the effects of such neglect have become clear. After just one week without contact from mother or other caregivers, these children begin to develop a notably glazed, depressed, non-responsive countenance. They sob uncontrollably. They rock themselves in an effort to pacify themselves. They stare for long periods at their hands, keeping them in front of their eyes in a desire to encounter another human being. But their hands eventually become deformed—twisted and bent—from these long periods of deprivation. Their faces eventually show changes in shape and appearance, developing sad and permanent blank stares. After a while they stop wailing and just moan to themselves. They come to be unable to stand, move their arms, roll over, or even lift their heads. They don't explore, nor can they engage with someone who tries to stimulate them. Seeming catatonic, they just stop growing; an 18-month-old child could be taken for a 6-month-old. Child development specialists liken them to concentration camp victims, and essentially they are. It is not good for babies to be alone.

A 2002 study on child abuse and neglect explains that children of abuse suffer not just physically but developmentally, and in their cognitive and verbal responsiveness. But there is a slight yet measurable difference between children who have been neglected and those who are neglected and physically abused. Astonishingly, one tends to show less responsiveness than the other. These researchers tell us which is which: "Neglect occurring alone is associated with more severe language problems than neglect occurring alongside abuse."[11] Remarkably, the researchers surmise that this is likely due to the fact that physical abuse is at least some kind of physical touch, even though evil in nature. Even this kind of malevolent physical touch can ironically reduce to a slight degree the psychological harm of absolute abandonment. Astounding.

It is a deeply powerful and true statement about the most basic part of being human: It is not good for man to be alone. The most sophisticated science available today illustrates the formidable implications of God's Second Definitive Statement in ways that we never could have imagined.

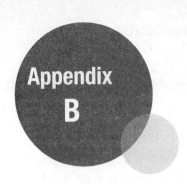

WERE JESUS AND PAUL
ANTI-FAMILY?

Many years ago I (Glenn) attended a sophisticated academic gathering at a large southern university on the topic of law and the family. I particularly wanted to hear one of the speakers because of his long and stellar reputation as a scholar—and because he was addressing the question of whether Christianity is pro-family.

Remarkably, his conclusion was that Christianity was *not* positive on the family. He chose a number of statements from Jesus and Paul to make his case. When you're talking about what Christianity believes, you can't do better than Jesus and Paul, can you?

But do Jesus and Paul really make statements that are "down" on the family? What most critics refer to, as the professor did that day, are passages like the following in which Christ tells His disciples,

> For I have come to set a man against his father, and a daughter against her mother, and a daughter-in-law against her mother-in-law. And a person's enemies will be those of his own household. Whoever loves father or mother more than

me is not worthy of me, and whoever loves son or daughter more than me is not worthy of me. (Matthew 10:35-37)

In Luke 14:26, Jesus says,

If anyone comes to me and does not hate his own father and mother and wife and children and brothers and sisters, yes, and even his own life, he cannot be my disciple.

These certainly don't seem like affirmations of family coming from our Lord's mouth. But we usually get it wrong when we pick out only one part of God's Word and interpret it apart from the rest of Scripture. To say that these statements mean that Christ was against family is painfully simplistic and wrong.

Nearly all Bible commentators agree that Christ was teaching here, in a dramatic way, that love of God must be our greatest love, overshadowing all our other loves, including that for mother, father, and family. God must be preeminent. If Jesus really did mean that we should hate and be at odds with our families, this would contradict Christ's own actions and His other teachings.

As we have seen in this book, Jesus maintained a strong relationship with His mother, caring for her, obeying her, and making sure she was cared for as He died on the cross. Jesus did not turn against His mother. He certainly didn't hate her. He wouldn't have taught one thing and done another.

And right in the middle of the Ten Commandments God gave to Moses is the directive to honor one's mother and father. Was Jesus at odds with God the Father and Moses? Hardly! Jesus actually affirmed this command, quoting it in His response to the Pharisees in Matthew 15:4.

What about Paul's words? One passage that exemplifies the

typical concerns some have about Paul's views on family occurs in
1 Corinthians 7:1 (NIV), where he wrote,

> Now for the matters you wrote about: It is good for a man
> not to marry.

This seems pretty straightforward. And even more verses later
in the chapter seem to indicate that Paul was sour on marriage in
general. But there are a number of things to consider about this
statement that show us Paul was not anti-marriage.

First, the translation is important. Some other Bible versions
don't say "marry"; the New American Standard, English Standard
Version, and King James Version say, "It is good for a man not to
touch a woman" or "not to have sexual relations with a woman."
Even if the latter is more correct, however, that would seem to contradict God's command to "be fruitful and multiply" (Genesis 1:28).

Clearly Paul was not giving us a universal directive, but merely
a statement in response to a question the Corinthian church asked
him earlier ("Now for the matters you wrote me about . . ."). We
don't know what they asked him, so we don't know what his answer
responded to. We are only hearing half the conversation.

So can we know what Paul believed about marriage?

Paul affirmed and encouraged marriage. In the very next verse
he declared, "Each man should have his own wife" (1 Corinthians
7:2), and later noted that those who desire to marry should do so
because "he is not sinning" (verse 36, NIV). In fact, Paul's emphasis
was really focused on devotion to the Lord, and he emphatically
declared that with the right heart before God, it is fine to remain
single or to marry.

Elsewhere, Paul strongly supported marriage as an institution
(Ephesians 5:22-33; Colossians 3:18-19; 1 Timothy 3:12; 5:14).

He warned against listening to "deceitful spirits" and "demons" who teach it is forbidden to marry (1 Timothy 4:1-3). If we interpret his answer to the Corinthians as rejecting marriage, wouldn't that make Paul a "deceitful spirit"?

And in the book of Hebrews, which most believe Paul authored, we are told,

> Let marriage be held in honor among all, and let the marriage bed be undefiled, for God will judge the sexually immoral and adulterous. (13:4)

It takes some pretty creative Scripture-twisting to conclude that Jesus or Paul took a dim view of marriage and family. Reading their words in full and in context against the larger text of Scripture makes it clear that both affirmed the virtue of marriage and the gift of family relationships. The professor's reading and presentation of Scripture that day was woefully simplistic.

Acknowledgments

For years, this book and the small-group curriculum that it laid the foundation for and supports has been an unfolding dream of ours, requiring much study, dreaming, planning, hitting a wall, backing up, and taking another run at it. It has been a humbling honor to labor at it and help bring it all together. A project of this magnitude cannot come together without an incredible amount of inspiration, support, and contributions.

We thank God for being, creating, and revealing. Without the Father, the Son, and the Holy Spirit, we would have no reason or inspiration to write this book. Our hope and our being are here alone.

We also want to thank our families for their support and patience during our absences of travel, long research, and seemingly constant writing. We are blessed to have our own imperfect families. And we are also inspired by the families of origin that we came from. We both have family histories that include many pains and many joys, and the blessings and truths that we have shared in this book have been in part revealed by our experiences there.

We've also been inspired by many teachers, researchers, and voices of the faith who have spurred us on toward this project by their important works. Of particular note we would mention Francis Schaeffer, John Paul II, John Zizioulas, Del Tackett, Marc Cardinal Oullet, Chesterton, Lewis, Roger Scruton, Matt Milliner, and Randy Alcorn. These and many other voices through the ages have pointed us toward important truths and gems of our Christian faith and the reality that faith reveals.

Many of our colleagues at Focus on the Family contributed thoughts, feedback, inspiration, and dedicated support for the development of this project: Clark Miller, Bob Dubberley, Rich Bennett, Derek Hanson, Greg Smalley, Roy Baldwin, Andrew Hess, Erin Berriman, Paul McCusker, Jim Mhoon, Mitch Wright, Nancy Shane, and Kathy DeMattee.

We especially appreciate the editorial touches that Larry Weeden's team brought to the book. We also want to thank Michael Hurka and Ron Wilson for maintaining a foundation of prayer support within the staff and supporters of Focus on the Family.

In the early stages of development, it was important that we find the right partners to bring these ideas to life in the video curriculum and film documentary. We were very blessed to have found remarkable partners in Mpower Pictures of Santa Monica. From that incredibly hard-working and highly talented team, we thank John Shepherd, Laurie Leinonen, Michael Balog, Megan Herrington, Catherine Fowler, and Michael Sajbel, who also introduced us to Tim Brygger (although he bailed to go to seminary!) and the saintly Gene Wohlberg. We are especially grateful for the faithful, ongoing support of prayer from Gene. This is a list of new friends that we hope will last a lifetime.

When it came time to select a host for the documentary and the curriculum, we found a gem in our dear brother Tim Sisarich, in the Focus on the Family offices of his home country, New Zealand. He caught the importance of this project years ago, and his strong grasp of the material, passion for family, and tender spirit represented the ideals of this project with grace and truth. And besides, he's a blast to work with.

And finally, we would like to acknowledge the role that great storytellers and artists have played throughout the ages in telling elements of this divine story over and over again through their gift. Perhaps you, like us, have found inspiration in masterful paintings, movies, novels, and music. Reflecting on great works of art often helps us see something of the divine story in them. We share the belief that all great art and its beauty point us back to the Great Artist. And we hope that like us, you will never be able to look at magnificent works of art again without seeing the echoes of the divine story that we share with the Creator.

About the Authors

GLENN T. STANTON is the director of Family Formation Studies at Focus on the Family and a research fellow at the Institute of Marriage and Family in Ottawa. Holder of a master's degree in Interdisciplinary Humanities from the University of West Florida, he debates and lectures extensively on gender, sexuality, marriage, and parenting at universities and churches across America. He served the George W. Bush administration for many years as a consultant on increasing fatherhood involvement in the Head Start program.

Glenn is the author of several books including *Secure Daughters, Confident Sons*; *The Ring Makes All the Difference*; *Marriage on Trial*; and *My Crazy, Imperfect Christian Family*. He and his wife have five endlessly growing and amazing children, and live in Colorado Springs.

LEON C. WIRTH is the former executive director of parenting and youth ministry at Focus on the Family. A speaker and writer, he has researched and participated in family ministry personally and vocationally for over 15 years. In 2012, as a founding board member, he helped establish the Fatherhood CoMission, a gathering of family and men's ministry organizations dedicated to championing the calling of fatherhood.

Leon co-wrote the documentary *Irreplaceable* with Glenn Stanton and launched Focus on the Family's fatherhood blog, *Dad Matters*, as a founding blogger. He has also contributed to the book *A Dad's Prayers for His Daughter* and co-authored *The One Year Father-Daughter Devotions*.

Leon earned a master's degree from Wheaton College. He, his wife, and their eight daughters enjoy life in Colorado Springs.

Notes

Introduction
1. We should not be scared or intimidated by the word "theology." It doesn't mean advanced, upper-level seminary study for a select few. It simply means seeking a greater understanding of who God is and what He should mean to us. The simple Sunday school ditty "Jesus loves me, this I know, for the Bible tells me so" and the bumper-sticker "God loves you!" are rich theological statements, are they not? Each of us is a theologian because we all ask questions and seek answers about who God is—even at the earliest ages.
2. When we use the word "story," we do not mean "fairy tale"—something made up. We're referring to something very real that actually did happen, is still taking place, and which we can know about. It's not "Tell us the *story* of Pinocchio again, Great Grandpa"; it's "Tell us the *story* again of how you and your friends freed those prisoners at Auschwitz."

Chapter 1: You Are Here
1. Meredith Bennett-Smith, "Davion Only, Teenage Orphan Asks Church for New Family," *HuffPost Parenting*, October 22, 2013.
2. Victoria Taylor, "Woman, 26, Posts Craigslist Ad Asking for Family for the Holidays," *New York Daily News*, December 7, 2013.
3. Brown is professor emeritus in the Department of Anthropology, University of California, Santa Barbara. His primary work on this topic is *Human Universals* (Temple University Press, 1991).
4. David Hart, *The Beauty of the Infinite: Aesthetics of Christian Truth* (Eerdmans, 2004), p. 161.
5. Alasdair MacIntyre, *After Virtue* (University of Notre Dame Press, 1981), p. 216.
6. James Bryan Smith, *The Good and Beautiful God* (InterVarsity Press, 2009), pp. 24–25.
7. Douglas Coupland, *Polaroids from the Dead* (Regan Books, 1996), pp. 179–80.
8. Flannery O'Connor, "The Fiction Writer and His Country," in *Mystery and Manners* (Farrar, Straus and Giroux, 1970), p. 35.

Chapter 2: Let Us Make Man (*Imago Dei*)

1. See, for instance, Alvin Schmidt, *Under the Influence: How Christianity Transformed Civilization* (Zondervan, 2001); Rodney Stark, *The Victory of Reason: How Christianity Led to Freedom, Capitalism, and Western Success* (Random House, 2006); and Rodney Stark, *For the Glory of God: How Monotheism Led to Reformations, Science, Witch-Hunts, and the End of Slavery* (Princeton University Press, 2004).

2. J.I. Packer and Thomas Howard, *Christianity: The True Humanism* (Word, 1985), p. 69.

3. C.S. Lewis, *Mere Christianity* (Macmillan, 1960), p. 152.

4. Timothy Ware, "The Trinity: Heart of Our Life," in *Reclaiming the Great Tradition: Evangelicals, Catholics & Orthodox in Dialogue*, James S. Cutsinger, ed. (InterVarsity Press, 1997), p. 126.

5. Colin E. Gunton, *The Promise of Trinitarian Theology* (T&T Clark, 1997), pp. 3, 7.

6. Ware, "The Trinity: Heart of Our Life," p. 136. See also footnote 21, Chapter 3, which explains an important difference that the Orthodox church has with other Christian traditions regarding the procession of the Holy Spirit from Father and Son.

7. Lewis, *Mere Christianity*, p. 152.

8. Francis A. Schaeffer, *Genesis in Space and Time: The Flow of Biblical History* (InterVarsity Press, 1972), p. 17.

9. John Calvin, *Genesis* (Crossway, 2001), pp. 24–25.

10. John Wesley, *Notes on the Entire Bible: Genesis* (Kindle edition, 2001), commentary on verses 26-28.

11. Leon Kass, *The Beginning of Wisdom: Readings in Genesis* (Free Press, 2003), p. 37.

12. Wesley, *Notes on Entire Bible: Genesis*, commentary on verses 26-28.

13. Martin Luther, *Lectures on Genesis, Chapters 1–5*, in *Luther's Works*, Jaroslav Pelikan, editor (Concordia, 1962), p. 60.

14. Schaeffer, *Genesis in Space and Time*, p. 46.

15. Schaeffer, *Genesis in Space and Time*, p. 18.

Chapter 3: It Is Not Good to Be Alone: How Family Completes the *Imago Dei*

1. Salimbene, "The House of Fame," in James Bruce Ross and Mary Martin McLaughlin, *The Portable Medieval Reader* (Penguin Books, 1977), p. 366.

2. John Calvin, *Genesis* (Crossway, 2001), p. 37.
3. John Paul II, *Male and Female He Created Them: A Theology of the Body*, trans. Michael Waldstein, Ph.D. (Pauline Books & Media, 2006), p. 147.
4. This story is dramatically told in a fascinating 2010 National Geographic documentary, *Solitary Confinement*.
5. Glenn T. Stanton, *Secure Daughters, Confident Sons: How Parents Guide Their Children into Authentic Masculinity and Femininity* (Multnomah, 2011).
6. John Paul II, *Male and Female He Created Them*, pp. 163–64, 203.
7. Robert Alter, *Genesis* (W. W. Norton, 1996), p. 9.
8. Anne Fausto-Sterling, "The Five Sexes: Why Male and Female Are Not Enough," *Sciences* (March/April 1993): 20–24; Anne Fausto-Sterling, "The Five Sexes, Revisited," *Sciences* (July/August 2000): 19–22.
9. Sylviane Agacinski, *Parity of the Sexes* (Columbia, 2001), pp. xxxiii, 3.
10. Timothy Keller, *The Reason for God: Belief in an Age of Skepticism* (Riverhead Trade, 2009), p. 224.
11. Hilary of Poitiers, *On the Trinity*, Book 3:1. This translation is from Philip Schaff, *Nicene and Post-Nicene Fathers*, 2nd ed., vol. 9 (Christian Literature Publishing, 1899).
12. C.S. Lewis, *Mere Christianity* (Macmillan, 1960), pp. 152–53.
13. Charles Williams, *The Image of the City and Other Essays* (Oxford University Press, 1958), p. xlv.
14. Timothy George, ed., *God the Holy Trinity: Reflections on Christian Faith and Practice* (Baker Academic, 2006), p. 12.
15. Colin E. Gunton, *The Promise of Trinitarian Theology* (T&T Clark, 1997), p. 7.
16. Francis A. Schaeffer, *Genesis in Space and Time* (InterVarsity Press, 1972), pp. 21–22.
17. Martin Buber, *I and Thou*, trans. Walter Kaufmann (Simon & Schuster, 1996), pp. 53, 62.
18. John Macmurray, *Persons in Relation* (Harper & Brothers, 1961), p. 211.
19. John Zizioulas, *Being as Communion: Studies in Personhood and the Church* (St. Vladimir's Seminary Press, 1997).
20. Michael Downey, *Altogether Gift: A Trinitarian Spirituality* (Orbis Books, 2000), p. 63.

21. We recognize that the Eastern church differs with the Western church on this point, with the East holding that the Holy Spirit does not proceed from the Father and the Son, but from the Father alone and rests upon the Son. It is an ancient, intricate, and complicated theological and historical matter referred to as the "filoque dispute"; *filoque* is a Latin word meaning "and the Son." But this difference has not caused either tradition of the church to denounce the other as heretical.

22. John Paul II, *The Role of the Christian Family in the Modern World, Familiaris Consortio*, given November 22, 1981 (Boston: Pauline Books & Media, 1981), p. 46.

Chapter 4: For This Reason

1. Angelo Scola, *The Nuptial Mystery* (Eerdmans, 2005), p. 12.

2. John Paul II, *Male and Female He Created Them: A Theology of the Body*, trans. Michael Waldstein, Ph.D. (Pauline Books & Media, 2006), p. 20.

3. John Zizioulas, *Being as Communion: Studies in Personhood and the Church* (St. Vladimir's Seminary Press, 1997), pp. 16–18.

4. John Donne, "Meditation XVII," *Devotions upon Emergent Occasions and Death's Duel* (Vintage Spiritual Classics, 1999).

5. Sam and Bethany Torode, *Aflame: Ancient Wisdom on Marriage* (Eerdmans, 2005), p. 27.

6. Torode, *Aflame*, p. 13.

7. Edward Westermarck, *The History of Human Marriage*, vol. 1 (Allerton, 1922), p. 27.

8. Alice Mathews and M. Gay Hubbard, *Marriage Made in Eden: A Pre-Modern Perspective for a Post-Christian World* (Wipf & Stock, 2004), p. 162.

9. Mathews and Hubbard, *Marriage Made in Eden*, p. 176.

10. Thomas Friedman, *The World Is Flat: A Brief History of the Twenty First Century* (Farrar, Straus and Giroux, 2005), p. 151.

11. C.S. Lewis, *Mere Christianity* (Macmillan, 1960), p. 91.

12. Karl Barth, *Church Dogmatics*, vols. 3/4 (T & T Clark, 1961), p. 133.

13. Of course, children can and do issue from various sexual unions— including those that are not loving, but deeply exploitive, such as rape. There are those that result from artificial reproductive technology outside of the union of a husband and wife, treating the male and female reproductive material as something it was

never intended to be: a market commodity to be sold and bought. These are facts, but they are not humanly or divinely ideal. When such an explanation of one's origin is shared with the child of any of these processes, it is not greeted with the response, "Oh, that's interesting," or "How exciting!" It changes the nature of that child's understanding of himself or herself in significant ways. In fact, we typically take great effort to avoid letting these children know of the nature of their creation either totally or at least until they reach maturity. We do not protect children from such information when they come from loving, marital unions.

14. Lewis, *Mere Christianity* (Macmillan, 1960), p. 96.
15. Robert T. Michael, et al., *Sex in America: A Definitive Survey* (Little, Brown and Company, 1994), p. 131.
16. Robert T. Michael, et al., *Sex in America*, pp. 127, 130.

Chapter 5: The Man Has Now Become Like One of Us

1. This desire of Satan to attack the essence and intimacy of the triune God takes on additional meaning when we enter Chapter 8 on fatherhood later in this book.
2. John Paul II, *Male and Female He Created Them: A Theology of the Body*, trans. Michael Waldstein, Ph.D. (Pauline Books & Media, 2006), 11:5, pp. 172–73.
3. Blaise Pascal, *Penseés* (Penguin Classics, 1966), Book VIII, *Diversion*, #136, p. 67.
4. Francis A. Schaeffer, *Genesis in Space and Time: The Flow of Biblical History* (InterVarsity Press, 1972), pp. 98–100.
5. C.S. Lewis, *Miracles* (Macmillan, 1960), p. 108.
6. Jacobus Petelin Gallus, *Mirable Mysterium*, a motet for five voices, published 1586.

Chapter 6: What God Has Joined Together

1. Daniel Patrick Moynihan, *The Negro Family: The Case for National Action*, Office of Policy Planning and Research, United States Department of Labor, March 1965, p. 1.
2. Nicholas Lemann, "Postscript: Daniel Patrick Moynihan," *New Yorker*, April 7, 2003.
3. Interview with James Q. Wilson, *The First Measured Century*, Public Broadcasting System, accessed February 2014, http://www.pbs.org/fmc/interviews/jwilson.htm.

4. Megan McArdle, "Europe's Real Crisis," *Atlantic*, April 2012, p. 35.

5. *The Sustainable Demographic Dividend: What Marriage and Fertility Have to Do with the Economy* (Social Trends Institute, 2011).

6. National Public Radio, *Morning Edition*, October 9, 2003; audio found at NPR Online, www.npr.org/templates.story.story.php?story Id=1459945.

7. George A. Akerlof, "Men Without Children," *Economic Journal*, March 1998; George Gilder, *Men and Marriage* (Pelican Publishing, 1987).

8. Joseph Henrich, Robert Boyd, and Peter J. Richerson, "The Puzzle of Monogamous Marriage," *Philosophical Transactions of the Royal Society* 367 (2012): 657–69.

9. The following is just a small sampling of such research: Glenn T. Stanton, *Why Marriage Matters: Reasons to Believe in Marriage in a Post-modern Society* (Pinon Press, 1997); Glenn T. Stanton, *The Ring Makes All the Difference: The Consequences of Cohabitation and the Rich Benefits of Marriage* (Moody Press, 2011); Kristin Anderson Moore, et al., "Marriage from a Child's Perspective: How Does Family Structure Affect Children, and What Can We Do About It?" *Child Trends Research Brief*, June 2002; Mary Parke, "Are Married Parents Really Better for Children?" *Center for Law and Social Policy Brief*, May 2003; Sara McLanahan and Gary Sandefur, *Growing Up with a Single Parent: What Hurts, What Helps* (Harvard University Press, 1994); Judith Wallerstein, *The Unintended Consequence of Divorce: A Landmark 30 Year Study* (Hyperion, 2000); Steven Stack and J. Ross Eshleman, "Marital Status and Happiness: A 17-Nation Study," *Journal of Marriage and the Family* 60 (1998): 527–36; Paul Amato, "The Impact of Family Formation Change on the Cognitive, Social, and Emotional Well-Being of the Next Generation," in *The Future of Children*, "Marriage and Child Wellbeing," vol. 15, no. 2 (Fall 2005), Woodrow Wilson School of Public and International Affairs at Princeton and the Brookings Institution; Linda J. Waite and Maggie Gallagher, *The Case for Marriage: Why Married People Are Happier, Healthier, and Better Off Financially* (Doubleday, 2000); Chris M. Wilson and Andrew J. Oswald, "How Does Marriage Affect Physical and Psychological Health? A Survey of the Longitudinal Evidence," *Institute for the Study of Labor Study Paper 1619* (Institute for the

Study of Labor, May 2005); Jonathan Gardner and Andrew Oswald, "How Is Mortality Affected by Money, Marriage, and Stress?" *Journal of Health Economics* 23 (2004): 1181–207; Christine M. Proulx, Heather Helms, and Cheryl Buehler, "Marital Quality and Personal Well-Being: A Meta-Analysis," *Journal of Marriage and Family* 69 (2007): 576–93; Amy Mehraban Pienta, et al., "Health Consequences of Marriage for the Retirement Years," *Journal of Family Issues* 21 (2000): 559–86; Hui Liu, "Till Death Do Us Part: Marital Status and U.S. Mortality Trends, 1986–2000," *Journal of Marriage and Family* 71 (2009): 1158–173; James S. Goodwin, William C. Hunt, Charles R. Key, and Jonathan M. Samet, "The Effect of Marital Status on Stage, Treatment and Survival of Cancer Patients," *Journal of the American Medical Association* 258 (1987): 3152–130; Catherine Reissman and Naomi Gerstel, "Marital Dissolution and Health: Do Males or Females Have Greater Risk?" *Social Science and Medicine* 20 (1985): 627–35; Robert Coombs, "Marital Status and Personal Well-Being: A Literature Review," *Family Relations* 40 (1991): 97–102; Jan Stets, "Cohabiting and Marital Aggression: the Role of Social Isolation," *Journal of Marriage and the Family* 53 (1991): 669–80; Lee A. Lillard and Linda J. Waite, "'Til Death Do Us Part: Marital Disruption and Mortality," *American Journal of Sociology* 100 (1995): 1131–156; Benjamin Malzberg, "Marital Status in Relation to the Prevalence of Mental Disease," *Psychiatric Quarterly* 10 (1936): 245–56; Susan L. Brown, "The Effect of Union Type on Psychological Well-Being: Depression Among Cohabitors Versus Marrieds," *Journal of Health and Social Behavior* 41 (2000): 241–55; David R. Williams, et al., "Marital Status and Psychiatric Disorders Among Blacks and Whites," *Journal of Health and Social Behavior* 33 (1992): 140–57; Laura Stafford, Susan L. Kline, and Caroline T. Rankin, "Married Individuals, Cohabitors, and Cohabitors Who Marry: A Longitudinal Study of Relational and Individual Well-Being," *Journal of Social and Personal Relationships* 21 (2004): 231–48; Kevin B. Skinner, et al., "Cohabitation, Marriage and Remarriage: A Comparison of Relationship Quality Over Time," *Journal of Family Issues* 23 (2002): 74–90; Claire M. Kamp Dush and Paul R. Amato, "Consequences of Relationship Status and Quality for Subjective Well-Being," *Journal of Social and Personal Relationships* 22 (2005): 607–27; Judith Treas and Deirdre Giesen, "Sexual Fidelity Among

Married and Cohabiting Americans," *Journal of Marriage and the Family* 62 (2000): 48–60; James Q. Wilson, *The Marriage Problem: How Our Culture Has Weakened Families* (HarperCollins, 2002); W. Bradford Wilcox, et al., *Why Marriage Matters: Twenty-Six Conclusions from the Social Sciences, 2nd ed.* (Institute for American Values, 2005).

10. William J. Goode, *The Family*, Foundations of Modern Sociology Series (Prentice Hall, 1963), pp. 3–5, 8.

11. Donald Brown, *Human Universals* (McGraw-Hill, 1991), p. 93.

12. Margaret Mead, *Male and Female: A Study for the Sexes in a Changing World* (William Morrow, 1949), pp. 188–89.

13. Bronislaw Malinowski, *Sex, Culture, and Myth* (Harcourt, Brace and World, 1962), pp. 3–4.

14. George Peter Murdock, *Social Structure* (Macmillan, 1949), pp. 1–2.

15. Pierre L. van den Berghe, *Human Family Systems: An Evolutionary View* (Waveland Press, 1979, 1990), pp. 45–46.

16. Edward Westermarck, *The History of Human Marriage*, vol. 1 (Allerton, 1922), pp. 26, 46.

17. Kathleen Gough, "The Origin of Family," *Journal of Marriage and the Family*, November 1971, 760–71.

18. Plato, *Republic*, Chapter 16, trans. Francis MacDonald Cornford (Oxford University Press, 1945), pp. 156, 159.

19. Noam Shpancer, "Child of the Collective," *Guardian*, February 18, 2011.

20. Maren Lockwood Carden, *Oneida: Utopian Community to Modern Corporation* (Syracuse University Press, 1998); Spencer Klaw, *Without Sin: the Life and Death of the Oneida Community* (Penguin Books, 1993).

21. Aristotle, *Politics*, trans. Peter L. Phillips Simpson (University of North Carolina Press, 1997), bk. 1, chap. 2, pp. 9–11.

22. Abraham Kuyper, *Lectures on Calvinism* (Eerdmans, 1943), p. 79.

23. Kuyper, *Lectures on Calvinism*, p. 80.

24. Kuyper, *Lectures on Calvinism*, p. 91.

25. Kuyper, *Lectures on Calvinism*, pp. 92–93.

26. Kuyper, *Lectures on Calvinism*, p. 96.

27. Kuyper, *Lectures on Calvinism*, p. 97.

28. Kuyper, *Lectures on Calvinism*, p. 104.

Chapter 7: Mothers as Image-Bearers

1. "Mother's Day Sees Highest Call Volumes of Year," *Reuters News Service*, May 7, 2010.
2. Pallavi Gogoi, "Father's Unspectacular Day," *Bloomberg Businessweek*, June 13, 2005.

Chapter 8: Fathers as Image-Bearers

1. This comes from a short, little-known book that C.S. Lewis wrote in tribute to the man who, he tells us, shaped his Christian understanding more than any other person. Lewis admits that if there is a nonfiction book of his that does not quote MacDonald, it doesn't readily come to his mind. Such is the debt Lewis owes MacDonald. See C.S. Lewis, *George MacDonald: An Anthology—365 Readings* (HarperCollins, 2009).
2. See James Barr's "Abba Isn't Daddy" in *Journal of Theological Studies* 39 (1988). Barr explains: "It is fair to say that *abba* in Jesus' time belonged to a familiar or colloquial register of language, as distinct from more formal and ceremonious language. . . . But in any case it was not a childish expression comparable with 'Daddy': it was a more solemn, responsible, adult address to a Father" (p. 46).
3. Margaret Mead, *Male and Female: A Study of the Sexes in a Changing World* (William Morrow, 1949), pp. 188–89.

Chapter 9: Children as Image-Bearers

1. Does it happen outside of marriage? Of course. But it should be remembered that not long ago, the sexual act, whether in marriage or not, was referred to as "marital relations"—as marriage is its proper place. Its nature and substance is a marital act, whether or not the individuals involved realize and honor it as such. Outside of marriage, this special communion is disrespected because it is out of its proper context.
2. Michael Downey, *Altogether Gift: A Trinitarian Spirituality* (Orbis Books, 2000), p. 63.
3. John Paul II, *Puebla: A Pilgrimage of Faith* (Daughters of St. Paul, 1979), p. 86.
4. Carl Sandburg, *Remembrance Rock* (Harcourt, Brace and Company, 1949), p. 7.

5. W. Bradford Wilcox and Carlos Cavallé, *The Sustainable Demographic Dividend: What Do Marriage & Fertility Have to Do with the Economy?* National Marriage Project, University of Virginia, 2012, pp. 5–23.

6. Herod was a bloodthirsty ruler, having killed his wife and at least two of his children—as well as beheading Jesus' cousin, John the Baptist.

Chapter 10: The Enemy

1. Helen E. Fischer, *Anatomy of Love: The Natural History of Monogamy, Adultery, and Divorce* (W. W. Norton, 1992).

2. David Popenoe and Barbara Dafoe Whitehead, "The State of Our Unions, 2006," National Marriage Project (Rutgers University, July 2006), p. 13.

3. Jonathan Last, *What to Expect When No One's Expecting* (Encounter Books, 2013).

4. Longman explains that 59 countries (44 percent of the world's population) are currently not producing enough children to avoid serious population decline. The U.N. projects that by 2050, 75 percent of all countries, even in underdeveloped regions, will face this problem. Of all countries above replacement level, only two saw an estimated rise in total number of children born, but the rise "was barely more than zero." Phillip Longman, *The Empty Cradle: How Falling Birthrates Threaten World Prosperity and What to Do About It* (Basic Books, 2004), pp. 8, 26, 30.

5. Charles Williams, *The Forgiveness of Sins* (Eerdmans, 1984), p. 117.

6. E. Mavis Hetherington, *For Better or for Worse: Divorce Reconsidered* (W. W. Norton, 2002); Judith Wallerstein, et al., *The Unexpected Legacy of Divorce: A 25 Year Landmark Study* (Hyperion, 2000); Elizabeth Marquardt, *Between Two Worlds: The Inner Lives of Children of Divorce* (Crown, 2005).

7. Joseph Henrich, Robert Boyd, and Peter J. Richerson, "The Puzzle of Monogamous Marriage," *Philosophical Transactions of the Royal Society* 367 (2012): 657–69.

8. Glenn T. Stanton, *The Ring Makes All the Difference: The Hidden Consequences of Cohabitation and the Strong Benefits of Marriage* (Moody Publishers, 2011).

9. Aleksandr Solzhenitsyn, *The Gulag Archipelago*, vol. 2 (Harper and Row, 1975), pp. 615–16.

Chapter 11: The Great Mystery and Destiny

1. For a well-researched and helpful paper on the similarities between the ancient wedding traditions of Christ's world and the wedding feast of the Lamb, from which much of this insight is gained, see Ellen Dooley, "Wedding Ceremonies in Ancient Palestine and the Wedding Feast of the Lamb," *Evangelical Journal* 26 (2008): 79–84.

Chapter 12: My Imperfect Family

1. G.K. Chesterton, "On Certain Modern Writers and the Institution of the Family," in *The Collected Works of G.K. Chesterton*, vol. 1 (Ignatius Press, 1986).
2. For example, see Isaiah 48:10; Zechariah 13:9; Job 23:10; Proverbs 17:3; Psalm 66:10.
3. For an excellent overview of the Christlike blend of grace and truth, see Randy Alcorn, *The Grace and Truth Paradox: Responding with Christlike Balance* (Multnomah Books, 2003).
4. T. Berry Brazelton and Stanley I. Greenspan, *The Irreducible Needs of Children: What Every Child Must Have to Grow, Learn, and Flourish* (Perseus Press, 2000); Council of Economic Advisers to the President, "Teens and Their Parents in the 21st Century: An Examination of Trends in Teen Behavior and the Role of Parental Involvement," May 2000; John DeFrain, "Strong Families Around the World," *Family Matters: Australian Institute of Family Studies* (1999), 53:6–13; Marla E. Eisenberg, et al., "Correlations Between Family Meals and Psychosocial Well-Being Among Adolescents" *Archives of Pediatric and Adolescent Medicine* 158 (2004): 792–96; Frank D. Fincham, "Spiritual Behaviors and Relationship Satisfaction: A Critical Analysis of the Role of Prayer," *Journal of Social and Clinical Psychology* 27 (2008): 362–88; Lawrence E. Gary, Lula A. Beatty, Greta L. Berry, et al., *Stable Black Families: Final Report* (Mental Health Research & Development Center, Institute for Urban Affairs & Research, Howard University, 1983); Robert B. Hill, *The Strength of Black Families* (Independent Publishers Group, 1971); Vincent Jefferies, "Religiosity, Benevolent Love and Long-Lasting Marriages," *Humboldt Journal of Social Relations* 30 (2007): 76–105; Jerry M. Lewis, *How's Your Family? A Guide to Identifying Your Family's Strengths and Weaknesses* (Brunner/Mazel, 1979); Kristen Anderson Moore, et al., "Family Strengths: Often Overlooked, but Real," *Child Trends Research Brief*, August

2002; National Center on Addiction and Substance Abuse, *The Importance of Family Dinners IV* (Columbia University, September 2007); David Olson, Hamilton I. McCubbin, Howard Barnes, et al., *Families: What Makes Them Work,* 2nd ed. (Sage Publications, 1989); Suzanna Smith, "Building a Strong and Resilient Family," University of Florida Extension Services (2005); Nick Stinnett and John DeFrain, *Secrets of Strong Families* (Little, Brown and Company, 1985); Brenda J. Thames, "Building Family Strengths: Overview," Clemson University Cooperative Extension Services, January 1998.

5. Christian Smith, *Souls in Transition: The Religious and Spiritual Lives of Emerging Adults* (Oxford University Press, 2009), pp. 220–24.

6. *Faith in Flux: Change in Religious Affiliation in the U.S.* (Pew Forum on Religion and Public Life, April 2009), p. 4.

Appendix A

. Dean Ornish, *Love and Survival* (Harper Perennial, 1998), pp. 2–3, 14.

2. James J. Lynch, *A Cry Unheard: New Insights into the Medical Consequences of Loneliness* (Bancroft Press, 2000), p. 1.

3. Lynch, *A Cry Unheard,* p. 5.

4. Joshua Wolf Shenk, "What Makes Us Happy?" *Atlantic,* June 2009.

5. Daniel Goleman, *Social Intelligence: The New Science of Human Relationships* (Bantam Books, 2006), pp. 4–5.

6. Allan N. Schore, *Affect Dysregulation and Disorders of the Self* (W. W. Norton, 2003), pp. xv, 7.

7. Daniel J. Seigel, *The Developing Mind: Toward a Neurobiology of Interpersonal Experience* (Guilford Press, 1999), p. 9.

8. Louis Cozolino, *The Neuroscience of Human Relationships: Attachment and the Developing Social Brain* (W. W. Norton, 2006), p. 22.

9. Sue Gerhardt, *Why Love Matters: How Affection Shapes a Baby's Brain* (Brunner-Routledge, 2004), pp. 10, 15.

10. Ashley Montagu, *Touching: The Human Significance of the Skin* (Harper & Row, 1972), pp. 61–62, 72.

11. Kathryn L. Hildyard and David A. Wolfe, "Child Neglect: Developmental Issues and Outcomes," *Child Abuse and Neglect* 26 (2002): 679–95, p. 686.